The
Complete Cat Book

RICHARD H. GEBHARDT
Former President, Cat Fanciers' Association

 **HOWELL**
BOOK HOUSE

New York

Maxwell Macmillan Canada
Toronto

Maxwell Macmillan International
New York   Oxford   Singapore   Sydney

Howell Book House
Macmillan Publishing Company
866 Third Avenue
New York, NY 10022

Maxwell Macmillan Canada, Inc.
1200 Eglinton Avenue East
Suite 200
Don Mills, Ontario M3C 3NI

Macmillan Publishing Company is part of the
Maxwell Communication Group of Companies.

Created and produced by Mirabel Books Ltd.,
P.O. Box 1214, London SW6 7ES

Special Photography by Bill Buckner
Editor: Phil Maggitti
Design by Chris McLeod and Peter Simmonett

Library of Congress Cataloging-in-Publication Data

Gebhardt, Richard H.

   The complete cat book/Richard H. Gebhardt.
   — 1st American ed.
      p. cm.
   Includes bibliographical references and index
      ISBN 0-87605-841-1
      1. Cats   2. Cat breeds.   I. Title.
   SF442. G43   1991
   636.8—dc20   91-13279

Macmillan books are available at special discounts for
bulk purchases for sales promotions, premium, fund-
raising, or educational use. For details, contact:

Special Sales Director
Macmillan Publishing Company
866 Third Avenue
New York, NY 10022

10 9 8 7 6 5 4 3 2 1

Separations by Oceanic Graphic Printing, Inc.
Printed and bound by C & C Offset Printing Co. Ltd
Printed in Hong Kong

Acknowledgements

As I wrote this book, there was never a doubt in my mind
about the person to whom it should be dedicated: my
lifelong partner, collaborator, and friend John Bannon,
whose loyalty and love of animals made possible my
achievements. John, who shared my heartaches and
highlights, has given me a sense of pride few people
experience.

I was fortunate to have been surrounded with persons
of great talent and achievement during my years in the
cat fancy, and I should like to acknowledge my mentors
in the Cat Fanciers' Association: Elsie Hydon, Rita
Swenson, Jean Rose, Lillias Bloem, Louise Sample, Matil
Rotter, and Robert Winn.

In addition, I have enjoyed lasting friendships with
some of England's legendary cat fanciers: Kathleen
Yorke, Joan Thompson, Grace Pond, and Brian Sterling-
Webb.

I must also mention my wonderful family, who
endured all my ambitions with their love and support—
and last but not least, the beloved four-legged members
of my household. Each and every one has been a special
part of my life.

Finally, I would like to acknowledge the help I received
from the following individuals who supplied information
or assistance in the preparation of this book: Carolann
Bannon, Bud and Betty Cowles, Tom Dent and Allene
Sergei of the Cat Fanciers' Association, Marna and Joe
Fogarty, the Garden Cat Club, the Garden State Cat Club,
Phil and Mary Ann Maggitti, Vicky and Peter Markstein,
Douglas Myers, Daphne Negus, John and Gina Philpot,
Lesley Pring and Eric Wickham-Ruffle of the Governing
Council of the Cat Fancy, Janice Reichle, Allen Scruggs,
Barbara St. Georges, Eric and Helena Thom, Betty White-
Ludden, and Herb Zwecker.

Contents

Preface by Betty White

It would be hard to imagine any species that has been surrounded by more misinformation, misunderstanding, and myth than the cat. Cats have ridden the roller coaster of popularity and rejection since they first entered a symbiotic existence with humans. In Egypt cats were worshipped as gods, and people often shaved their eyebrows to mourn the death of the family feline. In the Middle Ages and beyond, cats were hunted and cursed as the devil incarnate.

Today cats are back on top, having surpassed dogs as the most popular pets in America. Timing is everything, and cats have proven themselves totally adaptable to changing lifestyles in our fragmented society. They are willing to share affection when we are around, and able to be self-sufficient when we are not.

Too often this poise is misinterpreted as indifference by the uninitiated. Cats are deemed too independent, which can be something of an ego bender to people accustomed to the all-out effusiveness of a bounding dog. Subtlety is the name of the cats' game, and their dry wit is frequently unappreciated by those attuned to more obvious doggy humor. Unfortunately, many of these people have never spent any one-on-one time with a cat. If they did, their attitudes would probably be different.

Until relatively recent times the domesticated cat had made its way through the world almost unchanged. Only during the last one hundred years have humans begun to influence the basic appearance of the cat, creating a burgeoning number of varieties and officially recognized breeds. The total does not yet compare with the staggering diversity in dog breeds, but cat breeders haven't been at it as long.

Just as most felines seem to march to their own drums, so do the people who spend their lives around cats: the breeders, fanciers, and loving owners. And unlike the canine world, where the American Kennel Club reigns supreme, the cat fancy has no single, paramount organization to approve breed Standards, license judges, sanction shows, recognize new breeds and colors, and maintain records. Instead, there are *six* distinct cat registries in North America. Each is independent of the others, and all have different rules, requirements, procedures, and breed Standards.

Describing the growing number of purebred cats and accommodating the discrepancies among six different registries in one book seems a virtually impossible challenge, but my friend Richard Gebhardt has proven equal to the task. It has been my pleasure to have known Dick through the years. I have watched him in the judging arena, and have served with him on the board of directors of the Morris Animal Foundation.

Dick's many accomplishments—which include qualifying as the first international allbreed judge and serving for many years as president of the Cat Fanciers' Association—are overwhelming. Yet watching him handle cats, and seeing their response to him, says more than words possibly could. Dick not only knows cats, he respects them, understands them, and loves them inordinately. It is only fitting—and not at all surprising—that he should be the one to bring together this truly complete cat book.

Actress Betty White, a former president of the Morris Animal Foundation, remains one of its most popular spokespersons. The foundation provides funds for studies designed to improve the lives of all animals residing in households, zoos, or in the wild. Since it was organized in 1948, the foundation has allocated more than $7,500,000 in funds to more than five hundred research projects.

For additional information about the Morris Animal Foundation write to:
Morris Animal Foundation
45 Inverness Drive East
Englewood, CO 80112-5480

Before You Buy Your Cat

HOW TO LOCATE BREEDERS

People seeking a pedigreed kitten can find the names of breeders in the yearbooks published by cat associations, the breeders' ads in *Cats* or *Cat Fancy* magazines, and the classified section of the newspaper. Yearbooks, which contain the most pictures of different breeds, can be ordered from the executive offices of cat registries (See page 218). *Cats* and *Cat Fancy* are available at newsstands or at cat shows. Newspapers are available everywhere. Prospective buyers can meet breeders in person by visiting cat shows, which are advertised in newspapers and cat magazines.

HOW MUCH IS THAT KITTEN IN ...?

The price of a pet kitten is a function of breed, geography, supply, demand, and occasionally the number of surplus kittens a breeder has to feed. Between $300 and $400 is a reasonable range for most breeds in most parts of the country. Prices on either coast are sometimes higher, and breeders with new or exotic breeds often equate novelty with increased value, but there is little reason to pay more than $500 for a companion cat that is not going to be used for breeding.

Show kittens are another matter. Price will vary with breed, demand, and potential, but prices will start high and finish higher. Persian kittens are usually the most expensive. It is difficult to find one that will be competitive for less than $1,500. Of course, the more competitive a kitten is likely to be, the more a breeder is likely to ask for it.

The purchase price is not the only cost associated with buying a kitten. Anyone obtaining a kitten from a breeder who lives beyond driving distance must pay to have it shipped by plane. The buyer must also pay for the carrier in which the kitten is shipped—if the buyer does not have a carrier already—and for having the carrier sent to the kitten's breeder. Carriers that meet airline specifications can be purchased at cat shows, wholesale pet-supply stores, pet shops, or at some airline cargo offices. A sturdy, durable carrier costs about $25 to $35, depending on its size. Shipping costs, which vary with the length of the flight, the method of shipping, and the airline doing the shipping, can range from $30 to $40 for a short flight to more than $100 for a transcontinental journey.

BASIC CONCERNS

Contrary to their reputation for being aloof, cats are charming and devoted companions who provide us with affection and amuse us with their antics. What's more, they are meticulously clean and supremely self-sufficient—perfectly content to spend the day at home when we are away at work and delighted to see us when we return. Just as their ancestors have adapted to meet the earth's changing conditions over the last three million years, modern-day cats adapt well to the restrictions of urban living and the busy schedules of two-career families or single-parent homes.

Like people, kittens come in a variety of personalities, from shy to scintillating, and people who go to look at a kitten should observe carefully. Watch as a kitten plays with litter mates. If a kitten is right in the middle of the rolling and tumbling that kittens love, chances are he's in good health and developing normally. A wallflower that sits quietly while the others play might not be feeling well or might be the kind of kitten that requires a little more patience and attention than the average.

Two simple personality tests involve wiggling a few fingers along the floor about six inches in front of a kitten, or dangling a small toy back and forth. Does the kitten scamper over to investigate, or back away as though feeling threatened? A well-adjusted kitten will be curious to find out what this human is about. A nervous or a timid kitten will be more cautious. A poorly adjusted or immature kitten will disappear under the nearest chair.

For persons who have other pets or children at home, the curious, pleased-to-meet-you kitten is the best choice. This is the type more apt to adjust quickly and to get along with other family members. The timid kitten will probably make a fine companion, too, but

may need more time to adjust, and might prefer more quiet surroundings. As for the little one under the sofa, perhaps the perfect owner will come along one day, but chances are he doesn't think it's today.

No matter what personality suits a new owner best, a kitten is not suitable at all if it isn't healthy. While

Kittens love to climb and play in containers of all sorts

Kittens enjoy supervised outdoor play

making a kitten's acquaintance, a person should be making observations about the animal's health and general condition. Did the kitten follow alertly the toy that was waved about nearby? Are his eyes bright, shiny, and clear? Is his nose cool and slightly damp? Are his gums free of inflammation? Is the area around his tail clean?

Beware the kitten with a dry, warm-feeling nose or teary eyes. These are frequently signs of poor health. Inflammed gums are often an indication of gingivitis. Dirt or wetness in the area around a kitten's tail may signal diarrhea or urine scalding, which may in turn be signs of ill health.

A kitten's ears should be clean and free of wax or dirt. The body should be soft and smooth, a little lean, perhaps, but not skinny. The coat should be free of bald patches or flea dirt; skin should be free of scabs or scratches. Bald patches or scabs could mean ringworm. Flea dirt always means fleas.

Even if the prospective new member of the family appears healthy, a kitten should come with a money-back guarantee, and the new owner should have five working days in which to take a kitten to a veterinarian for an examination. The vet will check the kitten's temperature, test a stool sample for worms, listen to the kitten's heart and lungs, weigh the kitten, and test him for leukemia and other contagious diseases. If the vet discovers any serious, preexisting conditions such as leukemia or feline infectious peritonitis, the buyer should have the right to return the kitten and to have the purchase price refunded.

Though most cat breeders are reputable, kitten buyers should allow for the possibility that the person they're dealing with is not. If a breeder asks for a deposit on a kitten, the buyer should write "deposit for such-and-such kitten" on the memo line of the check.

At roughly eight to ten weeks, the young male's accoutrements (left) are quite visible; but even at birth the difference between the sexes is apparent. The male genital area resembles a colon (:), and the female's looks like an inverted exclamation mark (¡)

Buyers should also ask for a receipt for that deposit and should find out in advance—preferably in writing—if the deposit is refundable should they decide not to take the kitten. The same cautions apply when a person sends the check for the balance of the purchase price.

Many breeders will send the buyer a sales contract before they ship a kitten. Buyers should read the contract carefully and question any stipulations they do not understand or would not feel comfortable meeting.

Occasionally breeders who sell a kitten will say they haven't registered the kitten's litter yet, but when they do, they'll send along its "blue slip"—the application for registration (See box on page 11.) If buyers accept a kitten under this condition, they should ask the breeder to send them a note to the effect that "papers will follow within thirty to sixty days" after the breeder has shipped the kitten.

No matter how eager a person is to buy a kitten, a responsible breeder never lets a kitten go if it is more than a few days shy of twelve weeks. A kitten approaching twelve weeks has been properly weaned and has been eating solid food for some time. It is nursing infrequently, if at all, and has begun to make the transition from being a dependent to an independent creature. And by that time it has had all its vaccinations.

Kittens that are six to ten weeks old are still babies. If they're taken away from their mothers, the stress of going to a new home may cause them to become sick, to forget their litter training, or to chew on blankets or sofa cushions as a substitute for nursing—a habit they often keep the rest of their lives. So no matter how cute or tempting an eight-week-old might be, the kitten will adjust better—and so will the owner—if the transition to a new home is made when the kitten is at least three weeks older. Barring misfortune, the average cat will live ten to fourteen years, so the serious owner ought to be able to be patient for twenty-one extra days.

Many breeders like to economize by giving vaccinations themselves. If they do, the buyer should not accept a kitten that has not been to a veterinarian for at least one examination, preferably before its first vaccination was administered.

ABOUT BREEDS AND PERSONALITIES

There were forty-four breeds accepted for championship competition in at least one association at the time of this writing—early spring 1991. With so many breeds to choose from, a prospective owner should be able to find a kitten that suits any aesthetic taste, pocketbook, or living arrangement. As one might expect—and contrary to what one frequently hears—every breed does not have a unique personality distinct from every other breed's. There aren't that many distinct personalities among people, and there are far more breeds of people than there are of cats.

In truth, feline personality is more related to body type than it is to breed. For example, the slim, elegant Siamese is the most active, vocal, curious—and some would say the most intelligent—cat. Siamese share these traits to varying degrees with other svelte, tubular breeds like the Oriental Shorthair, Balinese, Abyssinian, and Cornish Rex. At the other end of the personality spectrum, the Persian is the most easygoing cat. It holds this trait in common with other foursquare, stocky breeds like the Sacred Cat of Burma, the British Shorthair, and the Exotic Shorthair.

In the middle of the spectrum for body type and personality is the pedigreed American Shorthair. A stylized version of its free-roaming relatives, the American Shorthair resembles a street cat about as much as steak tartare resembles ground chuck. On a personality scale of one to ten, the American Shorthair is a perfect, middle-of-the-road five.

No matter what the breed, the process of domestication retards the development of certain adult behaviors. Domesticated animals never, in short, quite grow up. We don't want them to. A lingering immaturity is part of their appeal. The self-sufficient, aggressive, urine-marking animal which is the adult of any feline species is not something we want running about in our homes.

The tendency of domesticated cats to be forever young is amplified by their socialization. In studies involving domestic cats conducted at Temple University in Philadelphia in the early 1980s, Eileen Karsh, Ph.D., found that kittens which were handled for as little as five minutes a day from the time they were three weeks old until they were fourteen weeks old became more attached to people than kittens which were handled daily from seven to fourteen weeks of age or kittens

This British Shorthair is sturdy and correct

An American Shorthair in a classic tabby pattern

which were not handled at all. Early handled kittens were more likely to tolerate being held ventral side up, and they approached humans almost four times as quickly as late or nonhandled kittens. These and other user-friendly characteristics are the traits one hopes to find in kittens that are advertised as having been "raised underfoot with lot of TLC (tender loving care)." The proof of the advertisement, however, is always in the handling.

TIPS ON SELECTING A SHOW CAT

Though some people prefer male or female cats as pets, either sex, if given love and attention and a place on the bed at night, will make a darling companion. Anyone planning to breed cats, however, should buy the best female he or she can find. This task is more complex, time consuming, and costly than locating a pet kitten. Some novices mistakenly believe that because a kitten can be registered it can automatically be shown. That's true, as far as it goes, but there's a difference between buying a cat that can be shown and buying a show cat. In fact, just because a kitten is said

to be show quality and is sold at a show-quality price do not always guarantee that it is good enough to be shown.

One way to find out how well a kitten is likely to do at a show—and to save oneself disappointment—is to buy a young adult or an older kitten that has been shown a few times. Some breeders like to show their kittens but do not have room to keep them all. Thus, a new owner might find a cat that's less than a year old and has a few final wins on its resume. If a person is willing to forgo the pleasure of watching a kitten grow up—and is willing to pay a little more for a proven winner—the older kitten or young adult might be a better choice than the untried adolescent.

In every case, it is better to wait until a show-quality kitten is older than twelve weeks before buying it. Kittens can change overnight, and it's difficult to predict how a kitten is going to develop when it is only twelve weeks old—no matter what glowing predictions a breeder might make. A five- or six-month-old kitten is less subject to change without notice.

No matter how old the show cat a person buys—or whether the cat is longhaired or short, male or female, adult or kitten—that person should do some homework before writing the check: visit shows, talk to breeders who are working with a particular breed, watch the cats in that breed being judged, and sit through several finals to see what the winning representatives of a breed look like. The prospective buyer should also consult the breed Standard (See Breeds Section), and take a copy of that Standard along when looking at kittens. The buyer should ask the kitten's breeder to show where a kitten meets the Standard and where it doesn't. If possible, the buyer should also take an experienced breeder along when looking at a prospective show kitten.

Anyone interested in buying a kitten from a breeder who lives too far away to visit, should ask to see pictures of the kitten. If the pictures are not clear, ask to see more. Ask the breeder to say, preferably in writing, where a kitten meets the Standard and where it falls short.

Persons buying kittens should also remember that they're buying the genetic influence of several generations. Buyers should look at a kitten's pedigree to see what titles its family members have won, especially those in the first two generations, for the parents and grandparents wield the greatest influence on a kitten's potential. If neither the parents nor the grandparents are grand champions, they either were not shown or they were not good enough to do well when they were shown. If they were not shown, ask why. If several of them were shown but did not "grand," think at least twice about buying the kitten. And ask the breeder how many grand champions the sire and dam of the kitten have produced. Just as thoroughbred breeders put great stock in equine families, so, too, should the prospective cat breeder or exhibitor.

Though pedigrees are written in English of a sort, they are manuscripts in a foreign tongue to many newcomers. Yet the breeder who does not learn the language might just as well be pondering graffiti on a dark wall under a bad light if he or she hopes to use pedigrees as an aid to acquiring or producing a cat.

Part of the knack of learning to understand pedigrees involves the ability to read between the lines, that is to say, seeing as many of the cats as possible in the first three generations of a pedigree, even if it is only in pictures. The astute buyer also tries to check out the littermates of the cats that are on a pedigree. This is particularly important if one is considering buying a cat that is inbred. While that cat may not have an extra ear, one should not consider buying it if one of its littermates did.

Nearly three hundred years ago William Penn remarked that "men are generally more careful of the breed of their [animals] than of their children." Penn's observation is, perhaps, too cynical to apply to modern-day cat breeders, but the touchstone of good breeding has remained the same since Penn's day: to buy a kitten with a pedigree that is stronger than either of its parents' pedigrees taken alone, one that will advance a breeder toward his or her goals.

REGISTRATION

Though all federations allow an exhibitor to show an unregistered kitten—and most make a one-time allowance for an unregistered adult—new owners should fill out the registration slip for an unregistered kitten or complete the transfer-of-ownership section on the owner's certificate if they bought a cat that was already registered. On these forms, new owners supply their name, address, cattery name, if they wish, and, if they bought a kitten, the name they want the kitten to have. The new owner should mail this document, with the correct fee, to the administrative office of the appropriate registry. Within two weeks after mailing the registration slip, the new owner's certificate should arrive by return mail.

Some breeders register their kittens in more than one association, so a new owner may receive more than one registration slip with a cat or kitten. But even if a cat is registered in only one association, an owner can register that cat in another one by mailing a photocopy of the cat's pedigree and of both sides of the registration slip from the association in which the cat is already registered, with the appropriate fee, to the "new" association's administrative office.

Choosing a cat or a kitten is like falling in love: the heart has the upper hand. The divorce rate being what it is, however, people should learn everything they can about their intended breeds before promising to love, honor, and support a cat in the manner to which it would like to become accustomed. Someone looking for a four-legged companion who requires little more than the occasional scratch behind the ears, for example, will not be satisfied with an in-your-face breed. Nor will the individual who craves constant fawning discover eternal wedded bliss with a prim, reserved cat who dresses for dinner.

The following chart contains evaluations of the activity level and grooming needs—high, medium, or low—of every recognized breed. These are important considerations to anyone buying a pedigreed cat. The chart also contains information of interest to anyone thinking about breeding cats. Are all the kittens in a breed showable? Are there genetic considerations that make one breed more challenging than others? These questions are answered Yes or No. Not all American Wirehair kittens, to mention one example, are showable. Some are born with straight coats. And Manx present a challenge to breeders because of the spinal problems and weak hindquarters that plague this breed.

	Activity Level	Grooming Needs	All Kittens Showable?	Genetic Concerns
Kashmir	L	H	Y	N
Korat	M	L	Y	N
Maine Coon	M	H	Y	N
Manx	M	L	N[15]	Y[16]
Norwegian Forest Cat	M	M	Y	N
Ocicat	M	L	N[17]	N
Oriental Longhair	H	L	N[18]	N
Oriental Shorthair	H	L	N[19]	N
Persian	L	H	Y	N
Peke-faced Persian	L	H	Y	N
Ragdoll	L	H	Y	N
Russian Blue	H	L	Y	N
Scottish Fold	M	L	N[20]	Y[21]
Scottish Fold Longhair	M	M	N[22]	Y[23]
Siamese	H	L	Y	N
Singapura	M	L	N[24]	N
Somali	M	M	N[25]	N
Sphynx	M	L	Y	Y[26]
Tonkinese	H	L	N[27]	N
Turkish Angora	M	L	Y	N
Turkish Van	M	M	Y	N

[1] Susceptibility to kidney problems is embedded in many lines.
[2] Produces some straight-eared kittens.
[3] Produces some straight-coated kittens.
[4] This breed is slow to develop an immune-system response, leaving cats prone to sneezing and other upper-respiratory symptoms.
[5] Produces some nonspotted kittens.
[6] Produces some brown kittens that cannot be shown in most associations.
[7] Cranial deformities occur frequently in many lines.
[8] Cranial deformities occur frequently in many lines.
[9] Has achieved provisional status only thus far.
[10] Produces some tailed and partially tailed kittens.
[11] Lethal gene prevents development of one fourth of all kittens in the womb. Spinal problems and weak hindquarters are also frequent in this breed.
[12] Produces straight-coated kittens when outcrossed to American or British shorthairs.
[13] Spasticity occurs in some lines.
[14] Produces some longhaired kittens that cannot be shown in most associations.
[15] Produces some tailed and partially tailed kittens.
[16] Lethal gene prevents development of one fourth of all kittens in the womb. Spinal problems and weak hindquarters are also frequent in this breed.
[17] Produces some nonspotted kittens.
[18] Can produce pointed kittens when outcrossed to Balinese.
[19] Can produce Siamese-colored kittens that cannot be shown in all associations.
[20] Produces some straight-eared kittens.
[21] Fold-to-Fold breedings produce a percentage of kittens with short, inflexible tails and hindquarter crippling.
[22] Produces some straight-eared kittens.
[23] Fold-to-Fold breedings produce a percentage of kittens with short, inflexible tails and hindquarter crippling.
[24] Produces nonticked kittens occasionally.
[25] Produces shorthaired kittens when crossed to an Abyssinian. These cannot be shown in most associations.
[26] Has had a tendency in the past to ineffective immune system development.
[27] Produces some colors and patterns which cannot be shown in most associations.

	Activity Level	Grooming Needs	All Kittens Showable?	Genetic Concerns
Abyssinian	H	L	Y	Y[1]
American Curl	M	M	N[2]	N
American Shorthair	M	L	Y	N
American Wirehair	M	L	N[3]	Y[4]
Balinese	H	L	Y	N
Bengal	M	L	N[5]	N
Birman	L	M	Y	N
Bombay	H	L	N[6]	Y[7]
British Shorthair	L	L	Y	N
Burmese	H	L	Y	Y[8]
Burmilla	M	L	Y[9]	N
Chartreux	M	L	Y	N
Colorpoint Shorthair	H	L	Y	N
Cornish Rex	H	L	Y	N
Cymric	M	M	N[10]	Y[11]
Devon Rex	H	L	N[12]	Y[13]
Egyptian Mau	H	L	Y	N
Exotic Shorthair	M	M	N[14]	N
Foreign Burmese	H	L	Y	N
Havana Brown	M	L	Y	N
Himalayan	L	H	Y	N
Japanese Bobtail	M	L	Y	N
Javanese	H	L	Y	N

Origins and Domestication of the Cat

THE WORLD'S FIRST CATS

All cats belong to the mammalian, carnivorous family known as *Felidae* or felids. About fifty-four million years ago felids began to evolve from miacids—small, tree-climbing creatures that resembled today's marten.

The Domestic Cat's Pedigree

Fossil remains suggest, however, that felids exhibiting close similarities to twentieth-century domestic cats did not appear until roughly twelve million years ago.

Felids can be classified most simply into three genera: *Panthera*, which includes cats that can roar—the lion, tiger, leopard, snow leopard, clouded leopard, and jaguar; *Felis*, which includes all non roaring cats but the cheetah; *Acinonyx*, a Genus awarded to

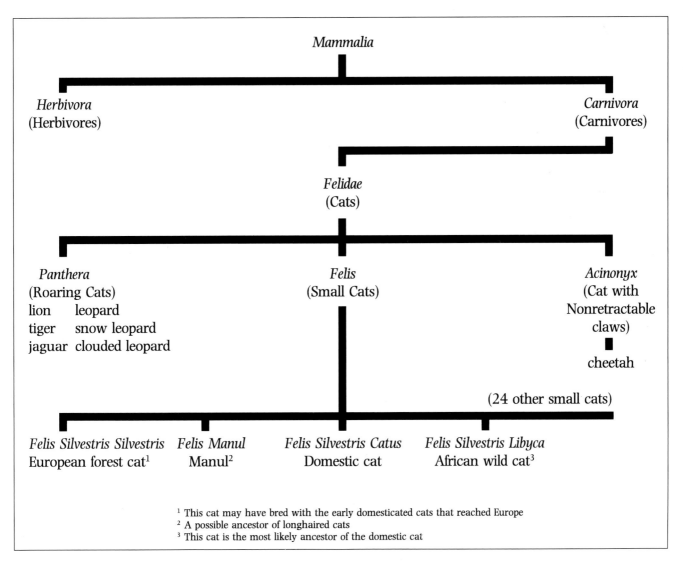

[1] This cat may have bred with the early domesticated cats that reached Europe
[2] A possible ancestor of longhaired cats
[3] This cat is the most likely ancestor of the domestic cat

the cheetah because its claws aren't fully retractable. The genus *Felis,* to which domestic cats belong, was well established when *Homo sapiens* appeared thirty thousand to thirty-five thousand years ago. In many places cats were contemporaries of prehistoric people, but were not domesticated by them. Our ancestors had domesticated at least a dozen animals—beginning with dogs, reindeer, goats, and sheep during the preagricultural phase more than ten thousand years ago—before coming to terms with the cat.

ANCESTORS OF THE DOMESTIC CAT

Most researchers believe that the African wild cat (*Felis silvestris libyca*)—a yellow, faintly striped animal somewhat larger than present-day felines, that is found primarily in deserts throughout Africa, Syria, Arabia, and parts of India—is the probable ancestor of the domestic cat. Chief among the reasons for this conclusion are correlations between human and feline habitats during the period when domestication is most likely to have occurred; morphological and behavioral adaptations in the domestic cat—including a hearing apparatus suited to open spaces like the desert; behavioral evidence—the African wild cat is docile and is still easily tamed today; and etymological evidence—the English word *cat,* the French *chat,* the German *Katze,* the Spanish *gato,* the fourth-century Latin *cattus,* and the modern Arabic *quttah,* appear to be derived from the Nubian word *kadiz,* meaning a cat.

Two other varieties may have contributed also to the cat's development: Pallas's cat (*Felis manul*), a long-coated resident of the steppes in Northern and Central Asia, is believed by some to be the longhaired cat's

Skulls from mummified Egyptian cats

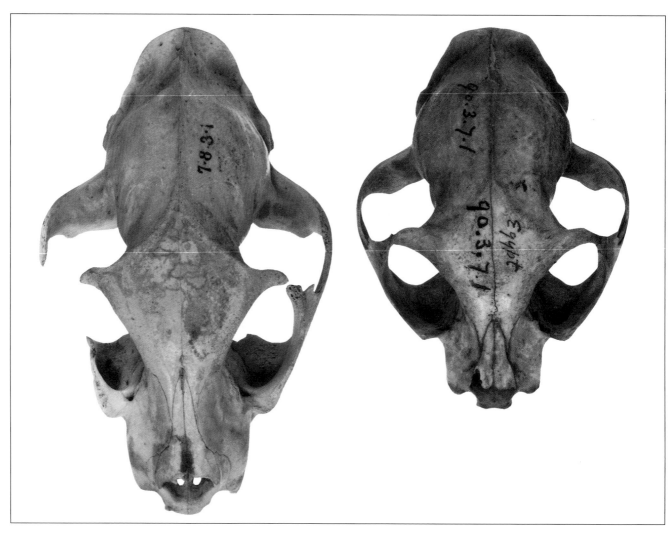

distant ancestor; and the never-domesticated European wild cat *(Felis silvestris silvestris)* may have interbred with domesticated cats once they had spread throughout Europe beginning in the fourth century, thereby contributing genes for darker tabby markings to the more lightly marked descendants of the African wild cat. The ancestors of the modern-day cat were either

ticked, mackerel, or spotted tabbies. The classic (or blotched) tabby pattern seen in the show ring does not occur in any other member of the cat family except *Felis catus,* the domestic cat, in whom it appeared as an ordinary gene mutation.

Egyptian cats in bronze (left) and earthenware

Dessins sans paroles des chats by Theophile Steinlen (1859-1923), a French lithographer

WHEN THE CAT WAS DOMESTICATED

"It is likely," says one animal behaviorist, "that the cat was first domesticated in Egypt, but the probable date of this event is, at best, an approximation. The earliest pictorial representations of cats from Egypt date from the third millennium B.C., but it is often difficult to ascertain whether these animals were wild or domestic. From about 1600 B.C. onwards [however] paintings and effigies of cats become increasingly abundant in Egypt, and it [seems] that these animals were fully domesticated."

HOW THE CAT WAS DOMESTICATED

Nearly all zoologists agree with their colleague Paul Leyhausen, who wrote: "There is no evidence that at any time during its history the cat's way of life and its reception into human homesteads were purposely planned and directed by humans, as was the case with all other domestic animals at least from a very early stage of their association. In every sense the cat domesticated himself—if with some unimagined assistance from man."

Cats were domesticated—whether by themselves or by humans—to hunt vermin and, to a lesser extent, for companionship. As agrarian societies developed, wild cats moved closer to towns and villages, attracted by food refuse and the large populations of rats and mice that thrived in granaries. When cats proved their skill at protecting grain, farmers began feeding them, hoping they would stay on the job.

IS THE CAT TRULY DOMESTICATED?

Although its ancestors formed an alliance with humans more than 3,500 years ago, the cat remains, according to one zoologist, "an instructive example of a species which is only in the first stage of domestication ... perfectly capable of still becoming feral, and comparatively little altered" by its association with humankind. Indeed, cats are the most wild among the tame animals and the most tame among the wild. Two circumstances unique to the cat have accounted for this development.

Except for the lion and the cheetah, all cats, unlike other domesticated animals, are solitary creatures. Their survival does not depend on membership in a well-structured group. Cats follow their own counsel. Horses, by comparison, follow the lead of the dominant member of the herd, usually the alpha mare. This ancient instinct allows humans to become the dominant animals in the horse's life once domestication occurs. The cat does not transfer its allegiance so easily.

Centuries of complete reproductive freedom have also influenced the cat's personality. Until the late nineteenth century humans exerted almost no control over the cat's choice of mates. Other domesticated animals had been subject to arranged marriages for thousands of years by then, and only the most docile animals were considered fit subjects.

One can argue, therefore, that the cat has been domesticated, if at all, for little more than a hundred years, that its domestication did not commence until people began to exert systematic control over its breeding activities, and that pedigreed cats—especially those of the longest standing—are the first truly domesticated felines. The more extensive the pedigree, the greater the evolution in that animal whose ancestors it records.

Though no one has formally studied differences in temperament between pedigreed and nonpedigreed cats, breeders who have both kinds make some interesting observations. An American Shorthair breeder once took a barn cat into her house and bred it to one of her pedigreed males. When that female had kittens, she would not use the litter pan in the same room where she was raising them. She preferred to eliminate away from the nest, like an animal in the wild. Nor was she comfortable about letting her owner handle her kittens, as females who have descended from generations of indoor cats normally are.

Compared to the tenure of the dog, the interval since the cat was first domesticated has been brief. We can only guess at the personalities of those earliest cats who accepted food from humans, then agreed to accept their companionship as well. In addition, we can only guess at how the cat's personality will be affected by continued selective breeding. One thing, however, is certain: those making the selections ought to base their choices at least as much on temperament as they do on type.

A cat receiving a deputation of mice, by Wenceslaus Hollar (1607-77).
From an 18th-century edition of Aesop's Fables

A Brief History of the Cat Fancy

THE BIRTH OF THE CAT FANCY IN ENGLAND

In 1598, the year that Shakespeare published *Much Ado About Nothing,* a cat show was held at the St. Giles Fair in England. Much apparently did not come of this event, for 273 years passed before the English cat fancy was born. The affair that inspired this birth was a cat show at London's Crystal Palace in 1871. This gathering was organized by Harrison Weir, an Englishman of various talents, who also wrote the Standards by which the entries were appraised, and served as one of the show's three judges.

The breeds exhibited at nineteenth-century British cat shows were the Abyssinian; Manx; Royal Cat of Siam, which included both pointed and solid-chocolate cats; shorthairs, which were no doubt the descendants of cats brought to England by the Romans nine centuries before; and longhairs, which were judged by one Standard and which included Persians, Angoras, and a few cats from Russia. There were also classes for hybrids between wild and domestic cats, the heaviest cats, gelded cats, and "Cats Belonging to Working

Harrison Weir with a prize-winning Persian cat

Men." The entrance fee in the latter was one third the fee in other classes, and the prize money offered to the first three finishers in the class was similarly reduced.

The popularity of cat shows in England led to the formation of the National Cat Club in 1887, Harrison Weir president. The NCC, whose motto was "Beauty Lives by Kindness," was both club and governing body. It established a national stud book and register to record the lineage of pedigreed cats.

The Cat Club, a rival to the NCC, was founded in 1898 by Lady Marcus Beresford and "some of the most important people in the land," according to one writer. Since TCC maintained its own stud book and register, persons who entered their cats in its shows had to enroll them in that association, too. After five years of stormy coexistence with the NCC, The Cat Club disbanded. Finally, in March 1910, the various clubs in England agreed to amalgamate. They formed the Governing Council of the Cat Fancy, which remains the oldest and the largest cat association in Great Britain today.

THE BIRTH OF THE CAT FANCY IN THE UNITED STATES

The cat fancy in the United States was officially born on May 8, 1895, when an Englishman named James T. Hyde organized a cat show in Madison Square Garden in New York. One hundred and twenty-five exhibitors—and 176 cats—endured temperatures as high as ninety-six degrees inside the Garden that day. This show—where the best cat was a brown tabby Maine Coon male—was the first to attract significant attention, but there had been other cat shows in the United States. For many years Maine Coon fanciers had promoted exhibitions of their cats in New England; and a handful of shows for all breeds of cats—frequently included as adjuncts to pigeon or poultry shows—had been held in Boston, Philadelphia, and Newburgh, New York.

Catalogs from cat shows in England

In 1896 the Madison Square Garden show attracted only 130 entries. Nevertheless, at the close of the show a group of cat fanciers created the American Cat Club, the first registry in the United States. Its functions included verifying pedigrees, maintaining a stud book, sponsoring shows, and promoting the welfare of cats. The club was disbanded a year later, and for several years there were no shows at Madison Square Garden.

Cat fanciers in Chicago organized two clubs in 1899. The first was the Chicago Cat Club. It was followed and eventually eclipsed by the Beresford club. Then, as now, no crown can be counted secure in the cat world.

THE CAT FANCY IN
EARLY TWENTIETH-CENTURY AMERICA

The Beresford Club, with a national membership of 170, began sponsoring shows in 1900, and in that year published the first stud book and register in the United States. The club's objectives were promoting the humane society and caring for all homeless or distressed cats—problems that more of the today's clubs should be concerned about.

Though the Beresford Club continued to put on shows, it eventually ceased to function as a registering body. That chore was assumed by the American Cat Association, generally referred to as the oldest registry in the United States. ACA was incorporated on May 11, 1904. Mrs. Clinton Locke, ACA's initial president, was the first woman in this country to operate a cattery. She had been importing and breeding cats since the late 1870s.

According to *The Cat Journal*, one of two cat publications available in the early 1900s, "a difference of opinion regarding some of the rules [led to] a break in the ranks" of ACA. The split occurred at the annual meeting in January 1906—the same month that Harrison Weir, the father of the cat fancy, died in England. The following month a group of ACA dissidents started the Cat Fanciers' Association, whose first president, Mrs. William Hofstra, had been vice-president of ACA. In December the Buffalo, New York, cat club sponsored the first CFA show, which drew an entry of 168 cats. CFA also began publishing its first stud book and register in *The Cat Journal* by the end of the year.

In early 1919 CFA withheld championship claims from certain exhibitors because of violations of its rules. The Silver Society, a Persian breed club, resigned because of this action. The Atlantic Cat Club, which had formerly resigned from ACA, resigned from CFA, too. Members of these clubs organized the United Cat Fanciers Association, a title that was changed to the Cat Fanciers' Federation a few months later.

"What is the American fancy coming to?" sniffed *The Cat Review* magazine disapprovingly. "Will ... all the clubs become little independent associations?"

By 1927 CFA had become the largest cat registry in

From the 1911 edition of the English Fur and Feather

the United States. That year CFA had thirty-two clubs, ACA twenty-six, and CFF eight. Two years later CFA passed the one-thousand mark in new registrations per year. In 1990 it registered more than eighty times that number.

THE SECOND WORLD WAR

World War II had a detrimental effect on the cat fancy, especially in Europe, yet fuel rationing and shortages of food restricted cat fancy activity in this country as well. The Pacific Cat Club in San Francisco sent a notice to *Cats* magazine in 1945 explaining that the club had been obliged to cancel several shows because of the war. Shortly after December 7, 1941, the only available hall for a cat show had been given over to military housing. As of January 1945 the Pacific club had not sponsored a show for three years, but the club kept on meeting nevertheless.

CFA licensed only ten shows for the year ending January 31, 1943, and the November board meeting that year had to be adjourned for lack of a quorum.

These Siamese were among the first ten of their breed to arrive in England. Mrs. Parker Brough's Tiam O'Shian IV (left) was imported from Bangkok in 1886 by Mrs. Vivian. Below: Mrs. Robinson's Champion Wankee, the first Siamese champion in England, was imported from Hong Kong. He earned his title in 1898 at the age of three.

Matters improved slightly by 1945. There were twenty-four shows scheduled from late August of 1945 through early February 1946. Of those, twenty-one were CFA shows, two were ACA shows, and one was a CFF show.

A person looking for a pedigreed cat today can choose from more than forty breeds. In 1945 that choice was limited to six: Abyssinian, Burmese (then recognized by ACA and CFF only), Manx, Persian, Siamese, and Domestic Shorthair. If the solid-chocolate Siamese shown in England fifty years earlier was actually a Burmese, the number of breeds available had not increased in the meantime. In addition, longhairs still dominated the final awards, prompting one writer to complain that few judges "have the courage to break the precedent of awarding 'Best Cat' to one of the longhaired felines. [As a result] silvers or solid-colored longhairs are most likely to go best in show."

Although the number of cat-registering bodies had remained constant for twenty-six years, Dr. W. A. Young, president of ACA in 1945, worried that three registries would "hold back the progress in the development of purebred cats" by creating "a somewhat confused public." Most cat fanciers disagreed.

Half a dozen new registries have been started since 1945. Only three of these—in addition to the three federations that existed when Dr. Young made his case

Catalogs from American shows

for unification—remain active today. These "newer" associations are: the American Cat Fanciers Association (1954), the Canadian Cat Association (1960), and The International Cat Association (1979).

The clubs that managed to hold shows during the later war years reported good entries. The Greater St. Louis Cat Club welcomed sixty-nine exhibitors and 231 entries on November 18 and 19, 1944. This CFA show was followed by an ACA show at the same location, the Hotel De Soto, on Monday and Tuesday, November 20 and 21, which attracted sixty-seven exhibitors and 173 entries. Three December 1944 shows—Empire in New York City, the Detroit Persian Society in the Motor City, and the Angel City Cat

Within the image (advertisement and article page):

C.F.A.   **FLAGSTONE**   A.C.A.

Creams   Silvers   Blue-eyed Whites

DBL. CH. LAS MONTANAS WALKIE TALKIE

All Southern Chinchilla Male, Best Novice, Angel City,
Cal. 1951-C.F.A.; Best Novice, New Orleans All-Breed
1953-A.C.A.; Best Novice, New Orleans, Longhair 1953-
A.C.A.; Best Cat and Best Champion, New Orleans All-
Breed 1953 - C.F.A.; Best Cat Opp., Best Champion
and Second Best Cat, Magic Valley All-Breed 1953-C.F.A.;
Second Best Cat, New Orleans All-Breed 1953-A C.A.

Flagstone's Wins this Year:

All American's	(2)	Best Champion	(3 times)
All Southern	(4)	Best Champion Opp.	(4 times)
Best Cat	(3 times)	Best Novice	(3 times)
Best Cat Opp.	(5 times)	Best Kitten	(4 times)
Second Best Cat	(3 times)	Second Best Kitten	(3 times)

All breeding stock Champions
and or Double Champions

MRS. HOWELL J. MUELLER
200 Torcido Drive, San Antonio, Texas, U.S.A.

Champion LAVENDER CHU-CHU, the Blue Longhair rated by
Miss Hydon as her "best cat ever."

Fanciers in Los Angeles—attracted entries of 194, 176, and 192 respectively. These numbers compare favorably with the average number of entries per show—179—for all six North American registries combined in 1990.

If the number of entries per show hasn't changed significantly in the last forty-five years, show formats and economics have. It cost $1 to $1.50 to enter a cat in a show then, it costs more than that for *people* to get into a show now—and as much as $55 to show a cat. Midweek shows, which were not uncommon then, are not offered today. What's more, shows in the 1940s consisted of one or two rings instead of the ten- and twelve-ring marathons now in vogue. And instead of selecting the ten best cats, kittens, alters, and household pets in a show, judges chose the best cat, kitten, champion, open, novice, Domestic Shorthair, and Foreign Shorthair. They also selected the best opposite sex cat in each of these categories, the best neuter, the

Cat association yearbooks are an important historical record of the comings and goings and goings on in the cat fancy

best spay, and, occasionally, the best cats in individual breeds such as Siamese or Manx.

THE EISENHOWER YEARS

Though the 1950s are considered a quiet interlude in American life, there was much unrest in the cat fancy then. A major disagreement erupted in 1954 over the question of representation. CFA was, and still is, run by a republican form of government. Each club sends one delegate to the annual meeting, and that delegate votes for the entire club. There are no individual votes or memberships in CFA. This arrangement did not suit many CFA members, who left the organization to form the American Cat Fanciers Association in 1954.

THE FREEWHEELING SIXTIES

A step in the direction of decorum was taken in 1961 when the CFA board of directors voted to prohibit stud service in the show hall and to make owners liable for the actions of their cats. Steps to unify the cat fancy were not as successful. At the annual meeting held in March 1966 in Columbus, Ohio, CFA's solicitor Robert Winn observed that "eight associations represents a situation which is intolerable." Indeed, there were scarcely more recognized breeds than there were associations in 1966. The breeds included the Abyssinian, American Shorthair, Burmese, Manx, Persian, Russian Blue, Siamese, Himalayan, Colorpoint Shorthair, Rex, and Havana Brown.

The most famous line of cats at the time on a national level was that of Grand Champion Silva-Wyte Trafari of JB. This black Persian female owned by John Bannon was CFA's top cat nationally in 1967 and *Cats* magazine's second-best and best-opposite-sex cat of the year. She was a daughter of Grand Champion Vel Vene Voo Doo of Silva-Wyte, the 1959 Cat of the Year.

His sire was Grand Champion Lavender Liberty Beau, the 1950 Cat of the Year. Trafari on her mother's side had the 1951 Cat of the Year, Grand Champion Pied Piper of Barbe Bleue. This was a line of tradition directly linked to the first notable cats of record.

Probably the greatest show cat of all time was the three-time cat of the year Grand Champion Shawnee Moonflight. He was a superb, copper-eyed white male that would bring tears to the eyes of those who judged him. His show career is unlikely to be surpassed.

The author amidst several generations of superb cats, among them three black Persians—1959 Cat of the Year Grand Champion Vel-Vene Voo Doo of Silva-Wyte, 1967 Cat of the Year Grand Champion Silva-Wyte Trafari of JB, and Grand Champion Silva-Wyte Elmer Fudd. Also represented are Grand Champion Silva-Wyte Pola, a white Manx. This portrait [24" x 36"] by Time *magazine cover artist, Roy Andersen, was presented to the author by the Cat Fanciers' Association in commemoration of thirty years of service.*

Grand Champion Silva-Wyte Trafari of JB

THE SEVENTIES AND BEYOND

In 1972 CFA was still seeking to unify the cat fancy into one central registry going as far as posting an announcement in *Cats* magazine, advertising a meeting to which representatives from all associations were invited. Unfortunately, no representatives of the other associations attended this meeting.

The idea of the establishment of a central registry was to provide better protection to cats and catteries. A cattery name is registered to insure that the same name is not used by another cattery, but that protection is available only if a cattery name is registered in all associations and that cattery is the first to register the name. One central registry would also prove to be more economical for breeders especially breeders trying to establish a new breed. Currently a cat must be registered in each association in which that particular cat is to be exhibited.

In 1979 The International Cat Association (TICA) was founded in Branson, Missouri. The immediate cause was an ACFA board of directors meeting at which disputes over show rules and other procedures

appeared beyond resolution. Consequently, ACFA's president, vice-president, and four of its regional directors resigned. Five weeks after this group had formed TICA, the new federation sponsored its first show. Within two years it was licensing more shows annually than anybody except CFA. This growth was made possible partially by the wholesale resignation of judges from ACFA: eighteen allbreed, seventeen specialty, and eleven trainees.

According to one of TICA's founders, so many ACFA members had resigned because they "wanted to eliminate bias in the judging format by removing cats' titles from the judges' books and [by adopting] more liberal registration rules." These and other innovations have made TICA a force to be reckoned with in the cat world.

The cat population in the United States grew by more than one third during the last decade, according to the Pet Food Institute, and sometime in 1985 cats overtook dogs as the most plentiful companion animals in the land. The increase in the number of cat shows has reflected this growth. In 1990 the six North American registries sponsored 824 shows that attracted 147,884 total entries.

NUMBER OF SHOWS*			
	1989-90	**1988-89**	**1987-88**
ACA	15	12	10
ACFA	144@	152	133
CCA	21	19	17
CFA	363+	335	317
CFF	38	49	48
TICA	243^	218	202
UCF			13x
TOTAL	824	785	740

* These figures are somewhat misleading because CFA and ACA count a show held on two consecutive days at the same location as one show, while ACFA, CCA, CFF, and TICA count each day of a weekend as a separate show, and, therefore, count each cat present on both days as two entries.
@ Includes 5 shows in Japan.
+ Includes 22 shows in Japan, 6 in Hawaii, and 13 in Europe.
^ Includes 1 show in France, 4 in Argentina, 1 in Brazil, and 5 in Japan.
x UCF, a small California association, has been inactive since 1988.

Design and Function of the Cat

ALL SYSTEMS GO

The cat is a remarkable collection of systems: nervous, endocrine, respiratory, lymphatic, digestive, reproductive, urinary, circulatory, and musculoskeletal.

The nervous system comprises the cerebrum, cerebellum, midbrain, spinal cord, twelve pair of cranial nerves, and paired sets of peripheral nerves that extend from the spinal cord to all parts of the body. Some functions governed by the agents of the nervous system are learning, reasoning, memory, judgment, and involuntary action—which are controlled by the cerebrum. Blood pressure, respiratory and heart rates are monitored by the midbrain.

The endocrine system comprises the glands that secrete hormones into the bloodstream. The master gland is the pituitary, at the base of the brain. Like a batch file in a computer, the pituitary gland controls the activities of other glands—including the thyroid and adrenal glands, the testicles and ovaries—which in turn control activities of the body. The pituitary gland also produces growth-stimulating hormone.

The respiratory system includes the nose, throat, larynx (voice box), trachea (windpipe), bronchial tubes, and lungs. A cat at rest completes twenty-five to thirty breaths a minute, about twice as many as a human does. In the cat, inhaling, the initial phase of respiration, takes about half as long as exhaling.

The lymphatic system, one of the main defensive systems of the cat's body, is a network of vessels that transport lymph—which is made up of excess tissue fluids, proteins, and other substances. This system functions without benefit of a pump, and carries out its mission through the venous side of the circulatory system. Lymph nodes, another component of the lymphatic system, filter out foreign particles found skulking throughout the body. Lymph nodes contain lymphocytes, a type of white blood cell, which produce antibodies that neutralize bacterial poisons.

The digestive system includes the mouth, teeth, esophagus, stomach, small and large intestines, liver, pancreas, and rectum. Of all carnivores, cats have the fewest teeth, thirty. Since these were not made for chewing, cats tear their food into small pieces, then swallow them whole.

The kidneys, ureters, bladder, and urethra make up the urinary or excretory system in both sexes. In close partnership is the reproductive system. The testicles and sperm ducts comprise the male reproductive system, while the female's ductwork includes fallopian tubes, uterus, womb, and vagina.

The remaining systems of the cat—circulatory and musculoskeletal—warrant some elaboration; the musculoskeletal system because it is the bedrock of conformation, body type at its most elementary, and the circulatory system because it is the medium through which many of the body's other systems function.

THE MUSCULOSKELETAL SYSTEM
THE MUSCLES

From the first time a kitten paddles toward its mother, it is seeking to command the voluntary muscles. These will soon enable the kitten to scuffle with its littermates for a place in the food line, knead contentedly against its mother's belly, crawl, wobble, stand, totter, fall, right itself, look about uncertainly, and then walk.

Voluntary muscles are sometimes called striped or striated muscles because they exhibit longitudinal stripes. They are also called skeletal muscles because their chief function is moving the cat's skeleton from place to place. Secured by tendons to bones, skeletal muscles are always arranged in pairs—antagonists and protagonists that work in cooperative opposition.

When a cat jumps, for example, it crouches on its heels by contracting two muscles: the hamstring, a flexor muscle located behind the thigh bone; and the tibialis, a flexor muscle in front of the tibia and fibula bones. At that point the corresponding extensor

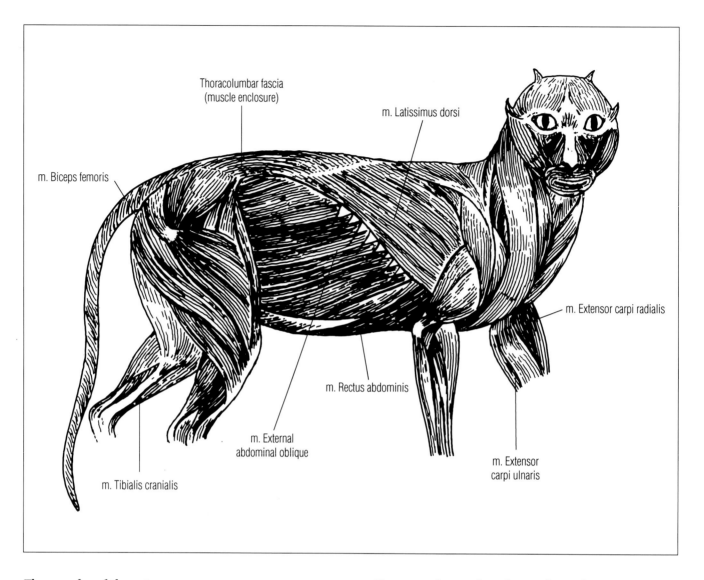

Thoracolumbar fascia
(muscle enclosure)

m. Latissimus dorsi

m. Biceps femoris

m. Extensor carpi radialis

m. Rectus abdominis

m. Extensor
carpi ulnaris

m. External
abdominal oblique

m. Tibialis cranialis

The muscles of the cat

muscles that were stretched while the hamstring and tibialis were contracting, contract powerfully themselves, hurling the cat temporarily beyond gravity's bounds.

Involuntary muscles, which are not consciously controlled by a cat, are already functioning when a kitten begins to crawl. Also known as smooth muscles, the involuntary muscles are found in the alimentary canal, the urinary tract, and the respiratory system.

THE SKELETON

There are 244 bones in the feline skeleton. Together with cartilage they comprise the skeletal system of the cat, and are officially classified as connective tissues that bear weight.

Bone can be cataloged into three classes according to shape: long, flat, and irregular. The radius and ulna in the front legs, as well as the tibia and fibula in the hind legs, are long bones. The scapula or shoulder blade is a flat bone. So are the bones of the skull and face. The metatarsals and metacarpals in the feet are irregular bones.

In addition to occurring in three shapes, bone is formed in three varieties of ossification: intramembranous, endochondral, and heterotopic. The latter, which occurs after birth and under pathologic (disease) conditions, is the formation of bone where bone isn't normally formed. Heterotopic ossification can result in harmless pieces of bone in scars or wounds, or it can result in harmful pieces of bone appearing in vital organs.

Endochondral ossification is the formation of new

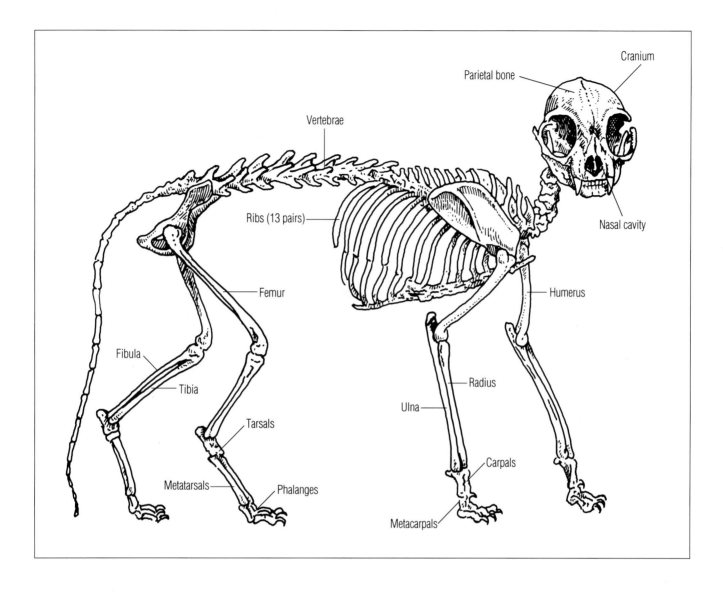

The cat skeleton

bone in an area of existing bone occupied by cartilage. In endochondral ossification, cartilage is removed and replaced by bone. The third type of bone formation, intramembranous ossification, is the development of bone under or within a connective-tissue membrane.

The flat bones in the skull are formed through intramembranous ossification. The bones at the base of the skull and in the face and trunk are formed through a combination of intramembranous and endochondral processes. Bone mass—that is, the compact bone of the shafts of the long and flat bones— is formed intramembranously, while bones grow in length endochondrally.

This means that body conformation in the cat is determined by the relative prominence of each type of bone growth. Some breeds, in which endochondral ossification is paramount, are long, lithe, and fine boned. Other breeds in which intramembranous ossification is prominent are more tanklike and substantial.

THE CIRCULATORY SYSTEM

The circulatory system comprises the heart, a network of arteries and veins, and a blood reservoir, the spleen. The cat's heart beats 110 to 140 times a minute, as much as twice the human heart rate. The circulatory system contains half a pint of blood that passes around the body once every eleven seconds. The blood loops first from the heart to the lungs, changing color from leaden blue to dazzling crimson. The iron atoms in

The cat's narrow chest and well-developed hindquarters confer agility and power

hemoglobin molecules of the red blood cells discharge carbon dioxide and latch on to oxygen molecules, freshly inhaled, like riders hooking the rings on a carousel.

That pulmonary circuit completed, blood gathers itself for its journey around the body. The pulsing of the heart sends blood into the aorta and from there into smaller arteries that subdivide in the body's nooks and fissures. The pace diminishes as blood enters smaller passages—called arterioles—that regulate its flow to the body's tissues.

Metarterioles are the conduits between arterioles and capillaries. By the time blood travels through metarterioles and into capillaries, whose walls are but one cell thick, it has been slowed from a torrent to a trickle. Changing courses and complexion in midstream, the blood is now purplish red after exchanging oxygen for carbon dioxide with cells adjacent to the capillary bed. The blood exits the capillaries through venules (tiny veins), which go to veins leading back to the heart, where the eleven-second journey commences again.

There are many workers in the cat's bloodstream: carrying out the oxygen-carbon dioxide exchange and shuttling back and forth between the brain and various tissues and organs. Elements in the bloodstream create the clots that patch up tears, control osmotic pressure and adjust the cat's thermostat toward cool when he is overheated, toward warm when he is in danger of freezing. Blood also defends the cat against invasion by disease, rushes to the stomach after meals, to the lungs during exertion, and (in humans at least) to the face in times of embarrassment.

The bloodstream is also the chief agent of thermoregulation in the body. Heat generated by bodily functions is unloaded into the blood, which conveys part of that heat to other body sites for redistribution and sends the rest on its way to the outside world. Blood's ability to speed to the surface of the skin in large volumes and at a high rate enables it to transport large quantities of heat outward. Conversely, when a cat is cold, it can create muscular heat by shivering; and that heat is carried by the blood to internal organs that cannot produce their own heat.

RED BLOOD CELLS

Red blood cells are the most numerous cells in the body. They exist in the cat in numbers that defy the mind to attach meaning to zeros. The production of red blood cells—which have a lifespan of two to six weeks—begins when tissue, anticipating a shortage of oxygen, dispatches a hormone called erythropoietin, via the bloodstream, to the bone marrow located in red blood cell construction sites. This hormone signals a number of primitive cells, so named because they have yet to develop fully, to begin growth.

These dormant cells quickly evolve into rubriblasts, the first recognizable harbingers of mature red blood cells. Each rubriblast divides into two. Three divisions later, the original pair of rubriblasts has turned into sixteen red blood cells (RBCs), composed mainly of water and hemoglobin. There are 270 million hemoglobin molecules in every red blood cell. Each hemoglobin molecule contains four atoms of iron. Therefore each molecule of hemoglobin can transport over 1 billion molecules of oxygen. When hemoglobin accounts for 95 percent of the dry weight of a red blood cell—about day three of the six-day RBC production process—the cell ejects its nucleus. This act of self-sterilization frees the cell from all distractions, leaving only the need to work, which the cell does until it works itself to death. The unperforated-doughnut shape of the mature red blood cell allows the cell to squeeze through the tiniest capillaries to deliver oxygen and haul away carbon dioxide.

GIVING CATS A HEAD START

In the cat fancy a headhunter is a judge whose examination of a cat is confined largely to the head. While the points allotted to the rest of the cat should be considered as well, there is no denying that the head sets the standard for the body in a physical sense.

The star pupil in the cat's head is the brain, the valedictorian of the central nervous system. Located in the cranial cavity, the brain is an enlarged, highly modified continuation of the spinal cord. It is divided into two egg-shaped hemispheres whose surfaces are marked by numerous, thick folds. These cerebral hemispheres make up the greater part of the fully developed brain, which is held by the snug-fitting cranial cavity. The posterior wall of this protective compartment (and a portion of its base as well) is formed by the occipital bone, whose lower section is perforated centrally by an almost circular opening. At this point the spinal chord blossoms.

Like wires running to the dashboard of a car, twelve pair of cranial nerves keep the brain informed of developments affecting the sensory and motor systems. Three of these twelve pair of nerves—the optic, olfactory, and auditory—serve as couriers of the special senses: sight, sound, and smell. Five pair of cranial nerves—the oculomotor, abducens, hypoglossal, trochlear, and spinal accessory—serve the motor functions; and the remaining four pair—the trigeminal, facial, glosso-pharyngeal, and vagus—serve both sensory and motor functions.

Gradually, the one-celled organisms that were the earliest forms of life banded together to form colonies. As cell colonies evolved into sponges, tubeworms, crustaceans, mollusks, fishes, and mammals, the head of each organism—besides playing host to the brain—began to partake in more of the body's functions. Thus, air intake, food intake, and excretory capabilities can all be found in the cat's head, which acts, in a sense, as the body in miniature. The head, for example, produces some digestive enzymes in the salivary glands, located on either side of the face and the adjacent parts of the neck. The largest of these glands is the parotid, named for its proximity to the ear.

Among the substances absorbed in the head are essential oils, which contribute much to the flavor of life. You can feel an example of this absorption when you suck on a cough drop and the tingling in your face tells you that your mucosa membrane is taking up the camphor in the drop. In similar manner, metallic salts and other relatively uncomplicated materials, including the rabies virus, are shed in saliva.

Besides directing sensory-motor activities and participating in vital functions of the body, the head, through the pituitary gland—the principal control gland of the body—influences the endocrine system, too. Nearly a dozen functions in the body are controlled by hormones manufactured, released, or stored by the pituitary gland at the base of the brain. These include everything from growth to the onset of estrus to the amount of urine secreted by the kidneys.

The head is the dominant part of the cat: because of its evolutionary history, its custody of the brain, its stewardship of the pituitary gland, and its access to feedback from all precincts of the body via the nervous and circulatory systems. Indeed, the cat's body can be thought of as a member of the servant class, dedicated to the needs of its headstrong master. The muscles of the legs and back, to cite an example, exist to transport the head so that it can obtain food and participate in the other functions essential to life.

The head also claims absolute priority to the body's oxygen and nutrient supplies and to its circulatory capacity. The circulatory system has nervous control mechanisms that deprive the guts, the legs, and the feet of blood to make sure that the cat's head gets an adequate supply. What's more, the brain lives on a diet of simple chemicals. Other cells throughout the body have to work harder for their nutrients—and they have the capacity to do so—but the brain lives well on simple fare.

CONFORMATION

Muscle and bone are the architects of conformation. The 244 bones in the feline skeleton lend support and substance to a cat's body while protecting its internal organs. In some breeds bone is sturdy as an oak; in others it is delicate as scrimshaw. In every breed bone is decorated in wreaths of muscle. By conducting an electrical impulse, and then—through a series of chemical transformations—converting that impulse into contractions, muscle produces movement and, ultimately, the gracefulness that characterizes the cat.

Japanese Bobtail

Devon Rex

Burmese

EARS

A cat's ears are decorative as well as functional. They make statements in addition to receiving them. There's no mistaking the message intended by a cat when its ears are pinned back. The upper limit of a cat's hearing is higher than a dog's and almost two octaves higher than ours. From a distance of three feet, cats can discriminate between sources of sound that are as little as three inches apart. They are also able to ignore the sound of their owners' voices from virtually any distance.

Colorpoint Shorthair

British Shorthair

Cornish Rex

EYES

Round, almond shaped, or in between, the cat's eye is a gem that reflects a mysterious luster. Cats are the most efficient gleaners of light. Their pupils can dilate to a soulful, half-inch width or narrow to the most inscrutable slit. Cats cannot see in absolute darkness, nor are they absolutely color blind, though they can see red only in the emotional sense. They are, in addition, somewhat farsighted. Their depth of field is in sharpest focus between seven and twenty feet.

Turkish Angora

Maine Coon Cat

Siamese

SIZE

Unlike dog breeders, who are able to work with a variety of sizes, cat fanciers are limited in design. The difference between the largest breed of cat, the Ragdoll, and the smallest, the Singapura, is little more than a dozen pounds and less than one square foot at the extreme; while the difference between the longest and the shortest facial profiles is about two inches. Most other breeds fall into the one-size-fits-all category. Yet within these frugal limits, more than forty breeds have been defined.

Exotic Shorthair

Ragdoll

Singapura

COAT LENGTH

There are twenty-seven shorthaired breeds and seventeen longhaired ones. Seven pair of breeds are separated by the gene for coat length: Abyssinian/Somali, Colorpoint Shorthair/Javanese, Exotic Shorthair/Persian, Manx/Cymric, Oriental Shorthair/Oriental Longhair, Scottish Fold/Scottish Fold Longhair, Siamese/Balinese. Coat length also relegates cats into shorthair or longhair specialty rings at shows, except in the Cat Fanciers' Association, where specialty rings are determined by facial type and body conformation.

American Shorthair

Persian

Bombay

COAT TYPE

Hair grows from tiny pits in the skin called follicles. Primary or guard hairs, the longest ones in a cat's coat, grow from individual follicles. Secondary hairs—usually classified as awn hairs (bristly tipped and medium in length) or down hairs (fine, crinkled, and short in length)—grow in groups from single openings. Grooming needs are determined not so much by coat length as by coat type. Breeds with thick undercoats (awn and down hairs) are more likely to mat—and hence require more attention—than breeds with less profuse undercoats.

Abyssinian

Birman

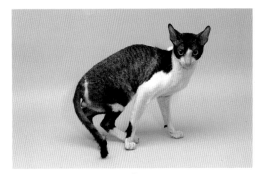

Cornish Rex

TAIL

Cats' tails range from long, thin, and whiplike to short, thick, and plumelike. The Siamese' tail ends somewhere over the rainbow; the Manx' tail stops before it begins. The Japanese Bobtail's tail is curled, corkscrewed, pom-pommed, and shaving brushed. It should not, however, be manipulated by a judge. Otherwise, judges check tails for kinks, proper length, and flexibility. They also check to see if a tail is swishing to and fro, which is not a sign of friendly barometric pressure. Cats don't see what all the fuss is about. They use their tails as balancing poles and to keep their noses warm when they sleep.

Oriental Shorthair

Scottish Fold

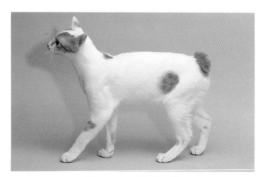

Japanese Bobtail

Introduction to the Breeds

At this writing there are forty-four cat breeds accepted for championship competition by at least one of the six registries in North America. Twenty-five breeds are accepted in every association: Abyssinian, American Shorthair, Balinese, Birman, Bombay, British Shorthair, Burmese, Chartreux, Cornish Rex, Devon Rex, Egyptian Mau, Exotic Shorthair, Havana Brown, Japanese Bobtail, Korat, Maine Coon Cat, Manx, Oriental Shorthair, Persian, Russian Blue, Scottish Fold, Siamese, Singapura, Somali, Tonkinese.

Seven breeds are recognized by at least half the associations: Cymric (5), Ragdoll (5), Turkish Angora (5), Ocicat (5), American Wirehair (3), Norwegian Forest Cat (3), and Scottish Fold Longhair (3).

Another seven breeds are accepted by only one or two associations: American Curl, Bengal, Foreign Burmese, Oriental Longhair, Snowshoe, Sphynx, and Turkish Van.

Three additional breeds are considered as separate entities in some associations, but as divisions of an existing breed by others: Himalayan, Kashmir, and Peke-faced Persian--all of which are considered as Persian divisions in some registries.

Finally, two breeds, the Colorpoint Shorthair and the Javanese, are recognized as separate breeds by some associations, but as colors of the Siamese and Balinese, respectively, by others.

In the following section, the reader will find photographs, breed Standards, and discussions of the origins and development of those thirty-two breeds accepted for championship competition by at least half the registries in North America. In addition, there are brief discussions and photographs of those breeds currently accepted by just one or two associations.

There are no Standards presented for those breeds, however, because of the possibility that their Standards will be altered if the breeds gain further acceptance. Nor are there breed Standards for the Colorpoint Shorthair and the Javanese, which are considered part of the Siamese and Balinese breeds, respectively, in the majority of associations.

Since the Cat Fanciers' Association is the largest registry, most people register their cats with CFA even if they choose to register and to exhibit their cats elsewhere. Therefore, CFA Standards are presented in every case where CFA recognizes a breed. In other cases, we have attempted to present the Standard of the association in the United States that recognized a breed first.[1] In all cases, where the Standards of other registries differ from the one being used to describe a breed, those differences are discussed in footnotes at the end of the Standard. Descriptions of the colors found in those breeds which occur in a handful of colors only are provided with the breed Standards. Several breeds occur in a multitude of colors, however. The colors for those breeds are listed, but not described, at the end of each breed Standard. A discussion of the colors for those breeds begins on page 170. Those breeds in which eye color must conform to coat color are identified—and the correspondences between eye color and coat color in those breeds are identified — on page 173.

---

[1] Since there is a British edition of this book, one breed, the Burmilla, which is recognized in England but not in North America, is discussed with the minority breeds; and the Turkish Van, recognized in only one North American registry so far, is accorded a full discussion and Standard because that breed is better established in the U.K.

Abyssinian

ORIGIN

Like its splendid coat pattern, the Abyssinian's history is composed of alternating theories. One band of believers claims that Abys descended from cats worshipped by the Egyptians more than four thousand years ago. Another group declares that Abys originated in the jungles of North Africa, from which they were brought to England by soldiers returning from the Abyssinian War during the late 1860s. Others argue that the Abys' ancestors were nothing more exotic than ticked tabbies roaming the fields and lanes of Great Britain. But whatever its country of origin, one thing about the Abyssinian is certain: it is obviously a definite and recognizable breed type.

As near as records indicate, the first Abyssinian to

Ruddy Abyssinian

reach England was a cat named Zula, who was imported by Mrs. Barrett-Lennard in 1868. According to one writer, Zula "and possibly other imports were bred with similarly marked cats of partly unknown origin," and thus the Abyssinian breed was born. By 1882 the Abyssinian was listed as a separate breed in England, and silver Abys, which were also known as chinchillas, were among the early Abyssinian colors. By 1900, however, many authorities declared that the Abyssinian was merely the result of chance matings

This Ruddy Abyssinian, bred in Great Britain, is shorter in the head, body, and legs than its American counterpart.

among ordinary tabbies, and the name Abyssinian was replaced for a time by "Ticks" or "British Ticks" or "Bunny Cats." This revisionist opinion was supported by the fact that each of the twelve Abyssinians registered in the Stud Book of the National Cat Club in England for 1900–1905 was descended from at least one parent of unknown origin.

DEVELOPMENT

The first Abys to arrive in the United States were owned by Jane Cathcart of Oradell, New Jersey. It is likely that they were silvers, since their names were Ch. Aluminum and Salt. They were exhibited in Boston in 1909. There is no record of additional imports until the 1930s—when a great many Abys were brought to this country—and the first recorded Aby litter in the United States was not born until 1935. The increased U.S. interest in the Abyssinian was important because World War II had a decided effect on the Abyssinian in Great Britain. Many breeders were forced to discontinue their efforts to preserve the Aby, and the list of stud cats in the 1947–48 Governing Council of the Cat Fancy records included just four Abyssinians, two of which were unproven.

The Abyssinian progressed rapidly in this country after the war. At first Abys were extremely difficult at the shows and did not adjust to being handled by strangers. Their temperament has improved greatly since then, and today the Aby classes are large and full of quality. An Aby standing tall on its toes, holding its head high with a look of superiority is like a living work of art.

Standard for the

ABYSSINIAN

Courtesy of the Cat Fanciers' Association. Differences in the Standards of other registries are indicated at the end of the text.

HEAD: (25)	**COAT:** (10)
Muzzle 6	Texture 10
Skull 6	
Ears 7	**COLOR:** (35)
Eye shape 6	Color 15
	Ticking 15
BODY: (30)	Eye color 5
Torso 15	
Legs and feet 10	
Tail 5	

GENERAL: the overall impression of the ideal Abyssinian would be a colorful cat with a distinctly ticked coat, medium[1] in size and regal in appearance. The Abyssinian is lithe, hard, and muscular, showing eager activity and a lively interest in all surroundings. Well balanced temperamentally and physically with all elements of the cat in proportion.

HEAD: a modified, slightly rounded wedge without flat planes; the brow, cheek, and profile lines all showing a gentle contour. A slight rise from the bridge of the nose to the forehead, which should be of good size, with width between the ears and flowing into the arched neck without a break.

MUZZLE: not sharply pointed or square. The chin should be neither receding nor protruding. Allowance should be made for jowls in adult males.

EARS: alert, large, and moderately pointed; broad, and cupped at base and set as though listening. Hair on ears very short and close lying, preferably tipped with black or dark brown on a ruddy Abyssinian, chocolate brown on a red Abyssinian, or slate blue on the blue Abyssinian.[2]

EYES: almond shaped, large, brilliant, and expressive. Neither round or oriental. Eyes accentuated by fine dark line, encircled by light–colored area.

BODY: medium long,[3,4] lithe, and graceful, but showing well-developed muscular strength without coarseness.[5] Abyssinian conformation strikes a medium between the extremes of the cobby and the svelte lengthy type. Proportion and general balance more to be desired than mere size.

LEGS and FEET: proportionately slim, fine boned. The Abyssinian stands well off the ground giving the impression of being on tiptoe. Paws small, oval, and compact. Toes five in front and four behind.

TAIL: thick at base, fairly long and tapering.

COAT: soft, silky, fine in texture, but dense and resilient to the touch[6] with a lustrous sheen. Medium in length but long enough to accommodate two or three dark bands of ticking.

PENALIZE: off-color pads. Long, narrow head; short, round head. Barring on legs; dark, broken necklace markings; rings on the tail. Coldness or gray tones in the coat.

DISQUALIFY: white locket, or white anywhere other than nostril, chin, and upper throat area. Kinked or abnormal tail. Dark, unbroken necklace. Gray undercoat close to the skin extending throughout a major portion of the body. Any black hair on red Abyssinian. Incorrect number of toes.

ABYSSINIAN COLORS

COAT COLOR: warm and glowing. Ticking: distinct and even, with dark–colored bands contrasting with lighter-colored bands on the hair shafts. Undercoat color clear and bright to the skin. Deeper color shades desired, however intensity of ticking not to be sacrificed for depth of color. Darker shading along spine allowed if fully ticked. Preference given to cats unmarked on the undersides, chest, and legs; tail without rings. Facial markings: dark lines extending from eyes and brows, cheekbone shading, dots, and shading on whisker pads are all desirable enhancements. Eyes accentuated by fine dark line, encircled by light–colored area. Eye color: gold or green, the more richness and depth of color the better.[7]

BLUE: coat warm beige, ticked with various shades of slate blue, the extreme outer tip to be the darkest, with blush beige undercoat. Tail tipped with slate blue. The underside and inside of legs to be a tint to harmonize with the main color. Nose leather: old rose. Paw pads: mauve, with slate blue between toes, extending slightly beyond the paws.

FAWN:[8] coat warm rose beige, ticked with light cocoa brown, the extreme outer tip to be the darkest, with blush-beige undercoat. Tail tipped with light cocoa brown. The underside and inside of legs to be a tint to harmonize with the main color. Nose leather: salmon. Paw pads: dark pink with light cocoa brown between the toes, extending slightly beyond the paws.

RED:[9] coat rich, warm, glowing red, ticked with chocolate brown, the extreme outer tip to be dark, with red undercoat. Tail tipped with chocolate brown. The underside and inside of legs to be a tint to harmonize with the main color. Nose leather: rosy pink. Paw pads: pink, with chocolate brown between toes, extending slightly beyond the paw pads.

RUDDY: coat ruddy brown (burnt sienna), ticked with various shades of darker brown or black; the extreme outer tip to be the darkest, with orange-brown undercoat. Tail tipped with black. The underside and inside of legs to be a tint to harmonize with the main color. Nose leather: tile red. Paw pads: black or brown, with black between toes, extending slightly beyond the paws.

LILAC:[10] a pale ivory, distinctly ticked with frosty gray. The extreme outer tip is to be the darkest, with a pale ivory undercolor. The undersides and forelegs (insides) to be unmarked pale ivory to harmonize with the undercolor. Ears and tail to be tipped with frosty gray. Paw pads—lilac pink, with dusky lilac between the toes and extending up the back of the hind legs, preferably to the hocks. Nose leather-mauve or pink.

CREAM:[11] a pale cream, distinctly ticked with a darker cream. The extreme outer tip to be the darkest, with a pale cream undercolor. The undersides and forelegs (insides) to be unmarked pale cream to harmonize with the undercolor. Ears and tail to be tipped with darker cream. Paw pads—pink, with dark cream between the toes and extending up the back of the hind legs, preferably to the hocks.

Abyssinian allowable outcross breeds:[12] none.

---

[1] ACA, ACFA: "Medium to large."
[2] TICA: "A thumb-print marking is desirable on the back of the ear."
[3] ACFA: "Medium."
[4] ACA: "Rather long."
[5] ACFA: "The back is slightly arched, giving the appearance of a cat about to spring."
[6] ACFA: "When thumbed backward, it should snap back into place."
[7] ACA, ACFA, CFF: "Gold, green, or hazel."
[8] ACFA does not recognize this color.
[9] TICA calls this color "sorrel (cinnamon)."
[10] ACA is the only association to recognize this color.
[11] ACA is the only association to recognize this color.
[12] In all associations where the breed is recognized.

American Shorthair

ORIGIN

Shorthaired cats arrived in North America with the early settlers. In fact, some historians believe there was at least one cat aboard the Mayflower when it landed in 1620. As they had for centuries before whenever they made their way from one land to another, cats earned their passage aboard ship by protecting stores of food and grain from rats and mice. After arriving in the New World, cats were expected to continue paying their own way and making their own breeding arrangements.

By 1900, domestic cats had begun to attract some notice from cat fanciers, but that attraction was minimal. Until then the Maine Coon Cat was the favorite son (and daughter) of cat fanciers in this country, and after the turn of the century most fanciers became interested in the more unusual and exotic foreign breeds. Not surprisingly, the first shorthaired "domestic" cat registered in the United States was from Great Britain: an orange tabby male with an unusual name, Champion Belle of Bradford, who had been imported around 1901. Belle was registered in a breed that was simply called "Shorthair." Sometime later, after American-born cats had been incorporated into breeding programs in this country, "Domestic" was added to the breed's designation.

Brown Classic Tabby American Shorthair

DEVELOPMENT

For many years there were few requirements that had to be met for registering Domestic Shorthairs. Most were of unknown origin, and they were frequently entered in household pet classes, which had been created for all cats that did not appear to be purebred or to have registered parents. When Domestics did compete in championship classes, they were not always treated kindly. Cat Fanciers' Association judge Kay McQuillen, who began showing cats in 1938, has written that there were often no cages provided for Domestic Shorthairs at shows and no trophies or rosettes for the winners in Domestic classes.

Once breeders began to realize the unusual colors and patterns they could develop by selectively breeding Domestic Shorthairs, they began to demand more respect for their breed. They voted to change the breed's name to American Shorthair beginning with the 1966 show season. What gained the breed even more respect, however, was the success of two silver tabbies. In 1964 a silver tabby male named Shawnee Sixth Son was CFA's Kitten of the Year, and in 1965 a silver tabby male named Shawnee Trademark was CFA's Best Cat. These were the first of their breed to achieve such status.

Over the years, the open registration of American Shorthairs has been an on-again-off-again practice. Open registration means that a person can register any shorthaired cat as an American Shorthair. Some breeders used this opportunity to introduce new colors

Silver Classic Tabby American Shorthair

to the American breed or new vigor to its gene pool by breeding street cats or farm cats to their registered Americans. Other breeders took advantage of the rule to introduce new breeds as outcrosses—mainly Persians, and the occasional Burmese. There is no question that a little Persian blood enhances the American Shorthair, producing a more stylized, rounded head and adding substance to bone and body. The silver tabby Americans competing today would not exist if it were not for outcrosses that have been made to chinchilla Persians under the generous terms of open registration. Indeed, the silver tabby is the most highly regarded American Shorthair and has enjoyed great popularity for many years.

American Shorthairs have made valuable contributions to other breeds as well. They were crossed with Siamese to lend new colors to the Colorpoint Shorthair. They were crossed clandestinely with Burmese to improve Burmese type and vigor. And thus the Bombay was born. Covert crosses between Americans and Persians produced the Exotic Shorthair. Americans also played a part in the foundation crosses that produced the Ocicat, Snowshoe, and Scottish Fold. And they were used to reintroduce calicos and bicolors to the Persian breed. What's more, American Shorthairs are still allowable outcrosses for the American Wirehair, Bombay, Devon Rex (until May 1, 1993), and Scottish Fold. Their endless supply and adaptability has benefitted many breeds in need of new blood, variety, strength, or vigor.

Standard for the
AMERICAN SHORTHAIR

Courtesy of the Cat Fanciers' Association. Differences in the Standards of other registries are indicated at the end of the text.

HEAD: 30
(includes eye shape and size; ear shape and set; nose structure)

TYPE: 25
(includes shape, size, bone, and length of tail)

COAT: 15

COLOR: 20
(tabby pattern = 10 points; color = 10 points)

EYE COLOR: 10

GENERAL: the American Shorthair is a true breed of working cat. The conformation should be adapted for this with no part of the anatomy so exaggerated as to foster weakness. The general effect should be that of a strongly built, well-balanced, symmetrical cat with conformation indicating power, endurance, and agility.
SIZE: medium to large. No sacrifice of quality for sake of size. Females may be less massive in all respects than males.
PROPORTIONS: slightly longer than tall. (Height is profile measure from top of shoulder blades to ground. Length is profile measure from tip of breastbone to rear tip of buttocks.) Viewed from side, body can be divided into three equal parts: from tip of breastbone to elbow, from elbow to front of hind leg, and from front of hind leg to rear tip of buttocks. Length of tail is equal to distance from shoulder blades to base of tail.
HEAD: large, with full-cheeked face giving the impression of an oblong just slightly longer than wide.[1] Sweet, open expression. Viewed from front, head can be divided in two equal parts: from base of ears to middle of eyes, and from middle of eyes to chin tip.
EARS: medium size, slightly rounded at tips and not unduly open at base. Distance between ears, measured from lower inner corners, twice distance between eyes.
FOREHEAD: viewed in profile, forehead forms smooth, moderately convex, continuous curve flowing over top of head into neck. Viewed from front, there is no dome between ears.
EYES: large[2] and wide with upper lid shaped like half an almond (cut lengthwise) and lower lid shaped in a fully rounded curve.[3,4] At least width of one eye between eyes. Outer corners set very slightly higher than inner corners. Bright, clear, and alert.[5]
NOSE: medium length,[6] same width for entire length. Viewed in profile, gentle concavely curved rise from bridge of nose to forehead.
MUZZLE: squared. Definite jowls in mature males.
JAWS: strong and long enough to grasp prey

successfully. Both level and scissors bites considered equally correct. (In level bite, top and bottom front teeth meet evenly. In scissors bite, inside edge of top front teeth touch outside edge of lower front teeth.)

CHIN: firm and well developed, forming perpendicular line with upper lip.

NECK: medium in length, muscular and strong.

BODY: solidly built, powerful, and muscular with well-developed shoulders, chest, and hindquarters. Back broad, straight, and level. Viewed in profile, slight slope down from hip bone to base of tail. Viewed from above, outer lines of body parallel.

LEGS: medium in length and bone, heavily muscled. Viewed from rear, all four legs straight and parallel with paws facing forward.

PAWS: firm, full, and rounded, with heavy pads. Toes: five in front, four behind.

TAIL: medium long, heavy at base, tapering to abrupt blunt end in appearance but with normal tapering final vertebrae.

COAT: short,[7] thick, even, and hard in texture. Regional and seasonal variation in coat thickness allowed.[8] Coat dense enough to protect from moisture, cold, and superficial skin injuries.

PENALIZE: excessive cobbiness or ranginess. Very short tail.

DISQUALIFY: any appearance of hybridization with any other breed—including long or fluffy fur, deep nose break, bulging eye set, brow ridge. Kinked or abnormal tail. Locket or button (white spots on colors not specifying same). Incorrect number of toes.

Undershot or overshot bite. Obesity or emaciation. Any feature so exaggerated as to foster weakness.

AMERICAN SHORTHAIR COLORS
(See page 170 for a full description of the colors listed below.)

Particolor colors: bicolor (white with unbrindled patches of black, white with unbrindled patches of blue, white with unbrindled patches of red, or white with unbrindled patches of cream), blue cream, calico, dilute calico, van bicolor (black and white, red and white, blue and white, or cream and white), van blue cream and white, van calico. **Shaded colors:** chinchilla silver, shaded cameo, shaded silver, shell cameo. **Smoke colors:** black smoke, blue smoke, cameo smoke, tortoiseshell smoke. **Solid colors:** black, blue, cream, red, white. **Tabby colors:** blue patched tabby, blue tabby (classic, mackerel), brown patched tabby, brown tabby (classic, mackerel), cameo tabby (classic, mackerel), cream tabby (classic, mackerel), red tabby (classic, mackerel), silver patched tabby, silver tabby (classic, mackerel).

American Shorthair allowable outcross breeds:[9] none.

---

[1] TICA: "Broad, rounded."
[2] TICA: "Medium to large."
[3] ACFA, CFF: "Eyes should be round." TICA: "Rounded."
[4] ACA: "Oval."
[5] ACFA, CFF, TICA: "[Eye] color must conform to requirements listed in coat-color descriptions."
[6] ACA, ACFA, TICA: "Medium short."
[7] CFF: "Medium length."
[8] CFF: "Allowance to be made for lack of luster in blues."
[9] In all associations where the breed is recognized.

American Wirehair

The American Wirehair grew out of a spontaneous mutation. The first wirehaired kitten appeared in a litter of barn cats that was born on March 5, 1966, in Verona, New York. Five of the kittens in that litter had ordinary coats. The sixth one, a red-and-white male, had sparse, wiry hair. When Joan O'Shea, a cat breeder living near Verona, heard about this kitten—whose every hair was crimped, coiled, and springy, even its whiskers—she went to visit the farmer who owned it. The farmer was not inclined to part with the kitten, but after its littermates had been killed by a weasel, he agreed to sell the red-and-white boy for fifty dollars to O'Shea, who named the kitten Adam.

One day when Adam was fourteen months old, O'Shea noticed a calico cat wandering in her yard. The cat, who belonged to the neighbors' daughter, appeared to be in season. O'Shea "invited the cat in" to meet Adam. This meeting produced four kittens, much to the neighbors' surprise. O'Shea offered to buy the kittens—two of which were red-and-white, wirehaired females. The others had normal coats.

By the time Adam became a father, O'Shea had mailed samples of his coat to the British geneticists Roy Robinson and A.G. Searle. Robinson replied that Adam's coat was unique, and that it was not related to either of the Rex mutations. All three types of Adam's hairs—down, awn, and guard—were twisted. In addition, the awn hairs were hooked at the tip. Though the Devon Rex possesses all three types of hairs, they are so foreshortened that they resemble down hairs (the shortest kind), while the Cornish Rex lacks guard hairs entirely (the longest type). Eventually, great variance developed among Wirehair coats. Some are sparse; some are close lying and tight; others are thick and springy—the most desirable kind. These variations occur because Wirehairs are crossed with American Shorthairs, many of which carry a recessive longhair gene that can influence coat texture.

Adam sired only three litters before dying of cystitis in 1970. Shortly after that Joan O'Shea stopped working with American Wirehairs. Fortunately, other breeders had taken up the cause. Mr. and Mrs. William Beck, who had worked with O'Shea in breeding Rex, had one of Adam's daughters. William Beck, a Cat Fanciers' Association judge, helped to secure registration status for Wirehairs. Rosemonde S. Peltz, M.D., at one time a CFA board member and a genetics consultant to the association, also became involved with the breed. The most active Wirehair advocate was CFA judge Bob Bradshaw. Most of today's breed stock descends from his Fesenbrad line.

CFA accepted Wirehairs for registration in September 1967, and the breed advanced to championship status on May 1, 1978. Although this breed is as truly American as the American Shorthair, from which the coat mutation sprang, American Wirehairs are registered as a separate breed. It would make more sense to consider the breed a variety of the American Shorthair, especially since the Shorthair is an allowable outcross breed for the Wirehair. This classification would allow straight-coated Wirehairs to be shown as American Shorthairs.

The Wirehair mutation is the work of a dominant gene. If a kitten inherits one gene for a wirehaired coat and another gene for a normal coat, the kitten will be a Wirehair. Breeding one Wire to another may produce a litter of all Wires, or some Wires and some straight-coated kittens, or all straight coats. The latter will only produce a Wire if they are bred to a Wire. One of the most disheartening experiences a Wirehair breeder must contend with is the surplus of straight-coated kittens. They are beautiful, normal kittens, and persons interested in breeding Wirehairs must be prepared to find good homes for them. Experienced breeders should inform prospective Wirehair fanciers about this responsibility.

RIGHT: Calico American Wirehair

BELOW: Calico American Wirehair (left) and Red-and-White American Wirehair (right)

Standard for the
AMERICAN WIREHAIR

Courtesy of the Cat Fanciers' Association. Differences in the Standards of other registries are indicated at the end of the text.

HEAD: 25
(including size and shape of eyes, ear shape and set)

TYPE: 20
(including shape, size, bone, and length of tail)

COAT: 45

COLOR and EYE COLOR: 10

GENERAL: the American Wirehair is a spontaneous mutation. The coat, which is not only springy, dense, and resilient, but also coarse and hard to the touch, distinguishes the American Wirehair from all other breeds. Characteristic is activity, agility, and keen interest in its surroundings.

HEAD: in proportion to the body. Underlying bone structure is round with prominent cheekbones and well-developed muzzle and chin. There is a slight whisker break.

NOSE: in profile the nose shows a gentle, concave curve.[1]

MUZZLE: well developed. Allowance for jowls in adult males.

CHIN: firm and well developed[2] with no apparent malocclusion.

EARS: medium, slightly rounded at tips, set wide and not unduly open at the base.

EYES: large,[3] round, bright, and clear. Set well apart.[4] Aperture has slight upward tilt.

BODY: medium to large.[5] Back level, shoulders and hips same width, torso well rounded and in proportion. Males larger than females.

LEGS: medium in length and bone, well muscled and proportionate to body.

PAWS: oval and compact. Toes, five in front and four behind.

TAIL: in proportion to body, tapering from the well-rounded rump to a rounded tip, neither blunt nor pointed.

COAT: springy, tight, medium in length.[6] Individual hairs are crimped, hooked, or bent, including hair within the ears. The overall appearance of wiring and the coarseness and resilience of the coat are more important than the crimping of each hair. The density of the wired coat leads to ringlet formation rather than waves. That coat which is very dense, resilient, crimped, and coarse is most desirable, as are curly whiskers.

PENALIZE: deep nose break. Long or fluffy fur.

DISQUALIFY: incorrect coat. Kinked or abnormal tail. Incorrect number of toes. Evidence of hybridization resulting in the colors chocolate, lavender, the Himalayan pattern, or these combinations with white.

AMERICAN WIREHAIR COLORS
(See page 170 for a full description of the colors listed below.)

Particolors: bicolors (black and white, blue and white, red and white, cream and white), blue cream, calico, dilute calico, tortoiseshell. **Shadeds:** chinchilla silver, shaded cameo, shaded silver, shell cameo. **Smokes:** black smoke, blue smoke, cameo smoke. **Solids:** black, blue, cream, red, white. **Tabbies:** (classic and mackerel patterns): blue tabby, brown tabby, cameo tabby, cream tabby, red tabby, silver tabby. **Other Wirehair colors:** any other color or pattern with the exception of those showing evidence of hybridization resulting in the colors chocolate, lavender, the Himalayan pattern, or these combinations with white.

American Wirehair allowable outcross breeds:[7] American Shorthair.

[1] TICA: "The nose and face are medium short."
[2] TICA: Chin is "moderately developed."
[3] TICA: "Medium to large."
[4] TICA: Set "moderately apart."
[5] TICA: "Medium size" body.
[6] TICA: "Short to medium short in length."
[7] In all associations where the breed is recognized.

Balinese

ORIGIN

During the 1930s and 1940s there had been many attempts to produce a longhaired, pointed cat. Among the byproducts of these experiments were shorthaired, pointed cats. Most of these were placed in pet homes, but some were registered as Siamese. All associations permitted the registration of cats of unknown origin.

Thus, a number of Siamese-Persian hybrids that carried a recessive gene for long hair made their way into Siamese breeding programs. Whenever two of these longhair carriers were bred, the chances of getting semilong haired Siamese kittens were one out of four on the average, and this happened frequently.

Blue Point Balinese

DEVELOPMENT

Most Siamese breeders treated semilonghaired kittens as if they didn't exist. "They were discarded or quietly given away as undesirables," one breeder reported. One hesitates to imagine what this person meant by "discarded," but a few breeders thought their semilonghaired kittens were desirable enough to make a breed out of them.

Perhaps these breeders were unfamiliar with basic genetics. Perhaps they were unable to admit that their longhaired Siamese were hybrids. Perhaps they feared the frenzy of Siamese breeders, who were even less able to admit that *their* breed was not entirely pure. But for whatever reasons, many Balinese breeders have always insisted—as the current Cat Fanciers' Association breed brochure declares—that the semilong coats on their cats are the result of a natural mutation.

The animosity of the Siamese breeders and the unromantic sound of *Longhaired Siamese* led Helen Smith of Merry Mews cattery, an early champion of the breed, to propose the name Balinese instead. Smith maintained that the graceful way her cats moved reminded her of the dancers on the island of Bali. Such a leap of the imagination may have been possible when the breed was first developed, but the use of Siamese outcrosses in Balinese breeding programs has shortened the Balinese coat considerably since the breed was first accepted for championship competition by the Cat Fanciers' Federation in 1963. There isn't much to distinguish a Balinese from a Siamese today except a wispy fringe on the underbelly and a meek plume of a tail. In fact, Balinese coats are so short—and the breed is so far removed from the original man-made source of its semilong hair—that it would seem logical for Balies to become a variety of Siamese instead of remaining a separate entity.

Standard for the
BALINESE

Courtesy of the Cat Fanciers' Association. Differences in the Standards of other registries are indicated at the end of the text.

HEAD: (20)
Long, flat profile 6
Wedge, fine muzzle,
   size 5
Ears 4
Chin 3
Width between eyes 2

EYES: (5)
Shape, size, slant, and
   placement 5

BODY: (30)
Structure and size,
   including neck 12

Muscle tone 10
Legs and Feet 5
Tail 3

COAT: (20)
Length 10
Texture 10

COLOR: (25)
Body color 10
Point color 10
Eye color 5

GENERAL: the ideal Balinese is a svelte cat with long, tapering lines, very lithe but strong and muscular. Excellent physical condition. Neither flabby nor bony. Not fat. Eyes clear. Because of the longer fur the Balinese appears to have softer lines and less extreme type than other breeds of cats with similar type.

HEAD: long, tapering wedge. Medium size in good proportion to body. The total wedge starts at the nose and flares out in straight lines to the tips of the ears forming a triangle, with no break at the whiskers. No less than the width of an eye between the eyes. When the whiskers and face hair are smoothed back, the underlying bone structure is apparent. Allowance must be made for jowls in the stud cat.

SKULL: flat. In profile, a long straight line is seen from the top of the head to the tip of the nose. No bulge over the eyes. No dip in nose.

NOSE: long and straight. A continuation of the forehead with no break.

MUZZLE: fine, wedge shaped.

CHIN and JAW: medium size. Tip of chin lines up with tip of nose in the same vertical plane. Neither receding nor excessively massive.

EARS: strikingly large, pointed, wide at base, continuing the lines of the wedge.[1]

EYES: almond shaped. Medium size. Neither protruding nor recessed. Slanted towards the nose in harmony with lines of wedge and ears. Uncrossed.[2]

BODY: medium size. Dainty, long, and svelte. A

distinctive combination of fine bones and firm muscles. Shoulders and hips continue same sleek lines of tubular body. Hips never wider than shoulders. Abdomen tight.[3] The male may be somewhat larger than the female.[4]

NECK: long and slender.

LEGS: long and slim. Hind legs higher than front. In good proportion to body.

PAWS: dainty, small, and oval. Toes: five in front and four behind.

TAIL: bone structure long, thin, tapering to a fine point. Tail hair spreads out like a plume.

COAT: long, fine, silky without downy undercoat.[5,6,7]

COLOR: body: even, with subtle shading when allowed. Allowance should be made for darker color in older cats as Balinese generally darken with age, but there must be definite contrast between body color and points. Points: mask, ears, legs, feet, and tail are dense and clearly defined. All of the same shade. Mask covers entire face including whisker pads and is connected to ears by tracings. Mask should not extend over top of head. No ticking or white hairs in points.

PENALIZE: lack of pigment in the nose leather and/ or paw pads in part or in total. Crossed eyes.

DISQUALIFY: any evidence of illness or poor health. Weak hind legs. Mouth breathing due to nasal obstruction or poor occlusion. Emaciation. Kink in tail. Eyes other than blue. White toes and/or feet. Incorrect number of toes. Definite double coat (i.e., downy undercoat).

BALINESE COLORS

BLUE POINT: body bluish white, cold in tone, shading gradually to white on stomach and chest. Points deep blue. Nose leather and paw pads: slate colored. Eye color: deep, vivid blue.

CHOCOLATE POINT: body ivory with no shading. Points milk-chocolate color, warm in tone. Nose leather and paw pads: cinnamon pink. Eye color: deep, vivid blue.

LILAC POINT: body glacial white with no shading. Points frosty gray with pinkish tone. Nose leather and paw pads: lavender pink. Eye color: deep, vivid blue.

SEAL POINT: body even pale fawn to cream, warm in tone, shading gradually into lighter color on the stomach and chest. Points deep, seal brown. Nose leather and paw pads: same color as points. Eye color: deep, vivid blue.

ADDITIONAL BALINESE COLORS

(See page 170 for a full description of the colors listed below.)

The following colors are recognized by some, but not necessarily all, of the other registries in North America. **Lynx point colors:** blue lynx point, blue-cream (or blue-tortie) lynx point, chocolate lynx point, chocolate-tortie lynx point, cream lynx point, lilac lynx point, lilac-cream lynx point, red lynx point, seal lynx point, seal-tortie lynx point. **Particolor point colors:** blue-cream (or blue-tortie) point, chocolate-tortie point, lilac-cream point, seal-tortie point. **Solid point colors:** cream point, red point.

Balinese allowable outcross breeds:[8] Siamese.

---

[1] ACFA: "Pricked slightly forward as if listening."
[2] CFF: "Slightly rounded eye allowable due to lack of extreme wedge."
[3] CFF: "And tucked up."
[4] ACFA: "The overall appearance should be that of a well-balanced Siamese cat with a long, flowing coat and a plumed tail."
[5] ACFA: "Short on head, medium length at shoulders, getting progressively longer toward the tail."
[6] ACFA: "Allowance can be made for lack of coat in a young cat."
[7] CFF: "Two or more inches in length."
[8] In all associations where the breed is recognized.

Birman

ORIGIN

This fabled breed is wrapped in the kind of legend that enthralls cat fanciers. According to that legend, the Birman—or Sacred Cat of Burma—was honored in its native land because people there believed that the souls of departed priests returned to their temples in the form of these beautiful cats. One of the holy places where the sacred cats lived was the temple of Lao-Tsun, located in western Burma between China and India. In this temple a priest named Mun-Ha knelt each night in adoration before a statue of Tsun-Kyan-Kse, a blue-eyed goddess who presided over the transmutation of souls. At Mun-Ha's side as he prayed was a sacred cat named Sinh.

One night the temple was ravaged by invaders from Siam, and Mun-Ha was killed. Sinh stood at once with his paws on his fallen master, facing the statue of Tsun-Kyan-Kse. As he did, a miraculous transformation came over Sinh. His coat, which had been white, took on the golden glow radiating from the statue. His

Blue Point Birman

yellow eyes turned a deep, sapphire blue; and his legs glowed with a brown-velvet radiance—except for his feet, which remained sparkling white, a sign of the purity of Mun Ha's soul. By the following morning, all the cats in the temple of Lao-Tsun had been transformed from white to seal pointed just like Sinh. For seven days he remained at his post. Then he died, carrying with him the soul of Mun-Ha.

Such a tale befits the Sacred Cat of Burma, adding to the stature of this breed. Unfortunately, it adds nothing to the explanation of the Birman's origin. Siamese and longhaired, bicolored Angoras are likely participants in that mysterious beginning. It is futile, however, to speculate whether this combination—if it was the one that produced the Birman—was intentional or whether it simply resulted from those cats interbreeding freely in an isolated setting. But whatever the parent breeds might have been—and wherever they might have joined forces—they had to have been carrying genes for point color, low-grade white spotting, and long hair.

DEVELOPMENT

Accounts of the arrival of the first Birmans in Western Europe are scarcely less fantastic than the temple legend. In two accounts, a male named Maldapour and a female named Sita were shipped from Burma to France in 1919. Maldapour did not survive the journey according to either report. Sita, who was pregnant, did. In the first narrative, the cats had been sent by a grateful temple priest to Major Gordon Russell, a British officer who had helped several priests and their cats to escape from the temple of Lao-Tsun into Tibet during an uprising in Burma. In the second account, "a Mr. Vanderbilt" obtained the sacred cats "for a price of gold" from a greedy servant who had stolen them from the temple. In both accounts, Sita's fate is unknown; but it is reasonable to assume that her kittens—including a perfectly marked daughter named Poupee—were the foundation stock used to create the Birman breed in France.

There is a third account of the Birman's arrival in France, this one contained in an article in the 1969 Cat Fanciers' Association Yearbook. Verner E. Clum, the author of that article, claimed to have "a magazine dated 1927 'Le Monde Felin,' in which there is a picture of a Mme. Marcelle Adam, first importer of [the Birman] breed in France in 1925." Mme. Adam's cattery name, incidentally, was Maldapour, and she was president of the Federation Feline Francaise. This seemed to have settled the issue, but in her next paragraph Clum recounted the Major Russell story without bothering to say which of the two individuals—Mme. Adam or Major Russell—she believed was truly the first Birman importer.

By 1925 the Sacred Cat of Burma was established well enough to be recognized for championship competition in France. Though its numbers were small, the Sacred Cat prospered until World War II. After the war there was a time when all that stood between the breed and extinction was one pair of cats. Through selective outcrossing the breed was reconstructed. The process was speeded up, no doubt, by the introduction of colorpoint longhairs with pedestrian type to Birman breeding programs.

The Sacred Cat of Burma was reestablished in France by 1955. Four years later the first pair of Sacred Cats arrived in the United States. By the mid-1960s the breed began to be accepted for championship competition in North America. At about the same time its name was changed—to Burman and then to Birman—and it was also accepted for championship competition in England.

Standard for the
BIRMAN

Courtesy of the Cat Fanciers' Association.
Differences in the Standards of other registries are indicated at the end of the text.

HEAD, BODY, TYPE & COAT: (65)	COLOR—INCLUDING EYE COLOR: (35)
HEAD: 30 (boning, nose, jaw, chin, profile, ear & eye shape & set)	**COLOR EXCEPT GLOVES:** 15 (body color, point color, eye color)
BODY/TYPE: 25 (boning, stockiness, elongation, legs, tail)	**GLOVES:** 20 (front & rear gloves, laces & symmetry)
COAT: 10 (length, texture, ruff)	

GENERAL: a cat of mystery and legend, the Birman is a colorpointed cat with long, silky hair and four pure white feet. It is strongly built, elongated and stocky, neither svelte nor cobby. The distinctive head has strong jaws, a firm chin, and a medium-length Roman nose with nostrils set low on the nose leather. There should be good width between the ears, which are medium in size. The blue, almost round eyes are set well apart, giving a sweet expression to the face.

HEAD: skull strong, broad, and rounded. There is a slight flat spot just in front of the ears

NOSE: medium in length and width, in proportion to size of head. Roman shape in profile.[1] Nostrils set low on the nose leather.

PROFILE: the forehead slopes back and is slightly convex. The medium-length nose, which starts just below the eyes, is Roman in shape (which is slightly convex),[2] with the nostrils set low on the nose leather.[3] The chin is strong, with the lower jaw forming a perpendicular line with the upper lip.

CHEEKS: full with somewhat rounded muzzle. The fur is short in appearance about the face, but to the extreme outer area of the cheek the fur is longer.

JAWS: heavy.

CHIN: strong and well developed.[4]

EARS: medium in length. Almost as wide at the base as tall.[5] Modified to a rounded point at the tip; set as much to the side as into the top of the head.

EYES: almost round[6] with a sweet expression. Set well apart, with the outer corner tilted VERY slightly upward. Blue in color, the deeper blue the better.

BODY: long[7] and stocky. Females may be proportionately smaller than males.

LEGS: medium in length and heavy.

PAWS: large, round, and firm. Five toes in front, four behind.

TAIL: medium in length, in pleasing proportion to the body.[8,9]

COAT: medium long to long,[10,11] silken in texture, with heavy ruff around the neck, slightly curly on stomach. This fur is of such a texture that it does not mat.[12,13]

COLOR EXCEPT GLOVES: body even, with subtle shading when allowed. Strong contrast between body color and points. Points except gloves: mask, ears, legs, and tail dense and clearly defined, all of the same shade. Mask covers entire face including whisker pads and is connected to ears by tracings. No ticking or white hair in points. Golden Mist: desirable in all point colors is the "golden mist," a faint, golden-beige cast on the back and sides. This is somewhat deeper in the seal points, and may be absent in kittens.

GLOVES: front paws have white gloves ending in an even line across the paw at, or between, the second or third joints. (The third joint is where the paw bends when the cat is standing.) The upper limit of white should be the metacarpal (dew) pad. (The metacarpal pad is the highest up little paw pad, located in the middle of the back of the front paw, above the third joint and just below the wrist bones.) Symmetry of the front gloves is desirable. Back paws: white glove covers all the toes, and may extend up somewhat higher than front gloves. Symmetry of the rear gloves is desirable. Laces: the gloves on the back paws must extend up the back of the hock, and are called laces in this area. Ideally, the laces end in a point or inverted "V" and extend 1/2 to 3/4 of the way up the hock. Lower or higher laces are acceptable, but should not go beyond the hock. Symmetry of the two laces is desirable. Paw pads: pink preferred, but dark spot(s) on paw pad(s) acceptable because of the two colors in pattern. Note: ideally, the front gloves match, the back gloves match, and the two laces match. Faultlessly gloved cats are a rare exception, and the Birman is to be judged in all its parts, as well as the gloves.

PENALIZE: white that does not run across the front paws in an even line. Persian or Siamese type head. Delicate bone structure. White shading on stomach and chest. Lack of laces on one or both back gloves. White beyond the metacarpal (dew) pad. (The metacarpal pad is the highest up little paw pad, located in the middle of the back of the front paw, above the third joint and just below the wrist bones.)

DISQUALIFY: lack of white gloves on any paw. Kinked or abnormal tail. Crossed eyes. Incorrect number of toes. Areas of pure white in the points, if not connected to the gloves and part of or an extension of the gloves. Paw pads are part of the gloves. Areas of white connected to other areas of white by paw pads (of any color) are not cause for disqualification. Discrete areas of point color in the gloves, if not connected to point color of legs (exception, paw pads). White on back legs beyond the hock.

BIRMAN COLORS

(The following colors are accepted in all associations.)

BLUE POINT: body bluish white to pale ivory, shading gradually to almost white on stomach and chest. Points, except for gloves, deep blue. Gloves pure white. Nose leather: slate color. Paw pads: pink. Eye color: blue, the deeper and more violet the better.

CHOCOLATE POINT: body ivory with no shading. Points, except for gloves, milk-chocolate color, warm in tone. Gloves pure white. Nose leather: cinnamon pink. Paw pads: pink. Eye color: blue, the deeper and more violet the better.

LILAC POINT:[14] almost white. Points, except for gloves, frosty gray with pinkish tone. Gloves pure white. Nose leather: lavender pink. Paw pads: pink. Eye color: blue, the deeper and more violet the better.

SEAL POINT: body even pale fawn to cream, warm in tone, shading gradually to lighter color on the stomach and chest. Points, except for gloves, deep seal brown. Gloves pure white. Nose leather: same color as points. Paw pads: pink. Eye color: blue, the deeper and more violet the better.

The following colors are accepted by CCA and TICA: red, cream, tortie, and lynx points.

The following colors are accepted in TICA only: cinnamon, fawn, seal tortie, blue tortie, chocolate tortie, cinnamon tortie, and frost tortie points. Seal, blue, chocolate, cinnamon, frost, fawn, red, and cream lynx points. Seal, blue, chocolate, cinnamon, frost, and fawn torbie points:

Birman allowable outcross breeds:[15] none.

[1] ACFA: "There is a definite stop between the eyes."
[2] TICA: " ... definite stop between forehead and Roman nose."
[3] TICA: The head is "slightly longer than wide in profile."
[4] TICA: " ... forming a perpendicular line with upper lip."
[5] ACFA and TICA: "moderately far apart."
[6] TICA: "large."
[7] ACA: "medium long."
[8] ACA: "rounded on end."
[9] CFF: " ... that is, not as long as the body."
[10] ACFA: "medium to long."
[11] ACA: "long."
[12] ACA: "or tangle."
[13] TICA: "Seasonal changes to be considered when judging coat length."
[14] ACA and TICA call this color "frost."
[15] In all associations where the breed is recognized.

Bombay

Everyone enjoys the wonderful fantasies and myths that have developed about the origins of cat breeds, but there are still many people who know the difference between fact and fantasy. The Bombay is a case in point. It is a manufactured breed if there ever was one, but it was not manufactured in quite the way its legend would have us believe.

During the late 1950s and early 1960s, Burmese breeders realized that they needed to outcross in order to produce a more compact body while retaining the dark, even coat their breed Standard required. Crossing to a Siamese would have lengthened the Burmese body, could have resulted in blue eye color, and would have eventually restored the darker points found on the original Burmese, which were themselves hybrid cats. Crossing to other breeds would have produced other unacceptable results. The logical candidate for an outcross, therefore, was the black American Shorthair. Many such crosses were made behind cattery doors. The kittens from these breedings were either black or brown.

Since there are no *allowable* outcrosses for the Burmese breed, anybody who wanted to use one of these nonpedigreed American-Burmese kittens in a breeding program (or in the show ring) had to falsify its pedigree. This was accomplished in several ways. Brown hybrids were added to legitimate sable Burmese litters, and black hybrids were registered as American Shorthairs in the same manner. In addition, there was open registration of American Shorthairs at the time—i.e., registries issued papers on American Shorthairs of unknown origin. Thus, black, hybrid kittens could also be registered as American Shorthairs, "particulars unknown."

There were several top-winning Burmese during the late 1950s and early 1960s that carried the resilient, thicker coats resulting from the Burmese-American cross. This was, indeed, a serious matter, causing much discussion among judges, breeders, and exhibitors. Clearly the need to outcross

Burmese was obvious; but the registration system, which did not allow outcrosses for this breed, actually encouraged the many frauds that breeders committed to get their hybrid cats registered and shown.

DEVELOPMENT

Nikki Shuttleworth Horner of Shawnee cattery in Louisville, Kentucky, worked with the Burmese-black American cross, eventually breeding black kittens to black kittens only. She was highly successful in establishing a truly black Burmese with excellent type and conformation. Everything about these cats was Burmese except their color. She realized, however, that it would be years before there could be any hope of adding a new color to the Burmese breed because of the strong position taken by Burmese breeders, who believed that sable was the only true Burmese.

Horner decided to request separate recognition for her black "Burmese," which she called Bombays—after the black leopard of India and the city of Bombay. By seeking recognition for these cats as a separate breed, she hoped to avoid any hostility from Burmese fanciers who obviously viewed the addition of a new color as a threat to their breed. In 1976 the Cat Fancier's Association accepted the Bombay for championship competition. To this day CFA still allows Bombay breeders to outcross their cats to sable Burmese for type and to black American Shorthairs for color. And to this day the problem of nonshowable kittens is still with us because all kittens from Bombay-to-Burmese crosses are considered Bombays—whether they are black or brown—by the majority of associations. The black kittens are no problem. They can be shown as Bombays if they are good enough. The brown ones can be used in Bombay breeding programs, but they cannot be shown—unless their breeders create bogus pedigrees for them, as some breeders do. The realistic approach to this situation—followed by The International Cat Association—is to show black kittens from Bombay-to-Burmese crosses as Bombays and brown kittens as Burmese.

Bombay

Standard for the
BOMBAY

Courtesy of the Cat Fanciers' Association. Differences in the Standards of other registries are indicated at the end of the text.

HEAD AND EARS: (25)	COAT: (20)
Roundness of head 7	Shortness 10
Full face and proper profile 7	Texture 5
Ears 7	Close lying 5
Chin 4	
	COLOR: (30)
EYES: (5)	Body color 20
Placement and shape 5	Eye color 10
BODY: (20)	
Body 15	
Tail 5	

GENERAL: due to its short, jet-black, gleaming coat and bright gold to vivid copper eyes, combined with a solid body and a sweet facial expression, the ideal Bombay has an unmistakable look of its own. It is a medium-sized cat, well balanced, friendly, alert, and outgoing; muscular and having a surprising weight for its size. The body and tail should be of medium length, the head round with medium-sized, wide-set ears, a visible nose break, and large, rounded, wide-set eyes, and be of excellent proportions and carriage.

HEAD: the head should be pleasingly rounded with no sharp angles. The face should be full with considerable breadth between the eyes, tapering slightly to a short, well-developed muzzle. In profile there should be a visible nose break;[1] however, it should not present a "pugged" or "snubbed" look.

EARS: the ears should be medium in size and set well apart on a rounded skull, alert, tilting slightly forward, broad at the base, and with slightly rounded tips.

CHIN: the chin should be firm, neither receding nor protruding, reflecting a proper bite.

EYES: set far apart with rounded aperture.[2]

BODY: medium in size, muscular in development, neither compact nor rangy.[3] Allowance is to be made for larger size in males.

LEGS: in proportion to the body and tail.

PAWS: round. Toes, five in front, four in back.

TAIL: straight, medium in length; neither short nor "whippy."

COAT: fine, short,[4] satinlike texture; close-lying with a shimmering, patent-leather sheen.

PENALIZE: excessive cobbiness or ranginess.

DISQUALIFY: kinked or abnormal tail. Lockets or spots. Incorrect number of toes. Nose leather or paw pads other than black. Green eyes. Improper bite. Extreme break that interferes with normal breathing and tearing of eyes.

BOMBAY COLOR

COLOR: the mature specimen should be black to the roots. Kitten coats should darken and become more sleek with age. Nose leather and paw pads black. Eye color ranging from gold to copper, the greater the depth and brilliance the better.

Bombay allowable outcross breeds:[5] black American Shorthair, sable Burmese.

---

[1] TICA: A "moderate stop."
[2] TICA, CFF, ACA: Eye aperture "in line with base of ear."
[3] TICA: "Slightly longer than Burmese."
[4] CFF, TICA: "Short to medium."
[5] In all associations where the breed is recognized.

British Shorthair

ORIGIN

The ancestors of the British Shorthair were brought to Northern Europe and then to Great Britain by Roman soldiers almost two thousand years ago. Despite these hardy cats' humble circumstances—they were called mongrel or street cats, and they bred freely without control—British Shorthairs appeared in great numbers in cat shows at London's Crystal Palace during the last quarter of the nineteenth century. Harrison Weir—the founder of the cat fancy, and the author of the first judging standards—"deemed it advisable ... to give special prizes" to blue British Shorthairs because of their beauty and popularity. As a result, British Blues were—and still are—listed separately from the other nonforeign shorthairs in Great Britain; and some people in the United States consider the British Blue a separate breed. It is not. It is, one of a large variety of colors occurring among the British Shorthair breed.

DEVELOPMENT

When longhaired cats began to appear at shows in England, they attracted a great deal of interest. "With the majority of fanciers, the long-haired cats are the most popular," wrote English breeder and judge Frances Simpson in 1903. By that time Persians and other longhaired cats—namely the Angora and the Russian—outnumbered shorthairs four-to-one at shows. After spending four and a half pages on longhairs, Simpson begins a two-page discussion of shorthairs with a less-than-enthusiastic "And now to consider ..." When she does consider black-and-white and tabby-and-white shorthairs, Simpson declares, "It seems almost a pity to so far encourage these cats as to give classes for them at our shows."

Bad came to worse for the British Shorthair during World Wars I and II. These had a ruinous effect on the cat fancy in England, and the British Shorthair suffered a devastating setback. Breeders had difficulty finding suitable studs for their females, and there is no doubt that in the interest of convenience and survival, they employed various outcrosses to keep their breeds alive. Some like to pretend that this never happened, but others admit that British Shorthairs were outcrossed to Persians, especially blues, in order to maintain eye color, type, and coat texture.

As happened with Domestic Shorthairs in this country, the longhaired cross seemed to enhance many an otherwise unappealing British Shorthair. What's more, judges rewarded these hybrid cats for their unusual beauty. Eventually a rule was instituted listing "any evidence of hybridization" as a cause for disqualification in British Shorthair classes; but by then so much hybridization had occurred that the regulation made little impact. Finally, the Persian was accepted as an allowable outcross for the British Shorthair in Great Britain. This caused problems for Americans who wanted to import British Shorthairs because registries in North America required at least three generations of British-to-British matings on a pedigree before they would register the cat it described.

Though a few shorthaired cats from Great Britain had been imported by American breeders not long after 1900, cat fanciers in this country had enough trouble gaining championship status for their own shorthairs without bothering about imports. For this reason, there was little American interest in pedigreed shorthairs from Great Britain until the mid-1960s. In 1970 the American Cat Fanciers Association became the first American registry to recognize British Shorthairs—in blue and black only. Eventually all other colors of the breed were accepted by all associations. Today, more British colors are being seen on the show bench than ever before, and the solid—or blue self color—is not as dominant as it once was. Because they have been developed out of such strong stock, British Shorthairs are free of known genetic defects. They require grooming as all cats do, and gentle brushing and bathing are necessary in showing a British Shorthair.

RIGHT: Blue-and-White Van British Shorthair

BELOW: Blue British Shorthair

Standard for the
BRITISH SHORTHAIR

Courtesy of the Cat Fanciers' Association. Differences in the Standards of other registries are indicated at the end of the text.

HEAD: (25)
Muzzle and Chin 5
Skull 5
Ears 5
Neck 5
Eye shape 5

BODY: (35)
Torso 20
Legs and Paws 10
Tail 5

COAT: (20)
Texture, length, and density 20

COLOR: (20)
Eye color 5
Coat color 15

GENERAL: the British Shorthair is compact, well balanced, and powerful, showing good depth of body, a full broad chest, short to medium, strong legs, rounded paws, tail thick at base with a rounded tip. The head is round with good width between the ears, round cheeks, firm chin, medium ears, large round and well-opened eyes, and a medium-broad nose. The coat is short and very dense. Females are less massive in all respects with males having larger jowls. This breed is slow to mature.

HEAD: round and massive. Round face with round underlying bone structure well set on a short, thick neck. The forehead should be rounded with a slight flat plane on the top of the head. The forehead should not slope.

NOSE: medium, broad.[1] In profile there is a gentle dip.

CHIN: firm and well developed.[2]

MUZZLE: distinctive, well developed, with a definite stop beyond large, round whisker pads.

EARS: ear set is important. Medium in size,[3] broad at the base, rounded at the tips. Set far apart, fitting into (without distorting) the rounded contour of the head.[4]

EYES: large, round, well opened. Set wide apart and level.[5]

BODY: medium to large, well knit and powerful.[6] Level back and a deep, broad chest.

LEGS: short to medium, well boned and strong. In proportion to the body. Forelegs are straight.

PAWS: round and firm. Toes: five in front and four behind.

TAIL: medium length in proportion to the body,[7] thicker at base, tapering slightly to a rounded tip.

COAT: short, very dense, well bodied, resilient and firm to the touch. Not double coated or woolly.

COLOR: for cats with special markings: 10 points for color and 10 points for markings. Shadow tabby markings in solid color, smoke, or bicolor kittens are not a fault.

PENALIZE: definite nose stop. Overlong or light undercoat. Soft coat. Rangy body. Weak chin.

DISQUALIFY: incorrect eye color, green rims in adults. Tail defects. Long or fluffy coat. Incorrect number of toes. Locket or button. Improper color or pigment in nose leather and/or paw pads in part or total. Any evidence of illness or poor health. Any evidence of wryness of jaw, poor dentition (arrangement of teeth), or malocclusion.

BRITISH SHORTHAIR COLORS
(See page 170 for a full description of the colors listed below.)

Particolors: bicolors (black and white, blue and white, red and white, cream and white), blue cream, calico, dilute calico, tortoiseshell. **Smokes:** black smoke, blue smoke. **Solids:** black, blue, cream, white. **Tabbies:** (classic, mackerel, and spotted tabby patterns): blue tabby, brown tabby, cream tabby, red tabby, silver tabby.

British Shorthair allowable outcross breeds:[8] none.

---

[1] TICA: "Short and snub."
[2] TICA: "Forms a perpendicular line with the nose."
[3] CFF: "Small to medium in size."
[4] ACA: "Broad at base with rounded tips and tilted forward."
[5] ACFA: "Eye color must conform to the requirements listed in coat color."
[6] TICA: "Semicobby."
[7] TICA: "Two thirds the length of the body."
[8] In all associations where the breed is recognized.

Burmese

ORIGIN

Probably no other breed has endured so much controversy and political conflict as the Burmese, which first arrived in the United States in 1930 in the person of a small brown cat. The cat's name was Wong Mau. She had accompanied a sailor, whose name has not been recorded, on a journey from Rangoon to San Francisco. There she was purchased by Dr. Joseph Thompson, a Navy psychiatrist. Wong Mau had a dark-brown body with still darker points—i.e., markings—on her face, ears, legs, and tail. She also had a somewhat rounded head and eyes. She was mated first to a seal point Siamese in an effort to establish her type. She produced typically pointed Siamese kittens and pointed kittens with darker-than-Siamese bodies like her own. When the darker-bodied cats were bred together—or when darker-bodied males were bred back to Wong Mau—they produced even-colored, dark-all-over kittens. All of which proved that Wong Mau was a hybrid with Siamese in her background.

DEVELOPMENT

Burmese were first registered in 1936. Their standard called for an "even, sable brown [color] shading to a trifle lighter on chest and abdomen [with] mask, ears, legs, and tail clearly defined and a darker brown than the body." The Cat Fanciers' Association, ever the purist among registries, required three generations of like-to-like breeding before it would enroll kittens as Burmese. There was no way this condition could be met because the Burmese gene pool was too small, and many breeders were still using seal point Siamese from Siamese-Burmese crosses in their breeding programs. The difference between Siamese and Burmese then was not so pronounced as it is today.

By 1940 Burmese had been accepted for championship competition by the three registries that existed at the time: CFA, the American Cat Association, and the Cat Fanciers' Federation. But on May 8, 1947, the CFA board of directors passed a motion which declared that "the recognition of the so-called Burmese breed ... is indefinitely suspended." CFA took this step because there weren't many Burmese that could meet its strict, three-generation breeding requirement. During their suspension Burmese were denied access to CFA shows, foundation records, and stud books. All existing registrations were suspended, and registration fees were returned. ACA and CFF continued to recognize Burmese during that time, which probably helped to save the breed from extinction. The CFA decision had been prompted by Siamese breeders, who claimed that Wong Mau had been nothing more than a Siamese with bad type and poor color, and who feared that the results of crosses between Burmese and Siamese cats would filter into their lines.

It was not until the 1956-57 show season that a Burmese met the requirements for stud book listing and the breed was reinstated by CFA. With the return of the Burmese a new standard was developed. It called for a solid, sable color without darker points on the extremities, and for a short, cobby body—surprisingly heavy for its size—a round head, and round, gold eyes. Theoretically, these requirements should have eliminated any interest in crossing Burmese with Siamese. Outcrosses were still needed, however, and the next logical choice was a black Domestic Shorthair. Some Burmese from this period reveal evidence of this practice, and, of course, many such clandestine matings were not recorded at all.

The new look in Burmese became popular. So did new, dilute colors—champagne, platinum, and blue—but only after bitter, life-and-death battles had been fought among Burmese breeders. Their resistance is puzzling because new colors add interest and vigor to a breed. This truth has been repeatedly demonstrated in the history of the Cat Fancy.

Today's Burmese are of top quality, but classes are not large considering the age of the breed. This is largely the result of problems that have developed within many Burmese lines. The "contemporary" look—with its extreme head type—that became popular during the 1980s has, in some cases, carried with it certain deformities.

Cleft palates, skulls that do not close, and other abnormalities occur frequently in contemporary Burmese kittens, along with improvements in type such as a shorter nose, more prominent eyes, and rounder muzzle. Some breeders claim that these

Sable Burmese

The British Burmese, seen here, has a longer nose and a longer body than the American version of this breed.

defects, nonexistent in "traditional" Burmese, can be bred away or minimized through judicious outcrossing. Others are not so optimistic.

These difficulties have not occurred in England. Because of the six-month quarantine regulation, there were few Burmese imported, and breeders were obliged to outcross in order to preserve the breed. They chose Siamese and British Shorthairs, which produced more colors than the few that exist in American Burmese, and a style of cat that is much more foreign-bodied and less extreme than the American version.

As of 1990, one North American registry, CFF, recognized a breed called the Foreign Burmese, which is less extreme in type and conformation and is available in more colors than the Burmese is.

Standard for the
BURMESE

Courtesy of the Cat Fanciers' Association. Differences in the Standards of other registries are indicated at the end of the text.

HEAD, EARS, and EYES: (30)

Roundness of head 7
Breadth between eyes
  and full face 6
Proper profile 6
(includes chin)
Ear set, placement,
  and size 6
Eye placement and
  shape 5

BODY, LEGS, FEET, and TAIL: (30)
Torso 15
Muscle tone 5
Legs and feet 5
Tail 5

COAT: (10)
Short 4
Texture 4
Close lying 2

COLOR: (30)
Body color 25
Eye color 5

GENERAL: the overall impression of the ideal Burmese would be a cat of medium size with substantial bone structure, good muscular development, and surprising weight for its size. This together with expressive eyes and a sweet expression presents a totally distinctive cat which is comparable to no other breed. Perfect physical condition, with excellent muscle tone. There should be no evidence of obesity, paunchiness, weakness, or apathy.

HEAD, EARS, and EYES: head pleasingly rounded without flat planes whether viewed from the front or side. The face is full with considerable breadth between the eyes, and blends gently into a broad, well-developed, short muzzle that maintains the rounded contours of the head.[1] In profile there is a visible nose break.[2] The chin is firmly rounded, reflecting a proper bite. The head sits on a well-developed neck. The ears are medium in size, set well apart, broad at the base and rounded at the tips. Tilting slightly forward, the ears contribute to an alert appearance. The eyes are large, set far apart, with rounded aperture.[3]

BODY: medium in size,[4] muscular in development, and presenting a compact appearance.[5] Allowance to be made for larger size in males. An ample, rounded chest, with back level from shoulder to tail.

LEGS: well proportioned to body.

PAWS: round. Toes: five in front and four behind.

TAIL: straight, medium in length.[6]

COAT: fine, glossy, satinlike texture; short and very close lying.

PENALIZE: distinct barring on either the front or rear outerlegs. Trace (faint) barring permitted in kittens and young adults.[7]

DISQUALIFY: kinked or abnormal tail, lockets or spots. Blue eyes. Incorrect nose leather or paw pad color. Malocclusion of the jaw that results in a severe underbite or overbite that visually prohibits the described profile and/or malformation that results in protruding teeth or a wry face or jaw. Distinct barring on the torso.

BURMESE COLORS

BLUE: the mature specimen should be a medium blue with warm fawn undertones, shading almost imperceptibly to a slightly lighter hue on the underparts, but otherwise without shadings, barring, or markings of any kind. Nose leather and paw pads: slate gray. Eye color: ranging from yellow to gold, the greater the depth and brilliance the better.

CHAMPAGNE: the mature specimen should be a warm honey beige, shading to a pale, gold tan underside. Slight darkening on ears and face permissible but lesser shading preferred. A slight darkening in older specimens allowed, the emphasis being on evenness of color. Nose leather: light warm brown. Paw pads: warm, pinkish tan. Eye color: ranging from yellow to gold, the greater the depth and brilliance the better.

PLATINUM: the mature specimen should be a pale, silvery gray with pale fawn undertones, shading almost imperceptibly to a slightly lighter hue on the underparts, but otherwise without shadings, barring, or markings of any kind. Nose leather and paw pads: lavender pink. Eye color: ranging from yellow to gold, the greater the depth and brilliance the better.

SABLE: the mature specimen is a rich, warm, sable brown; shading almost imperceptibly to a slightly lighter hue on the underparts but otherwise without shadings, barring, or markings of any kind. (Kittens are often lighter in color.) Nose leather and paw pads: brown. Eye color: ranges from gold to yellow, the greater the depth and brilliance the better. Green eyes are a fault.

Burmese allowable outcross breeds:[8] none.

---

[1] CFF: "Muzzle two thirds the length of the skull."
[2] CFF: "The stop should be moderate and well defined, but never indented or abrupt."
[3] CFF: "At least an eye's diameter apart."
[4] ACA: "Small to medium."
[5] ACFA, TICA: "A 'somewhat' compact appearance."
[6] CFF: "Thick with a blunt end."
[7] CFF: "An under or overshot jaw, green in the eye color. A break that is too extreme, heading toward an Exotic look, or a break that is not long enough, giving way toward the Tonkinese look. Muzzle too broad, giving a bulldog appearance, or too narrow, giving a wedge effect. Tail long and whiplike in appearance."
[8] In all associations where the breed is recognized.

Chartreux

ORIGIN

The Chartreux has been called "something of a national treasure" in France, where the breed was developed. References to blue, gray, or blue-gray cats can be found throughout French literature. The earliest recorded use of the name *Chartreux* to describe cats with blue fur has been found in the 1723 edition of the *Universal Dictionary of Commerce*, but we know from the work of the French poet Joachim du Bellay that "entirely gray" cats were common in France as early as 1558.

Legend, which often passes for fact in the cat fancy, credits the Carthusian monks with the development of the Chartreux. Members of this nine-hundred-year-old order, whose Le Grande Chartreux monastery is located near Grenoble, were known long ago as talented steel workers; and they also forged a potent,

Chartreux

66

green liqueur. There is no evidence, however, that they were cat breeders, that they obtained cats from monastic knights returning from the Crusades, or that they brought cats back to France from the Cape of Good Hope in the seventeenth century. Nor is there any evidence that the monks named the Chartreux. In fact, Carthusian archives do not mention cats at all.

DEVELOPMENT

The first Chartreux breeders of record are two sisters, whose surname was Leger. They lived on the small Brittany island of Belle-lle-sur-Mere off the northwest coast of France, where they originally bred Persians and Siamese in their de Guerveur cattery. The Legers became acquainted with the Chartreux in the late 1920s when they moved from the mainland to Belle-lle-sur-Mere. Shortly after they arrived on the island, they discovered a large population of blue-gray cats in Le Palais, the island's principal city. No one knows how or when the blue-gray cats migrated from the French mainland to Belle-lle-sur-Mere, but show records indicate that in 1931 at a show held in Paris, a Mlle. Leger became the first person to exhibit a Chartreux in France.

More than sixty years after making its debut, the Chartreux remains one of the cat fancy's rarest breeds, with a worldwide population scarcely more than one thousand. The principal reasons for this scarcity are World Wars I and II. Hostilities in France left many cats homeless, obliging them to fend for themselves and to arrange their own breedings in the streets. In addition, cats were sometimes killed for food when provisions were scarce, and several French observers have reported that Chartreux were also killed for their plush coats.

When breeders finally determined to preserve the Chartreux in the early 1950s, they attempted to strengthen the breed by outcrossing to other blue cats—Persians, British Shorthairs, and whatever non pedigreed cats they could find in France that approximated the Chartreux Standard. Fortunately, there is no lack of blue cats in the world. Chartreux fanciers had many breeds and varieties to choose from in their effort to revitalize the breed. Unfortunately, breed characteristics are compromised and the distinctions between breeds are erased by any but the most carefully planned and controlled outcrossing. By

1970, there was so little difference between the British Blue and the Chartreux that the Feline International Federation declared they had to be judged in the same category. This situation lasted for seven years until European breeders insisted that the Chartreux was a separate breed and deserved to be cultivated and judged as such. In England, however, there is still no distinction made between the two cats.

The Chartreux came to the United States in 1970 when a cat fancier from La Jolla, California, named Helen Gamon brought the first Chartreux to America. Three of the first ten imports by American breeders came from the Leger sisters, who had begun working with Chartreux more than forty years before. In the years since the breed arrived in the United States, the Chartreux has developed a style of its own that distinguishes it from the many breeds and varieties of blue cats.

Standard for the
CHARTREUX

Courtesy of the Cat Fanciers' Association. Differences in the Standards of other registries are indicated at the end of the text.

HEAD: (15)
Shape 4
Size 3
Profile/nose 5
Muzzle 3

NECK: (4)
Length 2
Size 2

EARS: (10)
Shape 3
Size 2
Placement 5

EYES: (10)
Shape 3
Size 3
Color 4

BODY: (20)
Shape 5
Size 5
Boning 5
Musculature 5

TAIL: (4)
Shape 2
Size 2

LEGS: (6)
Length 2
Boning 2
Musculature 2

FEET: (2)
Shape 1
Size 1

COAT: (14)
Length 4
Texture 10

COLOR: (15)
Uniformity 8
Brilliance 7

GENERAL: the Chartreux is a sturdy French breed coveted since antiquity for its hunting prowess and its dense, water repellent fur. Its husky, robust type is sometimes termed primitive, neither cobby nor classic. Though amply built, Chartreux are extremely supple and agile cats; refined, never coarse nor clumsy. Males are much larger than females and slower to mature. Coat texture, coat color, and eye color are affected by sex, age, and natural factors which should not penalize. The qualities of strength, intelligence, and amenability, which have enabled the Chartreux to survive the centuries unaided, should be evident in all exhibition animals and preserved through careful selection.

HEAD and NECK: rounded and broad but not a sphere.[1] Powerful jaw; full cheeks, with mature males having larger jowls. High, softly contoured forehead; nose straight and of medium length/width;[2] with a slight stop at eye level. Muzzle comparatively small, narrow, and tapered with slight pads.[3] Sweet, smiling expression. Neck short and heavyset.

EARS: medium in height and width;[4] set fairly high on the head;[5] very erect posture.

EYES: rounded and open; alert and expressive.[6,7] Color range is copper to gold; a clear, deep, brilliant orange is preferred.

BODY and TAIL: robust physique; medium long with broad shoulders and deep chest. Strong boning; muscle mass is solid and dense. Females are medium; males are large. Tail of moderate length; heavy at base; tapering to oval tip. Lively and flexible.

LEGS and FEET: legs of medium length; straight and sturdy; comparatively fine boned. Feet are round and medium in size (may appear almost dainty compared to body mass).

COAT: medium short[8,9] and slightly woolly in texture (should break like a sheepskin at neck and flanks). Resilient undercoat; longer, protective topcoat. NOTE: degree of woolliness depends on age, sex, and habitat, mature males exhibiting the heaviest coats. Silkier, thinner coat permitted on females and cats under two years.

PENALIZE: severe nose break, snubbed or upturned nose, broad, heavy muzzle, palpable tail defect, eyes too close together giving angry look.

DISQUALIFY: white locket, visible tail kink, green eyes.

CHARTREUX COLOR

COLOR: any shade of blue gray from ash to slate; tips lightly brushed with silver. Emphasis on color clarity and uniformity rather than shade. Preferred tone is a bright, unblemished blue with an overall iridescent sheen. Nose leather is slate gray; lips blue; paw pads are rose taupe. Allowance made for ghost barring in kittens and for tail rings in juveniles under two years of age.

Chartreux allowable outcross breeds:[10] none.

---

[1] ACA, ACFA, CFF, TICA: The head is "large and broad but not round."
[2] ACA, ACFA, CFF: "Nose short and straight."
[3] TICA: " ... but is not to be pointed."
[4] ACA, ACFA, CFF, TICA: "Small to medium in size."
[5] ACA, CFF: " ... with slightly rounded tips."
[6] TICA: "Large and set moderately wide apart."
[7] ACA: "At least the width of an eye between the eyes."
[8] ACA, TICA: "May be longer than that of other domestic shorthaired cats."
[9] ACFA, CFF: "Medium."
[10] In all associations where the breed is recognized.

Colorpoint Shorthair

ORIGIN

Years before the orthodox Siamese colors (seal, chocolate, lilac, and blue) had been granted championship status, breeders were producing the occasional odd-pointed variety. John Jennings, a British cat fancier, judge, and author wrote in 1893, that "experiments have been tried with a view to introducing another colour other than the characteristic dun (to the Siamese)." A geneticist in Sweden created tabby pointed Siamese in 1924; two red points were shown at a Siamese Cat Club show in England in 1934; and a few additional tabby pointed Siamese were bred in Scotland in 1940. Serious work on expanding the Siamese color scheme and gene pool did not begin, however, until the late 1940s. Naturally, this new interest infuriated the steadfast purist because additional colors could be produced only by outcrossing to other breeds—British or American shorthairs or Abyssinians, for example. As Jennings had warned fifty years earlier, "Any deviation from the pure, typical breed will, I opine, not be generally cared for, if for no other reason than its being incorrect." Then, as now, as always: the only thing more certain than change in the cat fancy is resistance to change.

DEVELOPMENT

Red and cream point Siamese were the first new colors to gain recognition. Along with the red and cream came the tortie points, and before long the tabby points followed. Indeed it was possible to produce any color and confine it to point restriction. In a short time breeders were producing remarkable Siamese type and deep blue eye color in hybrid Siamese.

In Great Britain the Governing Council of the Cat Fancy offered to recognized red and cream pointed Siamese as Pointed Foreign Shorthairs, but the breeders of these cats would not accept this designation. Meanwhile, in 1963 the Cat Fanciers Association voted to deny these cats recognition as Siamese. The following year, however, they were accepted as a separate breed called the Colorpoint Shorthair. England solved this what's-in-a-name problem by registering nontraditional Siamese under a different breed number from the four original colors.

To this day CFA and the Canadian Cat Association treat the Colorpoints as a separate breed, even though there is no longer a need to cross these cats to anything but other Colorpoints or Siamese, and the percentage of non-Siamese blood in today's Colorpoints is minuscule. This head-in-the-past classification system is a lingering consequence of the early Colorpoint breeders' belief that their cats resulted from a solemn and spontaneous mutation—despite written, genetic, and common-sense evidence to the contrary. Unfortunately, this unrealistic attitude led to the adaption of unrealistic rules which demand that any seal, chocolate, lilac, or blue point kittens born from Siamese-Colorpoint crosses be registered as Colorpoints. Such non Siamese Siamese cannot be shown legally, but the quality and type of these Colorpoints is so outstanding that many are being registered illegally with Siamese litters, a process known as paperhanging. This temptation does not exist in the four associations that recognize a wider variety of Siamese colors.

Associations that enforce artificial distinctions in any breed are creating a climate for fraud by not adopting registration rules based on genetics rather than exclusiveness. In registries that are genetically based, pedigrees are more likely to reflect the true background of a kitten, and buyers are free to accept or reject that kitten on the basis of an accurate pedigree. It is impossible to legislate morality, and the cat fancy must come to accept the fact that it is dealing with pedigreed, not purebred, cats.

Seal Lynx Point Colorpoint Shorthair

Cornish Rex

ORIGIN

The Rex cat is one of those rare developments that often result for some strange reason following a war or other period of massive change. On July 21, 1950, a curly coated, cream male kitten was born in a litter of five barn cats in Cornwall, England. The litter belonged to Nina Ennismore, who named the curly coated lad Kallibunker. Since she had formerly bred Rex rabbits, Ennismore assumed that Kallibunker's coat was the work of a spontaneous mutation, one that had also occurred in rats, mice, and horses.

Encouraged by cat fancier Brian Stirling-Webb and geneticist A.C. Jude, Ennismore bred Kallibunker to his mother—a tortie-and-white straighthaired cat named Serena—whom she also owned. This breeding produced two males and a female in August 1952. The female was normal coated, the males were both Rex. One of those died at seven months; the other, named Poldhu,

was eventually used to propagate Ennismore's new breed, called the Cornish Rex after its place of origin.

Meanwhile, in East Germany in 1951, a wavy-haired, black female cat—which had been observed on the grounds and in the basement of the Hufeland Hospital for five years—had been adopted by a cat lover named Dr. Rose Sheuer-Karpin. For the next seven years this German Rex, named Lammchen, produced numerous straighthaired kittens sired by local toms. When she was bred finally to one of her sons, two of their four kittens had wavy hair. This suggested that the gene behind the German Rex was recessive: i.e., the Rex coat pattern would be expressed only when a kitten inherited two copies of the gene for that trait, one from each parent.

Black-and-White Cornish Rex

DEVELOPMENT

After Nina Ennismore had inbred her strain of Rex as far as possible, she began to outcross to ordinary shorthaired cats so as not to risk her cats' health or reproductive ability. Though it would have been possible to introduce the Rex coat to any breed, she and other Rex fanciers chose to confine the gene to shorthairs. Longhaired Rex were most unappealing, and their coats were difficult to keep from matting.

As Ennismore's cat population grew—she had more than forty cats at one point—she was unable to sell enough kittens to defray expenses. She felt that she had no choice but to put a number of cats to sleep—Kallibunker and his mother Serena among them. Their son Poldhu came to grief of another sort when two veterinarians performed a testicular biopsy on him. The vets wanted to determine whether Poldhu was simply a blue-tabby-and-white stud or a rare, siring blue cream and white. The latter is a sex-linked color that appears virtually always in females. Males of this color are rare, and non sterile ones are more rare yet. The vets had assured Ennismore that this "slight operation would in no way affect" Poldhu's reproductive vigor, but after the biopsy he never sired again. Ironically, the tissue sample that had been taken from Poldhu was lost in the laboratory along with his virility.

By the late 1950s Ennismore had stopped working with Rex cats entirely, but Brian Stirling-Webb was determined to see the breed through. In 1961 he learned that a male Rex kitten had been born in Devon, one county east of Cornwall, the preceding year. The dam of this kitten was a tortie-and-white stray who had taken up with Beryl Cox. The sire was a feral, Rex-coated male who lived in a derelict tin mine near Cox's home.

When she learned of Stirling-Webb's interest in Rex, Cox offered to send her male kitten, whom she had named Kirlee, to live with Stirling-Webb so that Kirlee might provide some new blood for the new breed. Kirlee was bred to several Rex females from Cornwall, but every kitten from these matings had straight hair. Thus, Stirling-Webb concluded that Cornish Rex and the Rex from Devon were carrying separate mutation genes, and that the children of Kallibunker belonged to a different breed of cat than Kirlee did. Since, as Stirling-Webb knew, the Rex gene is recessive, all

kittens born from Cornish Rex females bred to Kirlee would have been wavy coated had the gene responsible for Kirlee's mutation been the same one responsible for Kallibunker's. Subsequent test matings between Cornish and German Rex in the United States proved that those two strains were compatible.

Before she was obliged to give up her cats in the late 1950s, Nina Ennismore had sent several Rex to American breeders. Most of these were Siamese breeders who used their own stock as outcrosses for the new Rex breed. This provided the fine bone, unusual head type, large ears, and racy, greyhound look that characterizes the best Cornish Rex today.

The Cornish Rex has been a straightforward success in the cat world. It is accepted for championship competition by all North American registries. The first two of the six currently active federations to grant championship status to the breed were the Canadian Cat Association and the American Cat Fanciers Association in 1963. At first, the Cat Fanciers' Association did not acknowledge the difference between Cornish and Devon Rex. CFA registered all Rex as Cornish until 1979, when it finally created a separate breed designation for the Devon Rex long after the other associations had done so.

Standard for the
CORNISH REX

Courtesy of the Cat Fanciers' Association. Differences in the Standards of other registries are indicated at the end of the text.

HEAD: (25)
Size and shape 5
Muzzle and nose 5
Eyes 5
Ears 5
Profile 5

BODY: (30)
Size 3
Torso 10
Legs and Paws 5
Tail 5
Bone 5
Neck 2

COAT: (40)
Texture 10
Length 5
Wave, extent of
   wave 20
Close lying 5

COLOR: 5

GENERAL: the Cornish Rex is distinguished from all other breeds by its extremely soft, wavy coat and racy type. It is surprisingly heavy and warm to the touch. All contours of the Cornish Rex are gently curved. By nature, the Cornish Rex is intelligent, alert, and generally likes to be handled.

PROFILE: a curve composed of two convex arcs. The forehead is rounded, the nose break smooth and mild, and the Roman nose has a high, prominent bridge.

HEAD: comparatively small[1] and narrow; length about one third greater than the width. A definite whisker break. Gently curved outlines.[2,3,4]

MUZZLE: narrowing slightly to a rounded end.[5]

EARS: large and full from the base,[6] erect and alert; set high on the head.[7]

EYES: medium to large in size,[8] oval in shape, and slanting slightly upward. A full eye's width apart. Color should be clear, intense, and appropriate to coat color.[9,10]

NOSE: Roman. Length is one third the length of the head. In profile a straight line from end of nose to chin with considerable depth and squarish effect.

CHEEKS: lean and muscular.[11]

CHIN: strong, well developed.

BODY: small to medium, males proportionately larger. Torso long and slender, not tubular; hips, muscular and somewhat heavy in proportion to the rest of the body.[12] Back is naturally arched with lower line of the body approaching the upward curve. The arch is evident when the cat is standing naturally.

SHOULDERS: well knit.

RUMP: rounded, well muscled.

LEGS: very long and slender. Hips well muscled, somewhat heavy in proportion to the rest of the body. The Cornish Rex stands high on its legs.

PAWS: dainty, slightly oval. Toes: five in front and four behind.

TAIL: long and slender, tapering toward the end and extremely flexible.[13,14]

NECK: long and slender.

BONE: fine and delicate.

COAT: short, extremely soft, silky, and completely free of guard hairs. Relatively dense. A tight, uniform marcel wave, lying close to the body and extending from the top of the head across the back, sides, and hips continuing to the tip of the tail. Size and depth of wave may vary. The fur on the underside of the chin and on chest and abdomen is short and noticeably wavy.

CONDITION: firm and muscular.

PENALIZE: sparse coat or bare spots.

DISQUALIFY: kinked or abnormal tail. Incorrect number of toes. Any coarse or guard hairs. Any signs of lameness in the hindquarters. Signs of poor health.

CORNISH REX COLORS

Particolor colors: bicolor (solid color and white, smoke and white, tabby and white, etc.), blue cream, calico, dilute calico, tortoiseshell, van bicolor, van blue cream and white, van calico. **Shaded colors:** chinchilla silver, shaded silver. **Smoke colors:** black smoke, blue smoke. **Solid colors:** black, blue, cream, red, white. **Tabby colors:** blue (classic, patched, and mackerel), brown (classic, patched, and mackerel), cream (classic and mackerel), red (classic and mackerel), silver (classic, patched, and mackerel). **Other Rex colors:** any other color or pattern.

Cornish Rex allowable outcross breeds:[15] none.

---

[1] TICA: "Medium."

[2] CFF: "The whiskers and eyebrows are unusually curly."

[3] ACA: "An indentation of outline appears between the point where the outer edge of the ear meets the head and the inner base of the ear meets the skull."

[4] TICA: "Egg shaped, with a pronounced roundness to the back of the skull."

[5] ACFA: "The muzzle break is important because it gives the distinctive Rex look to the head."

[6] CFF: "Taller than they are wide."

[7] ACFA, TICA: Viewed from the front, the ears present "a deep, conical appearance."

[8] ACA, CFF: "Medium in size."

[9] ACA: "Any color allowed and of secondary importance."

[10] ACFA: "The eye color for all colors, except pointed, to be green, hazel, or gold."

[11] ACA: "Prominent cheekbones contribute to the break at the muzzle."

[12] CFF: "The fine bones are covered with very firm muscle, giving the cat a well-rounded appearance, rather than an angular appearance."

[13] CFF: "The end of the tail is normally curved upward when carried down; when up, it is frequently topped."

[14] ACA, CFF: "No penalty for bare upper surface."

[15] In all associations where the breed is recognized.

Cymric

ORIGIN

The longhaired Manx or Cymric (*kim* rick) has appeared in Manx litters for as long as the breed has existed. There is no doubt that on the Isle of Man, where Manx originated, cats with long hair bred freely with the indigenous short-coated, tailless cats. The longhairs are thought to have arrived when the Vikings colonized this tiny island.

Red Classic Tabby-and-White Cymric

DEVELOPMENT

Beginning in the late 1930s and continuing for several decades, Manx breeders began to use Persians in their breeding programs, not from any deep desire to produce longhaired Manx, but in order to improve conformation and thickness of coat in their shorthairs. This was a convenient strategy because owners of stud Manx were few. It also served, though unintentionally, to increase the Manx gene pool. Cat fanciers, being what they are, will frequently seek recognition for

anything new or different that appears in their litters. Just as frequently they will attempt to explain the unique in terms of a rare mutation, and some people tried to use this as an explanation for the appearance of longhaired Manx kittens. Such was not the case.

Nor was it necessarily a good idea to promote the longhaired Manx as a championship breed. There are enough problems with Manx, and adding long hair to the picture—which could get in the way of the cats' toilet duties, and mat on their rear ends—should not be encouraged. With more and more of the longhaired Manx kittens appearing, however, some breeders

began to campaign to have them recognized as a breed. The Canadian Cat Association was the first to do so, granting championship status to Cymrics in the mid-1970s.

Cymrics tend to have the personality of the Manx. They are clownlike in behavior and really are true companions. Like other cats that are longhaired variants of what were originally shorthaired breeds, the Cymrics' coat does not seem to carry the fullness, thickness, or length exhibited by breeds where longhair-to-longhair breeding is done repeatedly.

Standard for the
CYMRIC

Courtesy of the Cat Fanciers' Association. Differences in the Standards of other registries are indicated at the end of the text.

HEAD and EARS: 25	LEGS and FEET: 15
EYES: 5	COAT LENGTH: 10
BODY: 25	COAT TEXTURE: 10
TAILLESSNESS: 5	COLOR: 5

GENERAL: the overall impression of the tailless Cymric is that of roundness; round head with firm, round muzzle and prominent cheeks; broad chest; substantial, short front legs; short back, which arches from shoulders to a round rump; great depth of flank; and rounded, muscular thighs. The heavy, glossy double coat of medium length is the main differentiating factor of the Cymric from its parent breed—the Manx. The Cymric should be alert, clear of eye, with a glistening, clean, well-groomed coat. It should have a healthy physical appearance, feeling firm and muscular, neither too fat nor too lean. It should be surprisingly heavy when lifted. Cymrics are slow to mature and allowance should be made in young cats.

HEAD and EARS: round head with prominent cheeks and a jowly appearance. Head is slightly longer than it is broad. Moderately rounded forehead, pronounced cheekbones, and jowliness (more evident in adult

males) enhance the round appearance. Short, thick neck. Definite whisker break, with large, round whisker pads. In profile there is a gentle nose dip.[1] Well-developed muzzle, slightly longer than broad, with a strong chin. Ears are wide at the base, tapering gradually to a rounded tip, with full interior furnishings. Medium in size in proportion to the head, widely spaced, and set slightly outward. When viewed from behind, the ear set resembles that of the rocker of a cradle.

EYES: large, round,[2] and full. Set at a slight angle toward the nose (outer corners slightly higher than inner corners). Ideal color conforms to requirements of coat color.[3,4]

BODY: solidly muscled, compact, and well balanced, medium in size with sturdy bone structure. The Cymric is stout in appearance, with broad chest and well-sprung ribs; surprisingly heavy when lifted. The constant repetition of curves and circles gives the Cymric the appearance of great substance and durability, a cat that is powerful without the slightest hint of coarseness. Males may be somewhat larger than females. Flank (fleshy area of the side between the ribs and hip) has greater depth than in other breeds, causing considerable depth to the body when viewed from the side. The short back forms a smooth, continuous arch from shoulders to rump, curving at the rump to form the desirable round look. Shortness of back is unique to the Cymric (and Manx), but is in proportion to the entire cat and may be somewhat longer in the male. Because of the Cymric's longer coat over the rump area, the body may appear longer.

TAILLESSNESS: absolute in the perfect specimen, with a decided hollow at the end of the backbone where, in the tailed cat, a tail would begin. A rise of the bone at the end of the spine is allowed and should not be penalized unless it is such that it stops the judge's hand, thereby spoiling the tailless appearance of the cat. The rump is extremely broad and round.

LEGS and FEET: heavily boned, forelegs short and set well apart to emphasize the broad, deep chest. Hind legs much longer than forelegs, with heavy, muscular thighs and substantial lower legs. Longer hind legs cause the rump to be considerably higher than the shoulders. Hind legs are straight when viewed from behind. Paws are neat and round, with five toes in front and four behind.

COAT LENGTH: the double coat is of medium length,[5] dense and well padded over the main body, gradually lengthening from the shoulders to the rump. Breeches, abdomen, and neck ruff are longer than on the main body. Cheek coat is thick and full. The collarlike neck ruff extends from the shoulders, being biblike around the chest. Breeches should be full and thick to the hocks in the mature cat. Lower leg and head coat (except for cheeks) should be shorter than on the main body and neck ruff, but dense and full in appearance. Toe tufts and ear tufts are desirable. Preference should be given to the cat showing full coating.[6]

COAT TEXTURE: coat is soft and silky, falling smoothly on the body yet being full and plush due to the double coat. Coat should have a healthy, glossy appearance. Allowance to be made for seasonal and age variations.

TRANSFER TO AOV: definite, visible tail joint. Short coat.

PENALIZE: coat that lacks density, has a cottony texture, or one that is of an overall even length.
SEVERELY PENALIZE: if the judge is unable to make the cat stand or walk properly.
DISQUALIFY: evidence of poor physical condition; incorrect number of toes; evidence of hybridization.

CYMRIC COLORS
(See page 170 for a full description of the colors listed below.)

Particolor colors: bicolors (black and white, red and white, blue and white, cream and white), blue cream, calico, dilute calico, tortoiseshell. **Shaded colors:** chinchilla silver, shaded silver. **Smoke colors:** black smoke, blue smoke. **Solid colors:** black, blue, cream, red, white. **Tabby colors:** blue tabby (classic, mackerel), blue patched tabby, brown tabby (classic, mackerel), brown patched tabby, cream tabby (classic, mackerel), red tabby (classic, mackerel), silver tabby (classic, mackerel), silver patched tabby. **Other Cymric colors:** any other color or pattern with the exception of those showing hybridization resulting in the colors chocolate, lavender, the Himalayan pattern, or these combinations with white.

Cymric allowable outcross breeds:[7] Manx.

[1] ACA: "Nose longer and broader than the American Shorthair's."
[2] ACA: "Almost" round.
[3] ACA: "Any eye color allowed and of secondary importance."
[4] TICA: Eye color should "conform to coat color, but should only be considered if all other points are equal."
[5] ACA: "Medium long."
[6] ACA: "Seasonal variation should not be penalized."
[7] In all associations where the breed is recognized.

Devon Rex

ORIGIN

In 1960 a kitten with wavy hair was discovered in a litter of straight-coated feral kittens in Devonshire, England. The father of this litter was believed to have been a tomcat with a similar wavy coat who lived in an abandoned tin mine near Buckfastleigh in Devonshire. The mother of the litter was a tortie-and-white, normal-coated stray that raised her kittens in a field at the foot of a garden belonging to Beryl Cox, who lived not far from the mine. Since the gene responsible for the Devon Rex coat is recessive—i.e., kittens will not develop this coat unless they inherit one copy of the curly-coated gene from each parent—many people assume that the tortie and white who produced the curly-coated youngster was herself an offspring of the tin-mine tom cat.

Beryl Cox named the wavy-haired kitten Kirlee, and he soon became her great favorite. She delighted in his

White Devon Rex

unique appearance, intelligence, and warmth and—it has been reported—his ability to walk a tightrope and to wag his tail like a dog when he was praised for this feat. For all Kirlee's charm, however, Cox had no inclination to create an entire curly-coated breed. Yet when she heard that a cat fancier named Brian Stirling-Webb was working to establish a curly-coated strain whose patriarch had been born in Cornwall, one county west of Devonshire, she offered to send Stirling-Webb her beloved Kirlee. After several breedings between Kirlee and the Cornish Rex produced nothing but normal-coated kittens, breeders concluded that the Devon and Cornish Rex were not on the same wave length. These were separate breeds caused by separate gene mutations. Thenceforward the two breeds were cultivated separately.

DEVELOPMENT

Since the Devon wouldn't mix with the Cornish—and since there weren't many Devons to mix with—their gene pool was established with help from other breeds. These outcrosses were chosen to produce as many colors and patterns as possible, including the restricted colorpoint pattern of the Siamese. The kittens from these outcrosses that were used to set Devon Rex type were selected for coat quality and conformation.

Kirlee, whom Cox had generously given to Stirling-Webb, was used throughout the early establishment of the breed. He was eventually neutered and sent to live as a pet with friends of Stirling-Webb.

By the late 1960s the Devon Rex had arrived in the United States, where it was first accepted for championship competition in 1972 by the American Cat Fanciers Association. Because of the breed's limited gene pool, breeders in this country are allowed to outcross to other shorthaired breeds: the British Shorthair, American Shorthair, Burmese, Bombay, and Siamese, depending on the individual federation, all of which now recognize the breed. The non-Rex off spring from these crosses, in addition to having straight coats, resemble ordinary household pets, which leads breeders to theorize that the Devon gene controls type and conformation as well as coat.

The Devon Rex can be distinguished from its next door neighbor from Cornwall in several ways: The Devon has a shorter coat that is less plush and less wavy than the Cornish coat, even though Cornish lacks guard hairs—the coarse, outer layer of a cat's coat. The Devon Rex has a decided stop to its nose; the Cornish has a Roman nose. Finally, the Cornish has a noticeable tuck up to its abdomen, and the Devon Rex does not.

Standard for the
DEVON REX

Courtesy of the Cat Fanciers' Association. Differences in the Standards of other registries are indicated at the end of the text.

HEAD: (35)
Size and shape 10
Muzzle and chin 5
Profile 5
Eyes 5
Ears 10

BODY: (30)
Torso 10
Legs and paws 10
Tail 5
Neck 5

COAT: (30)
Density 10
Texture and length 10
Waviness 10

COLOR: 5

GENERAL: the Devon Rex is a breed of unique appearance. Its large eyes, short muzzle, prominent cheekbones, and huge, low-set ears create a characteristic elfin look. A cat of medium-fine frame, the Devon is well covered with soft, wavy fur; the fur is of a distinctive texture, as the mutation which causes its wavy coat is cultivated in no other breed. The Devon is alert and active and shows a lively interest in its surroundings.

HEAD: modified wedge.[1] In the front view, the wedge is delineated by a narrowing series of three (3) distinct convex curves: outer edge of ears, cheekbones, and whisker pads. Face to be full cheeked with pronounced cheekbones and a whisker break. In profile, nose with a strongly marked stop; forehead curving back to a flat skull.

MUZZLE: short, well-developed muzzle. Prominent whisker pads.

CHIN: strong, well developed.

EYES: large and wide set, oval in shape, and sloping towards outer edges of ears. Color should be clear, intense, and appropriate to coat color.[2]

EARS: strikingly large and set very low, very wide at the base, so that the outside base of ear extends beyond the line of the wedge. Tapering to rounded tops and well covered with fine fur. With or without earmuffs and/or ear-tip tufts.

BODY: hard and muscular, slender, and of medium length. Broad in chest and medium fine in boning, with medium-fine but sturdy legs. Carried high on the legs with the hind legs somewhat longer than the front. Allowance to be made for larger size in males, as long as good proportions are maintained.

LEGS and PAWS: legs long and slim. Paws small and oval, with five toes in front and four behind.

TAIL: long, fine, and tapering, well covered with short fur.

NECK: medium long and slender.

COAT: density—the cat is well covered with fur, with the greatest density occurring on the back, sides, tail, legs, face, and ears. Slightly less density is permitted on the top of head, neck, chest, and abdomen. Bare patches are a fault in kittens and a serious fault in adults; however the existence of down on the underparts of the body should not be misinterpreted as bareness. Sparse hair on the temples (forehead in front of the ears) is not a fault. Texture: the coat is soft, fine, full-bodied, and rexed (i.e., appearing to be without guard hairs). Length: the coat is short on the back, sides, upper legs, and tail. It is very short on the head, ears, neck, paws, chest, and abdomen. Waviness: a rippled wave effect should be apparent when the coat is smoothed with one's hand. The wave is most evident where the coat is the longest, on the body and tail.[3]

PENALIZE: narrow, long, or domestic shorthair-type head; small or high set ears; short, bare, or bushy tail; straight or shaggy coat; bare patches.

DISQUALIFY: extensive baldness, kinked or abnormal tail, incorrect number of toes, crossed eyes, weak hind legs. Any evidence of illness or poor health.

DEVON REX COLORS

(See page 170 for a full description of the colors listed below.)

Particolor colors: bicolors (solid color and white, tabby and white, tortoiseshell and white, etc), blue cream, calico, fawn cream calico, lavender cream calico, cinnamon cream calico, chocolate tortoiseshell, cinnamon tortoiseshell, dilute calico, dilute van calico, fawn cream, lavender cream, tortoiseshell, van bicolor, van calico, fawn cream van calico, lavender cream van calico, cinnamon cream van calico. **Shaded colors:** blue cream shaded, blue shaded, cameo shaded, chinchilla, chocolate shaded, chocolate tortoiseshell shaded, cinnamon shaded, cinnamon tortoiseshell shaded, fawn cream shaded, fawn shaded, lavender cream shaded, lavender shaded, shaded silver, tortoiseshell shaded. **Smoke colors:** black smoke, blue smoke, blue cream smoke, chocolate smoke, chocolate tortoiseshell smoke, cinnamon smoke, cinnamon tortoiseshell smoke, cream smoke, fawn smoke, fawn cream smoke, lavender smoke, lavender cream smoke, red smoke cameo, tortoiseshell smoke. **Solid colors:** black, blue, cinnamon, chocolate, cream, fawn, lavender, red, white. **Tabby colors:** blue brown, cameo, chocolate, chocolate silver, cinnamon, cinnamon silver, cream, fawn, lavender, lavender silver, red tabby, silver tabby, blue silver, cream silver, fawn silver. **Other Devon Rex colors:** any other color or pattern. Examples: any color with one, two, three, or four white feet. Ticked tabbies. All point restricted colors such as seal point, chocolate point, blue point, lilac point, cream point, lynx points, cinnamon point, etc.

Devon Rex allowable outcross breeds: American or British shorthairs for litters born before May 1, 1993.[4]

---

[1] ACA, CFF, TICA: "Comparatively small."
[2] ACA: "Any eye color allowed, and of secondary importance."
[3] CFF: "Allowance should be made for lack of full development of coat until the cat matures, which is about eighteen months of age."
[4] CFA enforces these restrictions. Other associations are more liberal in their policy, allowing outcrosses to British Shorthair, American Shorthair, Burmese, Bombay, or Siamese, depending on the association.

Egyptian Mau

ORIGIN

ORIGIN

The Egyptian Mau gained recognition because of the efforts of Princess Nathalie Troubetskoy, one of the most accomplished and extraordinary persons ever associated with the cat fancy. A member of one of the oldest Russian families, the princess was born in Poland in 1897. She studied at the art theater and the medical school in Moscow, and served throughout World War I on Russian battle fronts. After living in England for twenty years, she went to Italy; and when the allied armies arrived, she served as chief nurse to the U.S. 2675th Regiment.

While the princess was living in Rome, a youngster whom she knew gave her a spotted silver, female kitten. The kitten had been given to him by a member of the diplomatic corps in one of the Mideast embassies. The princess named the kitten Baba, and realizing that she had unique qualities, sought to learn more about the kitten's background. After consulting with a veterinarian and several professors, the princess concluded that Baba was descended from Egyptian stock.

DEVELOPMENT

In December 1956 Princess Troubetskoy arrived in the United States with Baba and two other Egyptian Maus. Had she been able, as she had planned, to book passage on the Andrea Doria, which sank in the Atlantic off the coast of North America, the breed might never have been established. The cats that the princess brought to America were the first and only Egyptian Maus imported to this country.

When Baba was brought to the United States, the four-year-old Mau was a tall, elegant queen. Clear silver in color, she had black spotting, vivid necklaces and bracelets, and large eyes outlined in black. Another of the three Maus was Baba's three-year-old son Giorgio, called Jo-Jo, who was a larger,

stronger-looking bronze cat. An eleven-month-old female named Liza, ocher in color, completed the group. She was exhibited at the Empire Cat Show in 1957. Eleven years later the Cat Fanciers' Federation granted championship status to the Mau, which is now accepted in all associations.

Baba's offspring were, of course, the result of domestic crossing and much inbreeding. Like their mother they were most unpredictable, fiery, and wild natured. They did not accept other cats easily and were comfortable only on their own home territory. They would literally climb the walls in strange homes or at shows. Through selective breeding, those who pioneered the Mau have produced more docile cats—active and intelligent and great companions.

Standard for the
EGYPTIAN MAU

Courtesy of the Cat Fanciers' Association.
Differences in the Standards of other registries are indicated at the end of the text.

Point Score

HEAD: (20)
Muzzle 5
Skull 5
Ears 5
Eye shape 5

BODY: (25)
Torso 10
Legs and Feet 10
Tail 5

COAT: (5)
Texture and length 5

PATTERN: 25

COLOR: (25)
Eye color 10
Coat color 15

GENERAL: the Egyptian Mau is the only natural domesticated breed of spotted cat. The Egyptian's impression should be one of an active, colorful cat of

Silver Egyptian Mau

medium size with well-developed muscles. Perfect physical condition with an alert appearance. Well balanced physically and temperamentally. Males tend to be larger than females.

HEAD: a slightly rounded wedge without flat planes, medium in length. Not full cheeked. Profile showing a gentle contour with slight rise from the bridge of the nose to the forehead. Entire length of nose even in width when viewed from the front.

MUZZLE: neither short nor pointed. Allowance to be made for jowls in adult males.

EARS: medium to large,[1,2] alert and moderately pointed, continuing the planes of the head. Broad at base. Upstanding with ample width between ears. Hair in ears short and close lying. Inner ear a delicate, almost transparent, shell pink. May be tufted.

EYES: large[3] and alert, almond shaped,[4] with a slight slant towards the ears. Skull apertures neither round nor oriental.

BODY: medium long and graceful, showing well-developed, muscular strength. Loose skin flap extending from flank to hind leg knee. General balance is more to be desired than size alone. Allowance to be made for muscular necks and shoulders in adult males.[5]

LEGS and FEET: in proportion to body. Hind legs proportionately longer, giving the appearance of being on tiptoe when standing upright. Feet small and dainty, slightly oval, almost round in shape. Toes: five in front and four behind.

TAIL: medium long, thick at base, with slight taper.

COAT: hair is medium in length with a lustrous sheen. In the smoke color the hair is silky and fine in texture. In the silver and bronze colors, the hair is dense and resilient in texture and accommodates two or more bands of ticking separated by lighter bands.

PENALIZE: short or round head. Pointed muzzle.

Small, round, or oriental eyes. Cobby or oriental body. Short or whip tail. If no broken necklaces. Pencillings in spotting pattern on torso. Poor condition. Amber cast in eye color in cats over the age of 1½ years.
DISQUALIFY: lack of spots. Blue eyes. Kinked or abnormal tail. Incorrect number of toes. White locket or button distinctive from other acceptable white-colored areas in color sections of standard.

MAU PATTERN
(Common to all colors)

PATTERN: markings on torso are to be randomly spotted with variance in size and shape. The spots can be small or large, round, oblong, or irregular shaped. Any of these are of equal merit, but the spots, however shaped or whatever size, shall be distinct. Good contrast between pale ground color and deeper markings. Forehead barred with characteristic "M" and frown marks, forming lines between the ears which continue down the back of the neck, ideally breaking into elongated spots along the spine. The spinal lines, as they reach the rear haunches, meld together to form a dorsal stripe that continues along the top of the tail to its tip. The tail is heavily banded and has a dark tip. The cheeks are barred with "mascara" lines; the first starts at the outer corner of the eye and continues along the contour of the cheek, with a second line, which starts at the center of the cheek and curves upwards, almost meeting below the base of the ear. On the upper chest there are one or more broken necklaces. The shoulder markings are a transition between stripes and spots. The upper front legs are heavily barred but do not necessarily match. Spotting patterns on each side of the torso need not match. Haunches and upper hind legs to be a transition between stripes and spots, breaking into bars on the lower leg. Underside of body to have "vest buttons" spots; dark in color against the correspondingly pale ground color.

EGYPTIAN MAU COLORS

EYE COLOR: light green, "gooseberry green." Amber cast is acceptable only in young adults up to 1½ years of age.
BRONZE: warm, coppery-brown ground color across head, shoulders, outer legs, back, and tail, being darkest on the saddle and lightening to a tawny buff on the sides. Underside fades to a creamy ivory. All markings dark brown-black with a warm, coppery-brown undercoat, showing good contrast against the lighter ground color. Back of ears tawny pink and tipped in dark brown-black. Nose, lips, and eyes outlined in dark brown, with bridge of nose brown. Upper throat area, chin, and around nostrils pale, creamy white. Nose leather: brick red. Paw pads: black or dark brown, with same color between toes and extending beyond the paws of the hind legs.
SILVER: pale silver ground color across the head, shoulders, outer legs, back, and tail. Underside fades to a brilliant pale silver. All markings charcoal color with a white to pale silver undercoat, showing good contrast against lighter ground colors. Back of ears grayish pink and tipped in black. Nose, lips, and eyes outlined in black. Upper throat area, chin, and around nostrils pale clear silver, appearing white. Nose leather: brick red. Paw pads: black with black between the toes and extending beyond the paws of the hind legs.
SMOKE: pale silver ground color across head, shoulders, legs, tail, and underside. All markings jet black with a white to pale silver undercoat, with sufficient contrast against ground color for pattern to be plainly visible. Nose, lips, and eyes outlined in jet black. Upper throat area, chin, and around nostrils lightest in color. Nose leather: black. Paw pads: black with black between the toes and extending beyond the paws of the hind legs.
PEWTER (as described in the American Cat Association Standard): ground color suggesting pale fawn. Each hair to be composed of bands of pale silver and beige with black tipping. Loses ticking and lightens to cream on undersides. Chin, upper throat, and nose outlined in cream. Markings are charcoal to dark brown, with good contrast between ground color and markings. Paw pads–charcoal to dark brown. Nose leather–brick red. Eyes, nose, and lips outlined in charcoal to dark brown.

Egyptian Mau allowable outcross breeds:[6] none.

[1] TICA: "Medium to medium large."
[2] ACA, CFF: "Large."
[3] ACA, CFF: "Very large."
[4] TICA: "Rounded almond."
[5] ACA: "Neck is arched, proportionately long in relation to body."
[6] In all associations where the breed is recognized.

Exotic Shorthair

ORIGIN

Although it officially became eligible for championship competition on May 1, 1967, the Exotic Shorthair had been competing *sub rosa* as an American Shorthair for some time before that. In the days when American Shorthairs were still known as Domestic Shorthairs — i.e., prior to May 1, 1966—persons looking for an edge with this breed began crossing Persians to their Domestic Shorthair stock. The cats produced through this illegal scheme were far more pleasing than the Domestic Shorthairs with legitimate pedigrees. They were also far more successful in the show ring, where judges did not overlook them, even though the Domestic Shorthair Standard warned that "any evidence of hybridizing" was grounds for disqualification. Since evidence is in the eye of the beholder, judges always found a way to justify giving awards to these cats.

DEVELOPMENT

The Cat Fanciers' Association tried to stop people from using Persian-Domestic crosses by closing the Domestic Shorthair registry. When the modified Domestic Shorthairs had first appeared, breeders were allowed to register any domestic, non-pedigreed cat—real or imagined—for the price of a registration fee and a brief description of the cat. These foundation Domestics, spelled with an uppercase *D* once the registration fee had been accepted, could then be used in breeding programs. Or they could be used on paper as the nominal sires or dams of litters, while Persians capable of producing the same colors in a litter were doing the actual breeding. Obviously, closing the Domestic Shorthair registry was not going to put an end to this practice. If a breeder with a red tabby Domestic Shorthair male had a red tabby Persian male also, that breeder could still use the Persian for mating and claim on the application for litter registration that the Domestic cat was the father of the litter. Instead of putting a stop to hybridization, closing the Domestic Shorthair registry served only to make pedigrees less reliable. Before the registry was closed, anyone who saw "unknown" on a Domestic Shorthair pedigree generally assumed that "unknown" was code for "Persian."

Matters became more dicey with the appearance of silver American Shorthairs. Not only was their type and conformation suspect, their color was one that didn't exist in the Domestic Shorthair population. Silver had to have come from chinchilla or shaded silver Persians. Worse yet, some of these silver Domestic Shorthairs had no Domestic ancestors at all, having been produced from silver Persian-Abyssinian crosses. Judges of conscience withheld awards on silver Americans because the evidence of hybridization was as plain as the color on the cats. CFA, however, chose to deal with the problem by returning to open registration, thereby flinging open the barn doors to outside influences once again.

In 1966 this writer and Mrs. Jane Martinke, a CFA judge for many years, were cochairs of CFA's breed program. They suggested that CFA establish a new breed to accommodate the cats being produced and shown illegally as American Shorthairs. Martinke called this proposed new breed the Exotic Shorthair because *Exotic* accurately reflected the use of Abyssinians, Burmese, and other non-American breeds in its development. Breeders with hybrid Americans had the option of transferring their cats to this newly created breed, which was given championship status as of May 1, 1967. At that point the breeds that could be used legally to produce Exotics were limited to Persians and American Shorthairs.

The Exotic Shorthair has gained immense popularity with those who love Persian type but not the grooming required to maintain the Persian coat. In fact, the success of this breed, which ought to be called the Shortcoated Persian, has been so great that Exotics can now compete evenly with their longhaired counterparts, which was not always the case.

Once breeders had crossed an American Shorthair to a Persian to achieve a short coat, there was no reason to continue using Americans in Exotic Shorthair breeding programs. Nor is it advisable to breed Exotic to Exotic for more than one generation—two at most. Doing so invariably results in a loss of the desired Persian type and conformation. With so many Persians being used to produce Exotics—and with the longhaired gene being recessive—it is possible to produce longhaired kittens from two Exotics or from an Exotic-Persian cross. There is no difference between these longhaired Exotic Shorthairs and the so-called purebred Persians.

Longhaired Exotics present a problem to breeders and registries alike. Bred to a Persian or to another longhaired Exotic, these cats will produce only longhaired kittens, but such kittens cannot be shown in most registries. Eventually, the Exotic may become a variety of the Persian breed—just as Himalayans have. This would help to restore integrity to some Persian pedigrees. Just as Domestic Shorthair breeders once masked the used of Persians in their catteries, some Exotic breeders are illegally registering longhaired Exotics as Persians—and doing well with them in the show ring. As of 1991, the only registries with a realistic approach to this situation were the Canadian Cat Association and The International Cat Association, both of which allow longhaired Exotics to compete in championship classes.

Brown Classic Tabby Exotic Shorthair

Standard for the
EXOTIC SHORTHAIR

Courtesy of the Cat Fanciers' Association.
Differences in the Standards of other registries are
indicated at the end of the text.

HEAD: 30 (including size and shape of eyes; ear shape and set)	**COAT:** 10
	BALANCE: 5
	REFINEMENT: 5
TYPE: 20 (including shape, size, bone, and length of tail)	**COLOR:** 20
	EYE COLOR: 10

In all tabby varieties, the 20 points for color are to be divided 10 for markings and 10 for color. In all "with-white" varieties (calico, dilute calico, bicolor, van bicolor, van calico, van dilute calico, and tabby and white), the 20 points for color are to be divided 10 for "with-white" pattern and 10 for color.

HEAD: round and massive, with great breadth of skull. Round face with round underlying bone structure. Well set on a short, thick neck.

NOSE: short, snub, and broad. With "break."[1]

CHEEKS: full.

JAWS: broad and powerful.

CHIN: full, well developed, and firmly rounded, reflecting a proper bite.[2]

EARS: small, round tipped, tilted forward, and not unduly open at the base. Set far apart, and low on the head, fitting into (without distorting) the rounded contour of the head.

EYES: large, round, and full.[3] Set far apart and brilliant, giving a sweet expression to the face.[4]

BODY: of cobby type, low on the legs, deep in the chest, equally massive across shoulders and rump, with a short, well-rounded middle piece. Good muscle tone with no evidence of obesity. Large or medium in size. Quality the determining consideration rather than size.

BACK: level.

LEGS: short, thick, and strong. Forelegs straight.

PAWS: large, round, and firm. Toes carried close, five in front and four behind.

TAIL: short, but in proportion to body length.[5] Carried without a curve and at an angle lower than the back.

COAT: dense, plush, soft, and full of life. Standing out from the body due to dense undercoat. Medium in length.[6,7] Acceptable length depends on proper undercoat.

PENALIZE: for a flat or close-lying coat which falls over due to lack of support by a rich, thick undercoat. Cats with a ruff or tail feathers (long hair on the tail) shall be transferred to the AOV class.

DISQUALIFY: locket or button. Kinked or abnormal tail. Incorrect number of toes. Any apparent weakness in the hind quarters. Any apparent deformity of the spine. Deformity of the skull resulting in an asymmetrical face and/or head. For pointed cats, disqualify for crossed eyes, white toes, eye color other than blue. The above listed disqualifications apply to all Exotic Shorthair cats. Additional disqualifications are listed under "Colors."

EXOTIC SHORTHAIR COLORS[8,9]
(See page 170 for a full description of the colors listed below.)

Particolor colors: bicolors (black and white, blue and white, red and white, or cream and white), blue cream, calico, dilute calico, tabby and white, tortoiseshell, van bicolor, van calico, van dilute calico. **Pointed colors:** blue lynx point, blue point, blue-cream point, chocolate point, chocolate-tortie point, cream point, flame (red) point, lilac point, lilac-cream point, seal lynx point, seal point, tortie point. **Shaded colors:** chinchilla golden, chinchilla silver, shaded cameo, shaded golden, shaded silver, shaded tortoiseshell, shell cameo, shell tortoiseshell. **Smoke colors:** black smoke, blue smoke, blue-cream smoke, cameo smoke, smoke tortoiseshell. **Solid colors:** black, blue, chocolate, cream, lilac, peke-face red, red, white. **Tabby colors:** blue (classic, patched, and mackerel), brown (classic, patched, and mackerel), cameo (classic and mackerel), cream (classic and mackerel), peke-face red, red (classic and mackerel), silver (classic, patched, and mackerel).

Exotic Shorthair allowable outcross breeds:[10] Persian.

---

[1] ACA: " ... a decided break."
[2] TICA: "Forehead, nose, and chin in a straight line."
[3] ACFA: "However, the lids under certain gaze attentions of the cat may have a slight oriental, upward tilting appearance."
[4] CFF, TICA: "Eye color should conform to requirements for coat color."
[5] ACA, ACFA: " ... about as long as the distance between neck and tail root."
[6] ACA, TICA: "Short in length."
[7] CFF, TICA: "Slightly longer than other shorthairs." CFF: " ... but not long enough to flow."
[8] TICA recognizes the Exotic Shorthair in sepia and mink colors in addition to the colors listed below.
[9] CFF does not recognize the Exotic Shorthair in chocolate, lilac, or pointed colors.
[10] In all associations where the breed is recognized.

Havana Brown

ORIGIN

The Havana Brown was created in Great Britain during the 1950s, but brown cats first appeared at cat shows more than one hundred years ago. Some of the earliest cats imported from Siam by English cat fanciers were solid brown. An all-brown cat won first prize at a show in England in 1888. Six years later a brown cat said to belong to a breed called the Swiss Mountain Cat was exhibited in England. And in 1928 the Siamese Cat Club of Britain presented a special award to the cat with the best chocolate body in show.

By 1930, however, the Siamese Cat Club had decided that it was "unable to encourage the breeding of any but blue-eyed Siamese." Therefore, brown cats were not seen in England again until 1954, when photographs of two chestnut-colored kittens appeared in the August edition of the journal *Our Cats.* These kittens were called Bronze Leaf and Bronze Wing. They were from the Craigiehilloch cattery of Mrs. R. Clarke in Reading, County Berkshire. The mother of the kittens was a seal point Siamese named Our Miss Smith. Their father was Elmtower Bronze Idol, a brown hybrid who was the first Havana registered in England. Bronze Idol's mother was a black domestic shorthair by a seal point Siamese. Idol's father was also a seal point Siamese.

DEVELOPMENT

At first, chestnut-brown kittens with green eye color were called Havanas, though there is some disagreement about the origin of that name. Some people declare that the breed was named after the rabbit of the same color. Others say that Havana tobacco was the inspiration. When the Governing Council of the Cat Fancy in England recognized Havanas for championship competition in 1958, it assigned the name Chestnut Brown Foreign to the breed. A dozen years later GCCF reverted to calling the cats by their original name, Havana.

The first Chestnut Brown Foreigns arrived in the United States during the mid-1950s. By the end of the decade the United Cat Federation accepted the breed for championship competition under the name Havana Brown. While the American and the English versions of this breed ultimately shared the same name, they do not share the same conformation. In England the Havana is judged with foreign-bodied cats like the Siamese, Abyssinian, and Russian Blue. In the United States the general conformation is midway between the short-coupled, thickset breeds and the elongated, svelte ones. One unique characteristic of the Havana Brown is its corncob muzzle, which juts out from the end of the cat's face, dramatized by a definite whisker pinch.

Though it has been called by one British observer "a uniquely North American breed," the Havana Brown has gathered limited support in the United States and Canada. The subsequent development and instant popularity of the Oriental Shorthair, which shares a common ancestor or two with the Havana Brown, is

perhaps part of the reason for the Havana's slow progress. As happened with so many breeds in the early stages of their development, the Havana's temperament was a major problem for a time. As also happened with many other developing breeds, the Havana did not always breed true. The presence of Russian Blues and other shorthairs—some of unknown origin—in the Havana's background occasionally revealed itself in lavender Havana Brown kittens. The latter are accepted for championship competition in The International Cat Association and the Cat Fanciers' Federation.

The British version of the Havana Brown, seen here, resembles a medium-sized, Siamese-type cat more than the American rendition of the breed.

Havana Brown

Standard for the
HAVANA BROWN[1]

Courtesy of the Cat Fanciers' Association.
Differences in the Standards of other registries are
indicated at the end of the text.

HEAD: (25)
Shape 8
Ears 5
Muzzle 8
Chin 4

EYES: (10)
Shape & size 5
Color 5

COLOR: (30)
Coat color 20
Paw pads, nose leather
  & whiskers 10

COAT: 10

BODY and NECK: 15

LEGS and FEET: 5

TAIL: 5

GENERAL: the overall impression of the ideal Havana Brown is a cat of medium size with a rich, solid-color coat and good muscle tone. Due to its distinctive muzzle shape, coat color, brilliant and expressive eyes, and large forward tilted ears, it is comparable to no other breed.

HEAD: when viewed from above, the head is longer than it is wide, narrowing to a rounded muzzle with a pronounced break on both sides behind the whisker pads. The somewhat narrow muzzle and the whisker break are distinctive characteristics of the breed and must be evident in the typical specimen. When viewed in profile, there is a distinct stop at the eyes; the end of the muzzle appears almost square; this illusion is heightened by a well-developed chin, the profile outline of which is more square than round. Ideally, the tip of the nose and the chin form an almost perpendicular line. Allowance to be made for somewhat broader heads and stud jowls in the adult male. Allow for sparse hair on chin, directly below lower lip.

EARS: large, round tipped, cupped at the base, wide set but not flaring; tilted forward giving the cat an alert appearance. Little hair inside or outside.

EYES: aperture oval in shape.[2] Medium sized; set wide apart; brilliant, alert, and expressive. Color: any vivid and level shade of green; the deeper the color the better.[3]

BODY and NECK: torso medium in length, firm and muscular. Adult males tend to be larger than their female counterparts. Overall balance and proportion rather than size to be determining factor. The neck is medium in length and in proportion to the body. The general conformation is midrange between the short-coupled, thickset and the svelte breeds.

LEGS and FEET: the ideal specimen stands relatively high on its legs for a cat of medium proportions in trunk and tail. Legs are straight. The legs of females are slim and dainty; slenderness and length of leg will be less evident in the more powerfully muscled, mature males. Hind legs slightly longer than front. Paws are oval and compact. Toes: five in front and four behind.

TAIL: medium in length and in proportion to the body; slender, neither whiplike nor blunt; tapering at the end. Not too broad at the base.

COAT: short to medium[4] in length,[5] smooth and lustrous.[6]

DISQUALIFY: kinked tail, locket or button, incorrect number of toes, any eye color other than green, incorrect color of whiskers, nose leather or paw pads.

HAVANA BROWN COLORS

BROWN: a rich and even shade of warm brown throughout; color tends toward red brown (mahogany) rather than black brown. Nose leather: brown with a rosy flush. Paw pads: rosy toned. Whiskers: brown, complementing the coat color. Allow for ghost tabby markings in kittens and young adults.

LAVENDER[7] (as described in the Cat Fanciers' Federation Standard): Frost gray with a pinkish tone, sound and even throughout, the same shade to the skin. Nose leather and paw pads: lavender pink.

Havana Brown allowable outcross breeds:[8] none.

[1] TICA, which recognizes this cat in more than one color, calls the breed the Havana.
[2] ACA: "Set forward with a slight tilt toward the ears."
[3] TICA: "Allow for changing eye color up to one year."
[4] TICA: prefers a short coat.
[5] ACA, CFF: "Medium in length."
[6] TICA: "Allow for fuller coat on frosts."
[7] TICA also recognizes the Havana in this color.
[8] In all associations where the breed is recognized.

Japanese Bobtail

ORIGIN

The earliest written evidence of cats in Japan indicates that they arrived, most likely from China or Korea, at least one thousand years ago. Unfortunately, we cannot tell from records whether these immigrants had bobbed tails or whether the mutation that produces these tails first appeared in Japan. For hundreds of years bobtailed cats were highly valued and guarded, but in 1602 Japanese authorities decreed that all cats should be set free to cope with vermin which were threatening silk worms. Buying or selling cats was forbidden, and from that time forward bobtailed cats lived in the streets and on farms.

Red-and-White Japanese Bobtail

DEVELOPMENT

After World War II, United States military personnel stationed in Japan brought their families and their family pets with them. Some of these pets were pedigreed cats, and where there are pedigreed cats, there are eventually cat shows. At first, there was no interest, however, in registering the bobtailed cats of Japan. Ego, social structure, and pride of ownership among the Japanese dictated that foreign cats (as they generally are, no matter what the country) were the most prized. American-bred Persians, Siamese, or Abyssinians were much sought after, and Japanese brokers had a field day buying cats in the United States for resale at inflated prices back home.

There was no thought of registering the bobtailed cats of Japan until the early 1960s when American judges began officiating at Japanese shows. By the end of the decade there were a handful of bobtails in this country. In 1971 the Cat Fanciers' Association awarded the breed provisional status. Five years later Japanese Bobtails became eligible for championship competition in CFA, and they are now recognized in all associations.

There is a distinct difference between the Japanese Bobtail and the Manx. The Bobtail gene is recessive, and the cats, therefore, breed true. Furthermore, Bobtails are not plagued by the birth defects that occur in Manx. In order to insure the separation of these breeds, the Japanese Bobtail Breed Committee developed a Standard that would offer no advantage to anyone crossbreeding the two. Since the tail is not a physical structure that can be controlled by breeding, there is no set type required by the Standard—as long as the tail is present and is not more than three inches in length.

Long-coated kittens have appeared occasionally in some Bobtail litters, the result of deliberate or accidental crossing to other shorthaired cats carrying the recessive longhair gene. Half-tailed kittens have begun to appear, too. This demonstrates the truth of one of the oldest maxims in the cat fancy: In breeding cats it is wise to remember that what goes up, comes down. What you put in, you get out.

Standard for the
JAPANESE BOBTAIL

Courtesy of the Cat Fanciers' Association. Differences in the Standards of other registries are indicated at the end of the text.

HEAD: 20	**COLOR and MARKINGS:** 20
TYPE: 30	
	COAT: 10
TAIL: 20	

GENERAL: the Japanese Bobtail should present the overall impression of a medium-sized cat with clean lines and bone structure, well muscled but straight and slender rather than massive in build. The unique set of its eyes, combined with high cheek bones and a long parallel nose, lend a distinctive Japanese cast to the face, especially in profile, quite different from the other oriental breeds. Its short tail should resemble a bunny tail with the hair fanning out to create a pom-pom appearance which effectively camouflages the underlying bone structure of the tail.

HEAD: although the head appears long and finely chiselled, it forms almost a perfect equilateral triangle with gentle curving lines, high cheekbones, and a noticeable whisker break, the nose long and well defined by two parallel lines from tip to brow with a gentle dip at, or just below, eye level. Allowance must be made for jowls in the stud cat.

EARS: large, upright, and expressive, set wide apart but at right angles to the head rather than flaring outward, and giving the impression of being tilted forward in repose.

MUZZLE: fairly broad and rounding into the whisker break; neither pointed nor blunt.

EYES: large, oval rather than round, but wide and alert; set into the skull at a rather pronounced slant when viewed in profile. The eyeball shows a shallow curvature and should not bulge out beyond the cheekbone or the forehead.

BODY: medium in size, males proportionately larger than females. Torso long, lean, and elegant, not

tubular, showing well-developed muscular strength without coarseness. No inclination toward flabbiness or cobbiness. General balance of utmost importance.
LEGS: in keeping with the body, long, slender, and high, but not dainty or fragile in appearance. The hind legs noticeably longer than the forelegs, but deeply angled to bend when the cat is standing relaxed so that the torso remains nearly level rather than rising toward the rear. When standing, the cat's forelegs and shoulders form two continuous straight lines, close together.
PAWS: oval. Toes: five in front and four behind.
COAT: medium length, soft and silky, but without a noticeable undercoat. Relatively non-shedding.
TAIL: the tail is unique not only to the breed, but to each individual cat. This is to be used as a guideline, rather than promoting one specific type of tail out of the many that occur within the breed. The tail must be clearly visible and is composed of one or more curves, angles, or kinks, or any combination thereof. The furthest extension of the tail bone from the body should be no longer than three inches. The direction in which the tail is carried is not important. The tail may be flexible or rigid and should be of a size and shape that harmonizes with the rest of the cat.[1]
PENALIZE: short, round head, cobby build.
DISQUALIFY: tail bone absent or extending too far beyond body. Tail lacking in pom-pom or fluffy appearance. Delayed bobtail effect (i.e., the pom-pom being preceded by an inch or two of normal tail with close-lying hair rather than appearing to commence at the base of the spine).

JAPANESE BOBTAIL COLORS

COLOR: in the bicolors and tricolors (mi-ke) any color may predominate with preference given to bold, dramatic markings and vividly contrasting colors. In the solid-color cat the coat color should be of uniform density and color from the tip to the root of each hair and from the nose of the cat to the tail. Nose leather, paw pads, and eye color should harmonize generally with coat color. Blue eyes and odd eyes are allowed.

PARTICOLOR COLORS

Black and white; mi-ke (tricolor): black, red, and white; red and white; tortoiseshell: black, red, and cream.

SOLID COLORS

BLACK: dense, coal black, sound from roots to tip of fur. Shiny and free from any tinge of rust on tips. **RED:** deep, rich, clear, brilliant red, the deeper and more glowing in tone the better. **WHITE:** pure glistening white.

OTHER COLORS

OTHER JAPANESE BOBTAIL COLORS: include the following categories and any other color or pattern or combination thereof except coloring that is point restricted (i.e., Siamese markings) or unpatterned agouti (i.e., Abyssinian coloring). "Patterned" categories denote and include any variety of tabby striping or spotting with or without areas of solid (unmarked) color, with preference given to bold, dramatic markings and rich, vivid coloring. Other Solid Colors: blue or cream. Patterned self-colors: red, black, blue, cream, silver, or brown. Other bicolors: blue and white or cream and white. Patterned bicolors: red, black, blue, cream, silver, or brown combined with white. Patterned tortoiseshell: blue cream. Patterned blue cream. Dilute tricolors: blue, cream, and white. Patterned dilute tricolors: patterned mi-ke (tricolor), tortoiseshell with white.

Japanese Bobtail allowable outcross breeds:[2] none.

---

[1] CFF: "It should be noted that the tail of the Japanese Bobtail is very sensitive and should be handled very gently. No attempt should be made to straighten out the tail."

[2] In all associations where the breed is recognized.

Korat

ORIGIN

The first representation of the cat believed to be the ancestor of the modern-day Korat appears in the *Cat-Book Poems,* a manuscript preserved in the Thai National Library in Bangkok. This anonymous work contains verses that describe several kinds of cats. Among them is a solid blue presumed to be the ancestor of the Korat. Since the *Cat-Book Poems* was rescued from the Siamese city of Ayudha, which was 417 years old when it was leveled by Burmese invaders in 1767, we can assume that the Korat is more than two centuries old, and quite possibly older. Yet even though it is the namesake of the Siamese province of Korat, this silver-blue cat with the heart-shaped face and luminous green eyes can be found in most of the other provinces of Thailand (formerly Siam) as well.

In 1896 a blue cat was entered in the Siamese class at the National Cat Club show in England. The judge disqualified the cat because it did not look like the other Siamese. Its body was blue instead of biscuit colored. The cat's owner, who had recently returned from Siam, protested that his entry was indeed from that country, and that he had seen other cats like it on his journey. Whether this cat was a Korat or a blue point Siamese is not certain, but it has been established that the seal point Siamese, which is also common to Siam, carries the gene for blue color; and there surely had to have been some crossbreedings between Siamese and the self-colored blue cats in Siam, for it has also been reported that blue point kittens appeared in the litters born to the earliest Korats imported to this country. Thus it is safe to assume that the Korat began life in the United States as an established hybrid, which is how the Cat Fanciers' Association classified the breed when it was first recognized.

DEVELOPMENT

Although a Mr. Robins living in New York City in 1906 asserted that blue cats then existed in the province of Korat, little else was known about the breed in the United States until a pair of cats from Thailand arrived at Portland, Oregon, on June 12, 1959. These cats—a brother and sister named Nara and Darra—were a gift to Mrs. Jean Johnson of Gresham, Oregon, from a friend in Thailand. Jean and her husband Robert had lived in Thailand from 1947 to 1953. During their stay, Jean Johnson asked her Thai friends where she might find a Siamese cat, but she discovered that her friends had a different cat in mind than the Siamese she described.

As any American would have, Jean Johnson was referring to a buff-colored cat with dark-brown points: a seal point Siamese. When she eventually obtained one, her Thai friends informed her that while this was a Siamese cat, it was not *the* cat of the Siamese people: the Korat or *Si-Sawat* (see-sah-what) cat. In the Thai language the compound *Si-Sawat* means *a mingled color, with a smooth glossy shell*—a definition probably inspired by the silver sheen of the Korat's fur. And among *Sawat*'s several meanings are *good fortune* and *prosperity.* Thus, the Korat is also known as the good-luck cat.

Following its importation, the Korat attracted the attention of several cat fanciers in the United States. In September 1964 *The New York Times* reported the appearance of two Korats at the Empire Cat Club show, and the following year the Korat Cat Fanciers Association was formed. KCFA's preliminary membership list included twenty-six breeders and/or owners in North America. These Korat fanciers submitted a proposed Standard to various registries, and in 1966 Korats were accepted by the American Cat Association, the now defunct National Cat Fanciers Association, and the United Cat Federation. By the end of the decade, all other registries had followed suit.

This universal acceptance had been preceded by much discussion about whether the Korat might actually be a blue Burmese. There was a great similarity in body type between the two breeds at the time, and both had overly large eyes and close-lying fur. Consideration was given to registering the Korat as a Burmese color, not as a separate breed, but Burmese breeders would have rather died than accept any color other than sable into their breed. In fact, they would not even acknowledge the existence of the dilute colors of sable for the longest time.

The Korat has been a cat of good fortune indeed. There are no genetic deficiencies attached to this breed. Although some outcrosses were made to blue point Siamese in order to enlarge the Korat gene pool after it had first been brought to the United States, the overriding concern of the Korat breed club has been to keep this cat as pure—and as true to its original look—as possible. The breed club further requires that anyone wishing to register a Korat must show proof that the cat originated in Thailand.

Korat

Standard for the KORAT

Courtesy of the Cat Fanciers' Association. Differences in the Standards of other registries are indicated at the end of the text.

HEAD: (25)
Broad head 5
Profile 4
Breadth between
    eyes 4
Ear set and
    placement 4
Heart shape 5
Chin and jaw 3

EYES: (15)
Size 5
Shape 5
Placement 5

BODY: (25)
Body 15
Legs and feet 5
Tail 5

COAT: (10)
Short 4
Texture 3
Close lying 3

COLOR: (25)
Body color 20
Eye color 5

GENERAL: the Korat is a rare cat even in Thailand, its country of origin, and because of its unusually fine disposition, is greatly loved by the Thai people, who regard it as a "good luck" cat. Its general appearance is of a silver-blue cat with a heavy silver sheen, medium sized, hard bodied, and muscular. All smooth curves with huge eyes, luminous, alert, and expressive. Perfect physical condition, alert appearance.

HEAD: when viewed from the front, or looking down from just back of the head, the head is heart shaped with breadth between and across the eyes.[1,2] The eyebrow ridges form the upper curves of the heart, and the sides of the face gently curve down to the chin to complete the heart shape. Undesirable: any pinch or narrowness, especially between or across the eyes.

PROFILE: well defined with a slight stop between forehead and nose—which has a lionlike downward curve just above the leather. Undesirable: nose that appears either long or short in proportion.[3]

CHIN and JAW: strong and well developed, making a balancing line for the profile and properly completing the heart shape. Neither overly squared nor sharply pointed, nor a weak chin that gives the head a pointed look.

EARS: large, with a rounded tip and large flare[4] at base, set high on head, giving an alert expression. Inside ears sparsely furnished. Hairs on outside of ears extremely short and close.

BODY: semicobby, neither compact nor svelte.[5] The torso is distinctive. Broad chested with good space between forelegs. Muscular, supple, with a feeling of hard, coiled-spring power and unexpected weight. Back is carried in a curve. The males tend to be larger than females.

LEGS: well proportioned to body. Distance along back from nape of neck to base of tail appears to be equal to distance from base of tail to floor. Front legs slightly shorter than back legs.

PAWS: oval. Toes: five in front and four behind.

TAIL: medium in length, heavier at the base, tapering to a rounded tip. Nonvisible kink permitted.

EYES: large[6] and luminous. Particularly prominent with an extraordinary depth and brilliance. Wide open and oversized for the face. Eye aperture, which shows as well rounded when fully open, has an Asian slant when closed or partially closed. Undesirable: small or dull-looking eyes.

COAT: single. Hair is short in length,[7] glossy and fine, lying close to the body. The coat over the spine is inclined to break as the cat moves.

DISQUALIFY: visible kink. Incorrect number of toes. White spot or locket. Any color but silver blue.

KORAT COLOR

COLOR: silver blue all over, tipped with silver, the more silver tipping the better. Without shading or tabby markings. Where the coat is short, the sheen of the silver is intensified. Undesirable: coats with silver tipping on only the head, legs, and feet. Nose leather and lips: dark blue or lavender. Paw pads: dark blue ranging to lavender with a pinkish tinge. Eye color: luminous[8] green preferred, amber cast acceptable. Kittens and adolescents have yellow or amber to amber-green eyes. Color is not usually true until the cat is mature, usually two to four years of age.

Korat allowable outcross breeds:[9] none.

---

[1] ACFA, TICA: "Forehead large, flat."
[2] TICA: "With an indentation or crease (predominantly in the male) that accentuates the heart shape, giving the ideal head the appearance of a double heart or of a heart within a heart."
[3] ACFA: "Nose is short."
[4] ACFA: "Flair."
[5] ACFA: "Medium in size."
[6] ACA: "Extra large."
[7] ACFA, CFF: "Short to medium."
[8] ACFA, CFF: "Brilliant."
[9] In all associations where the breed is recognized.

Maine Coon Cat

ORIGIN

The Maine Coon Cat is a naturally occurring breed whose origins have been described in fantasies and legends that greatly add to its charm. According to some observers the Maine Coon descended from cats that had been sent to the United States from France by Marie Antoinette. Others believe that a sea captain named Coon brought Persian and Angora cats to this country, and Coon's cats, after jumping ship, introduced the longhair gene to the New World.

Persons knowing little about cat behavior and reproduction used the term Coon cats for another reason: they believed the Maine Coon resulted from a cross between a racoon and a cat. This is genetically impossible, even though many of the first longhaired domestic cats were brown ticked or seal brown in color and had tabby rings on their tails—much like the racoon.

Legends notwithstanding, early settlers undoubtedly brought the ancestors of the Maine Coon to America, and these were very likely the first domestic cats to arrive on the North American continent. They existed, no doubt, in much of the settled northeastern coast and on some coastal islands. It has not been established that Maine Coon Cats were more or less popular in Maine than they were anyplace else. Like most new breeds, they excelled in numbers and recognition where there were interested fanciers to promote them, and Maine seems to have been the first place where this occurred.

DEVELOPMENT

Maine Coon Cats were exhibited in shows as early as the 1860s. They were apparently very popular, and were frequent winners. In the 1895 Madison Square Garden Show, a brown tabby Maine Coon owned by Mrs. E.N. Baker was best cat. But as cat shows became more sophisticated and as more imported varieties came to this country, cats with long pedigrees and generations of like-to-like breeding gained preference with fanciers. Their goal was to produce cats of uniform color, without white markings or lockets. This new vogue caused the Maine Coon to take a back seat at shows and, eventually, to disappear from the show bench altogether.

Persian breeders continued to use Maine Coons for a time as outcrosses because they were especially strong and vigorous. In those days registries accepted cats of unknown parentage if they conformed to the colors recognized for a breed and if the person registering the cat provided a sworn affidavit testifying that it was a longhair or whatever else a breed Standard might require. Since Persian type then was very similar to the Maine Coon's, any solid white, blue, black, or red Coon Cats were quite acceptable in Persian breeding programs. The Cat Fanciers' Association registration form allowed longhairs to be of Persian or Angora "type." Persian type was preferred, but there was no distinction made between the two for registration purposes.

During the years when the Maine Coon was in decline, loyal fanciers attempted to gain recognition for the breed. Their efforts were always defeated by the snobbery of other breeders and the Coon fanciers' inability to develop a fitting Standard. Should it be a man-made, progressive Standard: the kind that allows a cat room to grow like the Persian and the Siamese? Or should it be designed to describe and preserve an existing cat? And if so, whose cats would be used to set the Standard to which all other breeders would have to conform? Furthermore, other opponents of Maine Coon recognition insisted that these cats did not possess desirable conformation and that the many colors occurring in the breed could not be controlled through selective breeding. No one would have dared to request recognition of any and all colors that appeared in litters. That would have made the breed appear too common.

Time and again the question came up: is the Maine Coon Cat simply the longhaired variety of the domestic, or American, Shorthair? Experience suggested that Maine Coons were originally the true Angora cats, and some books mention that New Englanders reported seeing Angora cats in the northeastern woods. In any case, the liberty to breed at random did produce a natural breed that is hail, hearty, and prolific. A breed whose wide variety of colors and markings appeals to everyone.

Many of the top-winning Maine Coons are a far cry from those still living on farms or in a semiwild condition. Today's show cats are much larger, longer, and in many cases too fine in bone and sparse in coat. The vast number of entries at the shows will result, in time, in a much more uniform cat; and it will, as with all other breeds, come together.

Though it is a longhair, the Coon Cat has a different texture and coat quality from the Persian. Maine Coons will mat if they are neglected totally, but they remain mat-free with little effort. A good metal comb and a bath will produce a strikingly handsome cat.

Standard for the
MAINE COON CAT

Courtesy of the Cat Fanciers' Association. Differences in the Standards of other registries are indicated at the end of the text.

HEAD: (30)
Shape 15
Ears 10
Eyes 5

BODY: (35)
Shape 20
Neck 5
Legs and Feet 5
Tail 5

COAT: 20

COLOR: (15)
Body color 10
Eye color 5

Brown Classic Tabby Maine Coon

GENERAL: originally a working cat, the Maine Coon is solid, rugged, and can endure a harsh climate. A distinctive characteristic is its smooth, shaggy coat. With an essentially amiable disposition, it has adapted to varied environments.

HEAD SHAPE: medium in width and medium long in length[1] with a squareness to the muzzle. Allowance should be made for broadening in older studs. Cheekbones high. Chin firm and in line with nose and upper lip. Nose medium long in length; slightly concave when viewed in profile.

EARS: large, well tufted, wide at base, tapering to appear pointed.[2] Set high and well apart.[3]

EYES: large, expressive, wide set.[4] Slightly oblique setting with slant toward outer base of ear. Eye color should be shades of green, gold, or copper,[5] though white cats may also be either blue or odd-eyed. There is no relationship between eye color and coat color.

NECK: medium long.

BODY SHAPE: muscular, broad chested. Size medium to large. Females generally smaller than males. Body should be long with all parts in proportion so appearance well-balanced, rectangular with no part of the anatomy so exaggerated as to foster weakness.[6] Allowance should be made for slow maturation.

LEGS and FEET: legs substantial, wide set, of medium length, and in proportion to the body. Paws large, round, well tufted. Five toes in front; four in back.

TAIL: long,[7] wide at base, and tapering. Fur long and flowing.

COAT: heavy and shaggy;[8] shorter on the shoulders and longer on the stomach and britches. Frontal ruff desirable. Texture silky with coat falling smoothly.[9]

PENALIZE: a coat that is short or overall even.

DISQUALIFY: delicate bone structure. Undershot chin. Crossed eyes. Kinked tail. Incorrect number of toes. Buttons, lockets, or spots.

MAINE COON CAT COLORS

(See page 170 for a full description of the colors listed below.)

Solid colors: white, black, blue, red, cream. **Tabby colors:** silver tabby (classic, mackerel, patched), red tabby (classic, mackerel), brown tabby (classic, mackerel, patched), blue tabby (classic, mackerel, patched), cream tabby (classic, mackerel), cameo tabby. **Tabby-with-white colors:** colors accepted are silver, red, brown, blue, or cream. **Patched-tabby-with-white colors:** colors accepted are silver, brown, or blue. **Particolors:** tortoiseshell, tortoiseshell with white, calico, dilute calico, blue cream, blue cream with white, bicolor (red and white, black and white, blue and white, cream and white. **Other Main Coon colors:** chinchilla silver, shaded silver, shell cameo (red chinchilla), shaded cameo (red shaded), black smoke, blue smoke, cameo smoke (red smoke), blue-cream smoke, tortie smoke.

Maine Coon Cat allowable outcross breeds:[10] none.

---

[1] ACFA: " ... slightly longer than wide."
[2] ACFA: " ... with lynxlike tipping and inner tufts extending beyond the outer edge of the ear."
[3] ACFA: "The distance between them being equal to the width of an ear at its base."
[4] ACA and ACFA prefer a round eye. TICA specifies oval. CFA and CFF state no preference.
[5] ACA, CFF, and TICA do not allow copper.
[6] ACFA: "When viewed from the rear, there is a definite squareness to the rump."
[7] ACFA, TICA: "At least the length of the body."
[8] ACFA: " ... and markedly subject to seasonal variation."
[9] ACFA: "Coat texture may vary with coat color."
[10] In all associations where the breed is recognized.

Manx

ORIGIN

It is difficult to think of the Isle of Man, located in the Irish Sea off the coast of England, without being reminded of the tailless cat so closely identified with this scenic place. Fanciful theories about the origin of the Manx run rampant, adding to the mystique of this unusual cat, which is so revered that it appears on a British coin. Yet no one knows how or when the Manx arrived on the Isle of Man. A logical explanation is that a Spanish ship with tailless cats on board foundered on Spanish Rock, which is close to the Manx shore. The cats swam to the rock and from there to the island at low tide.

DEVELOPMENT

The Manx was a popular, established breed in England long before the birth of the cat fancy in the 1870s, and Manx-type cats may have existed in other places as early as the 1500s. The spontaneous mutation that results in taillessness in cats can appear at any time in any location, but the size of the Isle of Man–221 square miles—insured that the gene responsible for taillessness was easily propagated. This gene is an incomplete dominant. If a kitten inherits one gene for taillessness and another for a normal tail, the kitten will be tailless.

While taillessness is the Manx trademark, the breed produces a variety of kittens: *rumpies,* which are completely tailless, with a hollow or dimple where the tail would normally be; *risers,* which have enough tail vertebrae to form a small knob at the end of the spine; *stumpies,* which have a definite, visible tail stump that's usually moveable but is often curved or kinked; and *longies,* or fully tailed cats. A Manx is at its finest, of course, when it is absolutely tailless. This is perfection highly prized, but risers may also be shown if the rise does not impede the progress of a judge's hand as it moves along the cat's back and over the spine.

Breeding two rumpy Manx together does not result in a complete litter of rumpies. This variety occurs because all Manx possess one gene for taillessness and another for full tails. Manx kittens that inherit two genes for taillessness—a lethal condition—die in the womb at an early stage of development. Genetic modifiers account for the differences in length on tailed Manx.

Manx are a very discouraging breed. It would be an injustice to the cat and to the new fancier not to mention the disappointments the prospective breeder should be prepared to cope with. Only those fanciers with a deep concern for the Manx' well being should be involved with them, for heartaches most frequently exceed triumphs.

There is good reason to argue that the Manx should not be a natural breed. True, it produces tailless kittens quite naturally, but a pure breed should not produce defects from like-to-like breedings. This happens all too often with Manx. Kittens may be born with a variety of spinal problems and weak hindquarters that lead to crippling. For as long as Manx have been recognized— and there were Manx taking prizes in British shows more than a century ago—the genetic defects have never been bred out of these cats.

A healthy Manx, however, is a joy to own, and anyone who does becomes totally devoted to the breed. Its rabbitlike gait and amusing antics bring endless pleasure and entertainment. It is important, therefore, to select for breeding those Manx that have the proper back and spine line. Too often Manx are seen on the show circuit that are swaybacked instead of possessing a rounded arch and a nice, high rump. Because of the potential for lameness in Manx, the conscientious judge will not place a win on a Manx that will not stand up. The cat should not rest on its hocks like a rabbit. It must be able to stand on all four paws.

There are many breeders inclined to link the Manx with the American or the British Shorthair by allowing the use of these breeds as outcrosses for the Manx. This would add to the Manx gene pool, a matter which the cat fancy will have to deal with if the Manx is to continue as a healthy, vigorous breed.

White Manx

Standard for the MANX

Courtesy of the Cat Fanciers' Association. Differences in the Standards of other registries are indicated at the end of the text.

HEAD and EARS: 25	**LEGS and FEET:** 15
EYES: 5	**COAT:** 10
BODY: 25	**COLOR and MARKINGS:** 5
TAILLESSNESS: 15	

GENERAL: the overall impression of the Manx cat is that of roundness; round head with firm, round muzzle and prominent cheeks; broad chest; substantial short front legs; short back which arches from shoulders to a round rump; great depth of flank; and rounded, muscular thighs. The heavy, glossy double coat accentuates the round appearance. With regard to condition, the Manx presented in the show ring should show evidence of a healthy physical appearance, feeling firm and muscular, neither too fat nor too lean. The Manx should be alert, clear of eye, with a glistening, clean coat.

HEAD and EARS: Round head with prominent cheeks and a jowly appearance. Head is slightly longer than it is broad. Moderately rounded forehead, pronounced cheekbones, and jowliness (jowliness more evident in adult males) enhance the round appearance. Definite whisker break, with large, round whisker pads. In profile there is a gentle nose dip.[1] Well-developed muzzle, slightly longer than broad, with a strong chin. Short, thick neck. Ears wide at the base, tapering gradually to a rounded tip, with sparse interior furnishings. Medium in size in proportion to the head, widely spaced and set slightly outward. When viewed from behind, the ear set resembles the rocker on a cradle.

EYES: large, round, and full. Set at a slight angle toward the nose (outer corners slightly higher than inner corners). Ideal eye color conforms to requirements of coat color.[2,3]

BODY: solidly muscled, compact, and well balanced, medium in size with sturdy bone structure. The Manx is stout in appearance, with broad chest and well-sprung ribs; surprisingly heavy when lifted. The constant repetition of curves and circles gives the Manx the appearance of great substance and durability, a cat that is powerful without the slightest hint of coarseness. Males may be somewhat larger than females. Flank (fleshy area of the side between the ribs and hip) has greater depth than in other breeds, causing considerable depth to the body when viewed from the side. The short back forms a smooth, continuous arch from shoulders to rump, curving at the rump to form the desirable round look. Shortness of back is unique to the Manx, but is in proportion to the entire cat and may be somewhat longer in the male.

TAILLESSNESS: absolute in the perfect specimen, with a decided hollow at the end of the backbone where, in the tailed cat, a tail would begin. A rise of the bones at the end of the spine is allowed and should not be penalized unless it is such that it stops the judge's hand, thereby spoiling the tailless appearance of the cat. The rump is extremely broad and round.

LEGS and FEET: heavily boned, forelegs short and set well apart to emphasize the broad, deep chest. Hind legs much longer than forelegs, with heavy, muscular thighs and substantial lower legs. Longer hind legs cause the rump to be considerably higher than the shoulders. Hind legs are straight when viewed from behind.[4] Paws are neat and round, with five toes in front and four behind.

COAT: double coat is short and dense, with a well-padded quality due to the longer, open outer coat and the close, cottony undercoat. Texture of outer guard hairs is somewhat hard; appearance is glossy. Coat may be thicker during cooler months of the year.

TRANSFER TO AOV: definite, visible tail joint. Long, silky coat.

SEVERELY PENALIZE: if the judge is unable to make the cat stand or walk properly.[5]

DISQUALIFY: evidence of poor physical condition; incorrect number of toes; evidence of hybridization.

MANX COLORS

(See page 170 for a full description of the colors listed below.)

Particolor colors: bicolors (white with unbrindled patches of black, white with unbrindled patches of blue, white with unbrindled patches of red, or white with unbrindled patches of cream); blue cream, calico, dilute calico, tortoiseshell. **Shaded colors:** chinchilla silver, shaded silver. **Smoke colors:** black smoke, blue smoke. **Solid colors:** black, blue, cream, red, white. **Tabby colors:** blue patched tabby, blue tabby (classic, mackerel), brown patched tabby, brown tabby (classic, mackerel), cream tabby (classic, mackerel), red tabby (classic, mackerel), silver patched tabby, silver tabby (classic, mackerel). **Other Manx colors:** any other color or pattern with the exception of those showing hybridization resulting in the colors chocolate, lavender, the Himalayan pattern, or these combinations with white.

Manx allowable outcross breeds:[6] none.

---

[1] ACA, ACFA, CFF: "The nose is slightly longer and broader than in the American Shorthair."

[2] ACFA, CFF, TICA " ... but in the Manx should be considered only if all other points are equal."

[3] ACA: "Any eye color allowed and of secondary importance."

[4] CFF: "In well-developed adults a slight pigeon-toed attitude is allowed when [the cat] is viewed from the rear. The hair will often be worn on the lower part of the leg below the hock because the Manx rests on this part as often as it does on its paws and should not be faulted for this."

[5] CFF: "The hopping gait should be allowed in kittens and very young, immature adults."

[6] In all associations where the breed is recognized.

Norwegian Forest Cat

ORIGIN

No one knows how long the Norwegian Forest Cat has existed in Norway or how it got there. In nature, the Forest Cat is most plentiful on the farms and in the woodlands of central Norway. This area lies north of every state except Alaska, and there is no doubt that Norway's harsh winter climate played an important role in the development of the Forest Cat's resourcefulness, vitality, and water-repellent coat.

Until the 1930s no one but the farmers of Norway, who prized the cat's superior hunting ability, paid any attention to the Forest Cat. The first Norwegian ever shown was a red-and-white male called Petten, exhibited in 1930 by Mrs. Holdis Rohlss, who later founded a short-lived club to promote the Forest Cat, which is known as the *Skogkatt* in its native land.

DEVELOPMENT

In the decades following World War II, the Norwegian Forest Cat was in danger of becoming extinct because of continued interbreeding with free-ranging domestic cats. Then, in the early 1970s Carl-Fredrik Nordane,

Brown Mackerel Tabby-and-White Norwegian Forest Cat

102

a former president of the Norwegian Cat Association, organized a breed club to champion the Forest Cat and to oversee its preservation through planned breeding programs. Because of Nordane's work, the general assembly of the Feline International Federation (FIFe) of Europe voted in late November 1977 to accept the Forest Cat for championship competition. When Nordane returned to Oslo from Paris the next day, he was greeted with music, flags, and a parade of grateful Norwegian Forest Cat fanciers.

Two years to the month after its acceptance in Europe, the Norwegian Forest Cat arrived in the United States. The breed is not yet accepted for championship competition by every association in the United States. Part of the reason is its resemblance to the Maine Coon, but Norwegian Forest Cat breeders insist that there are important differences between the two cats.

Some of these differences follow. The Maine Coon is long and rectangular; the Norwegian is boxy. The Maine Coon has a slight curve in its nose; the Norwegian, especially the male, has a straight nose. The Maine Coon has a prominent, squared-off muzzle; the Norwegian's muzzle fits neatly into its triangular face. The Maine Coon's ears sit upright on top of its head; the Norwegian's ears are wide spaced and tilted forward.

Standard for the
NORWEGIAN FOREST CAT

Courtesy of The International Cat Association. Differences in the Standards of other registries are indicated at the end of the text.

HEAD: 30
Shape and
  proportion 10
Ears 5
Eyes 5
Nose 5
Muzzle 5

BODY and TAIL: 30
Body 10
Legs and feet 10
Tail 10

COAT: 20

COLOR and MARKINGS: 10

CONDITION and BALANCE: 10

RECOGNIZED CATEGORIES / DIVISIONS / COLORS: Traditional category, all divisions, all colors.
HEAD: triangular shaped, leaning toward but not quite approaching an equilateral triangle (all three sides equal in length) from the outer base of the ear to the tip of the chin. The overall appearance should be as long as it is broad. The frontal skull is flat. The neck is medium short with heavy musculature, not in proportion to the body.
EARS: The ears are medium large, slightly rounded at the tip, set as much on the side of the head as on the top of the head; upright, alert, and arched forward as though listening. The ear furnishings are heavy. Lynx tips are desirable, but absence should not be considered a fault.
EYES: large, almond shaped, and expressive, set at a slight angle with the outer corner slightly higher than the inner corner.[1] Green-gold eye color is preferred although shades of green and gold are acceptable. White cats may be copper, blue, or odd-eyed.
NOSE: medium long, straight from the top of the forehead to the tip of the nose with no break. Females may exhibit a minimal curvature, but no break. Preference should be given to females with a straight nose.
MUZZLE: the muzzle shall be well developed. The end of the muzzle appears nearly square; this illusion is heightened by a well-developed chin; the profile outline is more square than round, not sharply pointed, and with no evidence of snippiness, foxiness, or a whisker pinch. Chin shall be firm with no malocclusion.
BODY: the body is of moderate length, heavily boned, with powerful appearance, showing a full chest and considerable girth without being fat. Males should be large and imposing; females are considerably smaller than males and are not faulted for their size. It should be noted that this breed is not fully mature until five years of age. The flank (fleshy area of the side between the ribs and the hips) has great depth, causing considerable depth to the body when viewed from the side.

LEGS and FEET: Legs are medium in length with the hind legs longer than the front legs, making the rump higher than the shoulders. The thighs are heavily muscled with substantial lower legs. When viewed from the rear, the legs are straight. The feet are large, round, firm, and well tufted. A distinguishing trait of this breed is that it walks on tiptoes, not flat footed.

TAIL: long and flowing. The desirable length should be equal to the body length from the base of the tail to the shoulders. When walking, the tail is carried high like a ship under full sail.

COAT: a distinguishing double coat; when pressed down with the finger tips, an impression will be left momentarily in the coat. The coat is long, smooth, soft, and not dry, with oily guard hairs hanging from the back down the sides covering the undercoat. The ruff consists of three separate sections: short back-of-the neck ruff; side mutton chops; and full front bib. There are full britches on the hind legs,[2] and the coat is uneven. Solid colors and bicolors have a smoother, softer coat than tabbies. The season of the year should be considered when judging these cats, as the overall coat is shorter and the mutton chops and breast collar are lacking in the summer; only the tail, ear, and toe tufts distinguish the cat as a longhair. Maturity must also be considered when judging these cats, for cats kept indoors year round or living in temperate climates exhibit coats which are softer and shorter than those spending time in cooler climates.[3]

COLOR and MARKINGS: All colors and combinations of colors are acceptable with or without white, with the exception of pointed cats. In the tabby group, white or off-white is allowable on the chin, breast, and stomach. Buttons, spots, and lockets are allowable in all colors.

CONDITION and BALANCE: the appearance of an alert, healthy, firm and muscular, well-proportioned cat is essential. The males should be large and imposing; females medium sized and well balanced. Good muscle tone with no evidence of obesity or emaciation is necessary. Lack of good condition is evidenced by dullness in the eyes and lack of coat luster. Well balanced physically and temperamentally; gentle and amenable to handling.

ALLOWANCES: button, spots, and lockets allowed in all colors. Females allowed minimal curvature in nose profile, but preference is given to those with straight nose. Allow for smoother, softer coat in solids and bicolors.

PENALIZE: short legs, cobby body, short nose with a break, round or square head, small ears, dry coat, matted fur, short tail, or any extreme variance from these set standards. Delicate bone structure is a cause for severe penalty.

WITHHOLD ALL AWARDS: See TICA show rules Article Sixteen for rules governing penalties/disqualification applying to all cats.

Allowable Norwegian Forest Cat outcross breeds:[4] none.

---

[1] ACFA, CFF: "It should be noted that between the ages of six months to a year, the cat goes through a stage in development where the eyes appear almost round; this should change around the time of their first birthday."

[2] ACFA: "Allowance should be made for less ruff and britches in younger cats under two years of age."

[3] ACFA: "It should be noted that it takes about two years for the coat to come in completely on colors other than tabbies. The season of the year should be considered when judging these cats as the overall coat is shorter and the mutton chops and breast collar are lacking or are much shorter in the summer; during hot weather the tail, ear, and toe tufts distinguish the cat as a longhair."

[4] In all associations where the breed is recognized.

Ocicat

The Ocicat was developed accidentally in the early 1960s by Virginia Daly, a Berkeley, Michigan, breeder. Daly worked with several breeds and was known, as she put it, to experiment with "rare, unusual, newly developed varieties." This experimentation did not always sit well with other breeders, one of whom said to Daly one day, "The next thing you'll be making will be an Abyssinian-pointed Siamese." Until then, said Daly, "I had never dreamed of such a thing, but I decided to take up the challenge."

Daly bred a seal point Siamese female to a ruddy Abyssinian male. The resulting kittens looked like Abyssinians, but they carried the recessive gene for the Siamese pattern. When Daly bred one of them—a female named She—to a Siamese, She produced the Aby-pointed Siamese that Daly had been looking for. She also produced a large, ivory cat with bright, golden spots and copper eyes. Daly named the cat Tonga. Daly's daughter called Tonga an Ocicat because of his resemblance to an Ocelot.

Tonga was sold for $10, with the agreement that he be neutered. Shortly afterward, Daly read an article in the *Journal of Cat Genetics* in which the author suggested that somebody ought to try to recreate the long-extinct Egyptian spotted fishing cat. Daly wrote to the author saying that she had and that the cat had just been sold.

The author wrote back saying that Tonga should be bred to his mother, but Tonga was never available when She was in season. Tonga's father was, and a breeding between him and She produced a second Ocicat. At this point, Daly gave up on the Aby-pointed Siamese. "There are enough Siamese in the world," she said. "So why continue with bread when you can make cake?"

DEVELOPMENT

At the 1966 Detroit Persian Society Show, Tonga caught the eye of a Cat Fanciers' Association judge.

CFA soon announced that the Ocicat would be accepted for registration. Yet by October 15, 1970, only two Ocicats had been registered. Personal obligations in the Daly family and a pet-limitation ordinance in Berkeley, Michigan, delayed the further development of the Ocicat, and the breed did not advance from registration to provisional status until February 1986. The following year it was accepted for championship competition by CFA and The International Cat Association. At that point, the Ocicat became an overnight sensation.

Between 1986 and 1989, annual Ocicat registrations jumped 292 percent. In fact, three out of four Ocicats registered between 1958 and 1990 in CFA were registered in the last five years of the 1980s.

"For a long time the Ocicat just didn't have the right sort of promotion," says Bill McKee, who was instrumental in getting the breed accepted. But once a new breed club was started, "a lot of people came out of the woodwork who had had Ocicats but weren't doing anything with them."

**Standard for the
OCICAT**

Courtesy of the Cat Fanciers' Association. Differences in the Standards of other registries are indicated at the end of the text.

HEAD: (25)
Skull 5
Muzzle 10
Ears 5
Eyes 5

BODY: (25)
Size 5
Torso 10
Legs and feet 5
Tail 5

COAT and COLOR: (25)
Texture 5
Coat color 5
Contrast 10
Eye color 5

PATTERN: 25

Cinnamon Ocicat

GENERAL: the Ocicat is a medium to large, well-spotted, agouti cat of moderate type. It displays the look of an athletic animal: well muscled and solid, graceful and lithe, yet with a fullness of body and chest. It is alert to its surroundings and shows great vitality. The Ocicat is found in many colors with darker spots appearing on a lighter background. Each hair (except on the tip of tail) has several bands of color. It is where these bands fall together that a thumbprint-shaped spot is formed. This powerful, athletic, yet graceful, spotted cat is particularly noted for its "wild" appearance.

HEAD: the skull is a modified wedge showing a slight curve from muzzle to cheek, with a visible, but gentle, rise from the bridge of the nose to the brow. The muzzle is broad and well defined with a suggestion of squareness, and in profile shows good length. The chin is strong, and the jaw firm with a proper bite. The moderate whisker pinch is not too severe. The head is carried gracefully on an arching neck. An allowance is made for jowls on mature males.

EARS: alert, moderately large, and set so as to corner the upper, outside dimensions of the head. If an imaginary horizontal line is drawn across the brow, the ears should be set at a 45-degree angle, i.e., neither too high nor too low. When they occur, ear tufts extending vertically from the tips of the ears are a bonus.

EYES: large, almond shaped, and angling slightly upwards toward the ears with more than the length of an eye between the eyes.

SIZE: medium to large.[1] The Ocicat should have a surprising weight for its size. It should be noted that females are generally smaller than males. The overall structure and quality of this cat should be of greater consideration than mere size alone.

TORSO: solid, rather long bodied, with depth and fullness but never coarse. Substantial bone and muscle development, yet with an athletic appearance. There should be some depth of chest with ribs slightly sprung, the back is level to slightly higher in the rear, and the flank reasonably level. Preference is given to the athletic, powerful, and lithe, and objection taken to the bulky or coarse.

LEGS and FEET: legs should be of good substance and well muscled, medium long, powerful and in good proportion to the body. Feet should be oval and compact with five toes in front and four in back, with size in proportion to legs.

TAIL: fairly long, medium slim with only a slight taper and with a dark tip.

COAT TEXTURE: short, smooth, and satiny in texture with a lustrous sheen. Tight, close lying, and sleek, yet long enough to accommodate the necessary bands of color. There should be no suggestion of woolliness.

TICKING: all hairs except the tip of the tail are banded. Within the markings, hairs are tipped with a darker color, while hairs in the ground color are tipped with a lighter color.

COAT COLOR: all colors should be clear and pleasing. The lightest color is usually found on the face around the eyes, and on the chin and lower jaw. The darkest color is found on the tip of the tail. Contrast is scored separately.

CONTRAST: distinctive markings should be clearly seen from any orientation. Those on the face, legs, and tail may be darker than those on the torso. Ground color may be darker on the saddle and lighter on the underside, chin, and lower jaw. Penalties should be given if spotting is faint or blurred, though it must be remembered that pale colors will show less contrast than darker ones.

EYE COLOR: all eye colors except blue are allowed. There is no correspondence between eye color and coat color. Depth of color is preferred.

PATTERN: there is an intricate tabby "M" on the forehead, with markings extending up over the head between the ears and breaking into small spots on the lower neck and shoulders. Mascara markings are found around the eyes and on cheeks. Rows of round spots run along the spine from shoulder blades to tail. The tail has horizontal brush strokes down the top, ideally alternating with spots, and a dark tip. Spots are scattered across the shoulders and hindquarters, extending as far as possible down the legs. There are broken bracelets on the lower legs and broken necklaces at the throat–the more broken the better. Large well-scattered, thumbprint-shaped spots appear on the sides of the torso, with a subtle suggestion of a classic tabby pattern–a spot circled by spots in place of the bull's eye. The belly is also well-spotted. The eyes are rimmed with the darkest coat color and surrounded by the lightest color. Penalties should be given for elongated spots following a mackerel pattern.

DISQUALIFY: white locket or spotting, or white anywhere other than around eyes, nostrils, chin, and upper throat (except white agouti ground in silvered colors). Kinked or otherwise deformed tail. Blue eyes. Incorrect number of toes. Due to the spotted, patched-tabby (torbie) cats resulting from the sex-linked O gene, no reds, creams, or torbies are allowed. Very rufous cinnamons and fawns may resemble red or cream, but never produce female torbies.

OCICAT COLORS

BLUE: blue spotting on a pale blue or buff agouti ground. Nose leather: blue rimmed with dark blue. Paw pads: blue.

BLUE SILVER: blue spotting on a white agouti ground. Nose leather: blue rimmed with dark blue. Paw pads: blue.

CHOCOLATE: chocolate spotting on a warm-ivory, agouti ground. Nose leather: pink rimmed with chocolate. Paw pads: chocolate pink.

CHOCOLATE SILVER: chocolate spotting on a white agouti ground. Nose leather: pink rimmed with chocolate. Paw pads: chocolate pink.

CINNAMON: cinnamon spotting on a warm-ivory, agouti ground. Nose leather: pink rimmed with cinnamon. Paw pads: pink or rose.

CINNAMON SILVER: cinnamon spotting on a white agouti ground. Nose leather: pink rimmed with cinnamon. Paw pads: pink or rose.

FAWN: fawn spotting on a pale-ivory, agouti ground. Nose leather: pink rimmed in fawn. Paw pads: pink.

FAWN SILVER: fawn spotting on a white agouti ground. Nose leather: pink rimmed in fawn. Paw pads: pink.

LAVENDER:[2] lavender spotting on a pale-buff or ivory agouti ground. Nose leather: pink rimmed with dark lavender. Paw pads: lavender pink.

LAVENDER SILVER:[3] lavender spotting on a white agouti ground. Nose leather: pink rimmed with dark lavender. Paw pads: lavender pink.

SILVER: black spotting on a pale, silver/white agouti ground. Nose leather: brick red rimmed with black. Paw pads: black.

TAWNY (BROWN SPOTTED TABBY):[4] black or dark-brown spotting on a ruddy or bronze agouti ground. Nose leather: brick red rimmed with black. Paw pads: black or seal.

Ocicat allowable outcross breeds:[5] Abyssinian for litters born before January 1, 1995.

---

[1] ACA, TICA: "Large."
[2] TICA does not recognize this color.
[3] TICA does not recognize this color.
[4] TICA calls this color brown.
[5] In all associations where the breed is recognized.

Oriental Shorthair

ORIGIN

The Oriental Shorthair was born on a winter's night in 1950 when a British cat fancier named Baroness von Ullman decided to create a new variety of cat: a brown shorthair with green eyes and Siamese body type. Nearly four years later photographs of two kittens answering to this description appeared in the August 1954 issue of the British journal *Our Cats*. The kittens were called Bronze Leaf and Bronze Wing, and even though they had not been produced by the baroness, their color and conformation met her original design. The mother of these kittens was a seal point Siamese named Our Miss Smith. Their father was a brown hybrid called Elmtower Bronze Idol. He was by a seal point Siamese male out of a black domestic shorthair female who had a seal point Siamese father. At first the chestnut-brown kittens were called Havanas after the rabbit of the same color, according to some authorities; after Havana tobacco, according to others. For some reason, when the Governing Council of the Cat Fancy in England recognized the rabbit/tobacco-colored cats for championship competition in 1958, it issued the name Chestnut Brown Foreign to this breed instead.

DEVELOPMENT

Four years after Chestnut Browns had been accepted, a British cat breeder and geneticist named Patricia Turner began working to produce a blue-eyed white cat of the same foreign type. Two other breeders started similar programs at about that time, and they began pooling their resources in 1964. The preliminary result of their work was exhibited at a cat show in York, England, the following year. Before long these sound-hearing, blue-eyed white cats became "the talk of the cat fancy," wrote one observer. They were eventually accorded championship status under the name Foreign White in England, where individual colors are often registered as separate breeds.

Persons working with Foreign Whites combined Siamese with a variety of shorthaired breeds to achieve their goal. In addition to the blue-eyed whites they sought, they also produced cats of Siamese conformation whose color was not restricted to their points—i.e., face, ears, legs, and tail. In 1972 Peter and Vicky Markstein, two of the United States' better-known Siamese breeders, went to England in search of new Siamese lines. To the Marksteins' surprise they found the Siamese type they wanted in the newly emerging Foreign Whites and associated, nonpointed colors. The Marksteins were so taken with these cats that after returning to the United States, they decided to seek the acceptance of all Foreign shorthairs as one breed that would be called the Oriental Shorthair in this country. They set up a program unlike any previous approach to developing a breed. It was well thought out and executed. No detail was overlooked. The foundation for the Oriental Shorthair was the Siamese, which provided the type, and American Shorthairs as well as Abyssinians, which provided additional color and the all-important gene for head-to-toe color distribution. This formula produced an endless assortment of colorful, attractive cats that benefitted in many ways from the expanded Siamese gene pool from which they had been derived. Hybridizing produced vigorous, healthy cats with strong, hard bodies, and excellent muscle tone.

By May 1, 1977, the Oriental Shorthair was competing in championship classes in the Cat Fanciers' Association, and the breed was soon accepted by the other associations in the fancy. Its emergence, however, brought to light an issue that had first been raised with the introduction of colors other than seal, chocolate, lilac, and blue to the Siamese breed in the 1960s: viz., Is it type and body conformation or restrictive point coloring or specific point colors that define the Siamese breed? Eventually all cat federations will have to resolve this question.

Pointed kittens do and will continue to appear in Oriental Shorthair litters. These kittens look like Siamese, and they breed like Siamese. Bred to one another—or to a so-called purebred Siamese—they can never produce a solid-colored cat. Yet the majority of registries exclude these Siamese-type Oriental Shorthairs from the show ring. The federations that continue to do this will slowly paint themselves into a corner. Those registries like The International Cat Association, which is willing to accept all kittens that occur naturally in an Oriental Shorthair breeding and to allow these kittens to be shown, deserve congratulations. There is always someone who will cherish these kittens. To persist in enforcing a registration policy that can result in the culling of such kittens for purely cosmetic reasons reduces cat breeding to the level of an inhumane act.

White Oriental Shorthair

Standard for the
ORIENTAL SHORTHAIR

Courtesy of the Cat Fanciers' Association. Differences in the Standards of other registries are indicated at the end of the text.

HEAD: (20)
Long, flat profile 6
Wedge, fine
   muzzle, size 5
Ears 4
Chin 3
Width between eyes 2

EYES: (10)
Shape, size, slant,
   and placement 10

BODY: (30)
Structure and size,
   including neck 12
Muscle tone 10
Legs and Feet 5
Tail 3

COAT: 10

COLOR: (30)
Coat color 20
   (color 10; pattern 10)
Eye color 10

GENERAL: the ideal Oriental Shorthair is a svelte cat with long, tapering lines, very lithe but muscular. Excellent physical condition. Eyes clear. Strong and lithe, neither bony nor flabby. Not fat.

HEAD: long tapering wedge, in good proportion to body. The total wedge starts at the nose and flares out in straight lines to the tips of the ears forming a triangle,[1] with no break at the whiskers. No less than the width of an eye between the eyes. When the whiskers are smoothed back, the underlying bone structure is apparent.[2] Allowance must be made for jowls in the stud cat.

SKULL: flat. In profile, a long straight line is seen from the top of the head to the tip of the nose. No bulge over eyes. No dip in nose.

NOSE: long and straight. A continuation of the forehead with no break.

MUZZLE: fine, wedge shaped.

CHIN and JAW: medium sized. Tip of chin lines up with tip of nose in the same vertical plane. Neither receding nor excessively massive.

EARS: strikingly large, pointed, wide at the base, continuing the lines of the wedge.

EYES: almond shaped, medium sized. Neither protruding nor recessed. Slanted towards the nose in harmony with lines of wedge and ears. Uncrossed.

BODY: long and svelte.[3] A distinctive combination of fine bones and firm muscles. Shoulders and hips continue the same sleek lines of tubular body. Hips never wider than shoulders. Abdomen tight. Males may be somewhat larger than females.

NECK: long and slender.

LEGS: long and slim. Hind legs higher than front. In good proportion to body.

PAWS: dainty, small, and oval. Toes: five in front and four behind.

TAIL: long, thin at base, tapered to a fine point.

COAT: short, fine textured, glossy, lying close to body.

COAT COLOR: the Oriental Shorthair's reason for being is the coat color, whether it is solid or tabby patterned. In the solid-color cat, the coat color should be of uniform density and color from the tip to the root of each hair and from the nose to the tail. The full coat color score (20) should be used to assess the quality and the correctness of the color. In the tabby-patterned cat, the quality of the pattern is an essential part of the cat. The pattern should match the description for the particular pattern and be well defined. Pattern should be viewed while the cat is in a natural standing position. Ten points allotted to the correctness of the color; it matches the color description. The division of points for coat color applies only to the tabby-colors class.

PENALIZE: crossed eyes. Palpable and/or visible protrusion of the cartilage at the end of the sternum.

DISQUALIFY: any evidence of illness or poor health. Weak hindlegs. Mouth breathing due to nasal obstruction or poor occlusion. Emaciation. Visible kink. Miniaturization. Lockets and buttons. Incorrect number of toes.

EYE COLOR: green. White Orientals may have blue or green eye color, but not odd eyed.[4,5]

ORIENTAL SHORTHAIR COLORS
(See page 170 for a full description of the colors listed below.)

Particolor colors: blue cream, cinnamon tortoiseshell, chestnut tortie, fawn cream, lavender cream, tortoiseshell. **Shaded colors:** blue cream silver, blue silver, cameo, chestnut silver, chestnut tortie silver, cinnamon silver, cinnamon tortie silver, ebony silver, fawn silver, lavender cream silver, lavender silver, tortoiseshell silver. **Smoke colors:** blue smoke, cameo smoke, chestnut smoke, cinnamon smoke, ebony smoke, fawn smoke, lavender smoke, particolor smoke (white undercoat deeply tipped with ebony, chestnut, blue, or lavender with clearly defined, unbrindled patches of red and/or cream tipped hairs). **Solid colors:** blue, chestnut, cinnamon, cream, ebony, fawn, lavender, red, white. **Tabby colors:** blue silver, blue, cameo, cinnamon silver, cinnamon, chestnut silver, chestnut, cream, ebony, fawn, lavender silver, lavender, red, silver.

Oriental Shorthair allowable outcross breeds:[6] Siamese or Colorpoint.

---

[1] ACFA: "An isosceles triangle."
[2] ACFA: "There will be no probing for a whisker pinch."
[3] ACA, CFF, TICA: "Medium in size."
[4] TICA: "Odd eyes in the particolors and whites are acceptable."
[5] TICA: "Allowance should be made for lighter eye color in dilute-colored cats; tabby markings on solid cats up to twelve months."
[6] In all associations where the breed is recognized.

Persian

ORIGIN

The Persian is certainly the most prized—and plentiful—of all pedigreed cats. Nearly three out of four cats registered belong to the Persian/Himalayan family; and new registrations of a single Persian color—black—regularly outnumber all but a handful of individual breeds. Because Persians comprise such a large entry at most major shows—and because Persians are recognized in nearly fifty colors and patterns—this breed is grouped into seven color divisions in the Cat

Fanciers' Association to allow for greater mechanical ease in judging. Those divisions are: solid, tabby, shaded, smoke, particolor, bicolor, and pointed.

All this diversity may have started with a single color more than 350 years ago. According to the Italian traveler Pietro della Valle (1586-1652), who is credited with introducing the Persian to Europe, there was in Persia "a species of cats which properly belong to the province of Chorazan." The beauty of these cats, said della Valle, "consists in the color of their hair, which is gray [and] soft as silk, and so long that, though not frizzled, it forms ringlets in some parts, and particularly under the throat." Della Valle described these gray, longhaired cats as "very tame," and observed that "the Portugese have brought them from Persia into India."

Commenting on della Valle's description of the gray cats from Chorazan province, the French naturalist Count de Buffon (1707-1778) wrote, "It appears that the Persian cats resemble, in color, those we call Chartreux cats, and that, except in color, they have a perfect resemblance to the cat of the Angora. It is probable, therefore, that the cat of Chorazan in Persia, the cat of Angora in Syria, and the Chartreux cat

Calico Persian

constitute but one race, whose beauty proceeds from the particular influence of the climate."

What de Buffon ascribed to climate—"the most beautiful and longest hair" on the Persians and Angoras—is actually the result of a spontaneous mutation preserved through interbreeding in the confined mountain areas of Turkey and Persia. Eventually, through the efforts of della Valle, who wrote that he planned to bring home "four couple" of these cats, longhairs were imported from Chorazan province to Italy. Other travelers then brought other longhaired cats to France and, finally, to England, where they were known as French cats until the middle of the nineteenth century.

Though de Buffon wrote that the Persian had "a perfect resemblance" to the Angora, by the time the cat fancy was founded in Great Britain in the 1870s, there were noticeable differences between the two types. The Angora had a smaller, more narrow, less rounded head, less rounded eyes, and finer bone than the

Copper-eyed White Persian kitten

Red Classic Tabby Persian

Persian. The Angora's tail was more fanlike and pointed at the tip; and the Angora's coat—frilly on the chest and longer on the underparts—was not so heavy nor immense as the Persian's.

Despite these differences, no fancier cared to separate the two types, and they were used interchangeably to breed cats that were classified generically as longhairs and judged according to that classification. When the Points of Excellence, the first Standards by which cats were judged, were drawn up by Harrison Weir in England, they contained descriptions of Abyssinians, Manx, Siamese, "long-haired" cats, and "short-haired" cats. Neither the Persian nor the Angora was mentioned by name. Nevertheless, in his seminal work *Our Cats and All About Them*, published in 1889, Weir included a short chapter on Angoras and another on Persians,

and in these chapters he described the differences between the two.

He also included a chapter about longhaired cats from Russia, which "differed from the Angora and the Persian in many respects, [being] larger in the body with shorter legs" and having eyes that were "large and prominent, of a bright orange, slightly tinted with green." The tail was short and wooly. Weir had little experience breeding Russians, but C.H. Lane, writing in 1903, warned against crossing Persians with Russians because any increase in size obtained by this cross, "would be more than counterbalanced by coarseness and want of clearness in markings."

Gradually the Angora began to fade from prominence (the Russian never really attained it), and by 1903 Frances Simpson, an English cat breeder, author, and judge declared, "There are two distinctive breeds, viz., the *Long-haired* or Persian Cats, and *Short-haired* or

English and Foreign Cats." Be that as it was, when the Governing Council of the Cat Fancy (GCCF) was organized in England in 1910, it was decided that Persians should continue to be called *longhairs*, a practice that survives in England to this day.

In addition, GCCF treats each longhaired color as a separate breed: White Longhair, Blue Longhair, Black Longhair, and so forth, with blacks enjoying the status of breed Number 1 in the British registry. This classification scheme enlarges on the one started by Harrison Weir, whose *Points of Excellence* contained one Standard that applied to "black, blue, gray, red, or any self- or solid-coloured long-haired" cats and a separate Standard for judging "White, long-haired" cats. Weir also had a Standard for "brown, blue, silver, light gray, and white tabby" longhairs.

One British writer has observed that classifying colors as separate breeds "recognizes the practical fact that body type does tend to differ slightly from one colour to another" among Persians. Perhaps Weir's classification also recognizes the fact that most of the French cats imported to England before 1850 were white. "Coloured long-haired cats were then rare," said Weir, "and but little cared for or appreciated."

By the turn of the century the cat fancy was established in the United States, and American fanciers had been importing Persians and other cats from Great Britain for several years. (As early as 1885 a brown tabby male named King Humbert was exported to America, where his new owner subsequently refused $1,000 for him.) Until the 1900s the Maine Coon Cat had been the dominant longhair at shows in the United States, but the Persian soon claimed that distinction.

When Frances Simpson wrote *Cats and All About Them* in 1903 (a title similar to the one Weir used for his earlier book), there were already separate Standards in this country for blue Persians, orange Persians (both self and tabby), creams (also known as fawns), and orange-and-white cats (longhaired and short). Furthermore, white Persians were being judged in two classes—one for blue-eyed-whites, the other for golden-eyed whites. There were also separate Standards for shaded silvers, chinchillas, and tortoiseshells.

In longhairs, as in all other breeds, imported cats set the standard in this country during the first decades of

Chinchilla Silver Persian kitten

this century. In 1930 the Cat Fanciers' Association established the rank of Grand Champion—the highest, show-ring title a cat could attain. The first cat to achieve that designation was Eastbury Trigo, a red tabby Persian male imported from England. Not until World War II had brought devastation to the cat fancy in England did American breeders begin to assert their independence from British influence.

DEVELOPMENT
SOLID PERSIANS

While Persians have improved considerably since World War II, improvement has not been unilateral. The British writer who observed that body type differs among Persian colors might have added that facial type varies among colors as well. The first Persian color to gain dominance was blue. Queen Victoria was a patron of blues; a Blue Persian Society was founded in England in 1901; the first entry in the first stud book published in the United States was a "golden-eye Blue Female Longhair"; and by the middle of this century and beyond, blue Persians excelled so much in type that it was difficult to see anything other than a blue take best-in-show or best-kitten awards.

Such was the quality of blue Persians that many breeders would not consider mating anything but a blue to another blue for one generation after the next. This practice was known as color breeding, and it occasioned great debates about whether a cat was

This Cream Cameo Longhair, bred in England, typifies the British preference for a more moderate nose and ear set.

LEFT: Known as a Blue Point Colorpoint Longhair in England, where it was bred, this cat would be called a Blue Point Himalayan/Persian in the United States.

BELOW: Blue Longhair, bred in England

eligible to be called colorbred after three or after five generations of like-color-to-like-color breeding. The question was moot for all but the blues, however, because blues were the only cats for whom color breeding resulted in an increase rather than a decrease in overall quality.

Many of the outstanding blues produced in the 1940s and 1950s eventually became the breeding stock of catteries in the United States. Breeders who could not hope to compete with blues in the ring directed their attention to other colors, often using blues to improve the type of reds, blacks, blue creams, shadeds, torties, tabbies, and smokes. Some of these colors—at first the creams and blue creams and then others—began rivaling blues, which ultimately surrendered their dominance at shows.

Black Smoke Persian kitten

Blue Cream Longhair, bred in England

TABBY PERSIANS

Though tabbies were present at the creation of the cat fancy in England and had competed at the first shows there, Harrison Weir did not believe that tabbies had been among the original longhaired cats imported to Europe and subsequently to England from the Middle East. He suggested that tabby patterns had been introduced by crossing longhairs with shorthaired tabbies in England or with the longhaired Russian cats, which were also tabbies. Judging from Weir's Standards and illustrations, the original tabbies shown were mackerel longhairs, mackerel shorthairs, or spotted

shorthairs. Today the classic (or blotched) tabby pattern is the most popular. This pattern, which is recessive to the mackerel and which does not occur in the wild, was a development exclusive to the cat fancy.

It was extremely difficult from the beginning to produce tabbies of any quality. Surely, this discouraged many breeders, and it serves to explain why tabbies have never enjoyed great popularity. The most important consideration in breeding tabbies is to produce the boldest, most clearly defined markings possible. Breeding tabby to tabby, strangely enough, may result in a muddled pattern that contains too many markings and irregularities. To avoid this problem and to improve type in their tabbies, breeders have crossed them with blues, blacks, reds, creams,

Tortoiseshell Longhair, bred in England

and tortoiseshells, thus producing new tabby colors, including blue and cameo, and a new tabby pattern, the patched tabby (or torbie), which is a tortoiseshell cat with the usual patches of red and cream but whose predominant color is tabby instead of black.

Of all the tabbies, the reds have achieved type comparable to the best Persians today. Red tabbies, however, are frequently neither-nors: cats that have too many markings to qualify as solid reds but fewer and less distinct markings than the tabby Standard calls for.

The peke-faced Persian, a seldom-seen variety, competes in the regular solid and tabby divisions in some associations, but is judged as a separate class or breed by the others. The Cat Fanciers' Federation, which considers the peke a separate breed, explains in its Standard that peke-faced Persians "resemble the Pekinese dog. There is a cascading of skin under the eyes ... an indentation or depression in the bone on each side of the nose [and] the muzzle is broad and decidedly wrinkled." In addition, "the eyes are large, very round, set wide apart, and very prominent and have a different expression from the standard Persian."

SHADED PERSIANS

There has always been a great deal of confusion regarding shaded Persians. At present the colors in the shaded division are: chinchilla silver, shaded silver, chinchilla golden, shaded golden, shell cameo, shaded cameo, shell tortoiseshell, and shaded tortoiseshell. Most observers believe that the first shaded cats, a

Tortoiseshell Persian kitten

silver-colored variety that came to be known as chinchillas, were produced in the early 1880s in Great Britain by breeders who crossed silver tabbies of unsound markings to lightly tipped smokes; and although no one knows where the name *chinchilla* came from, there may well have been some connection with the South American rodent so prized for its coat, which was similar in color.

It is interesting that Weir's only mention of *chinchilla* in *Our Cats and All About Them* (1889) is in reference to a silver-gray Abyssinian color. When a specialty club for silver Persians was formed in England a few years later, it included self-silvers, shaded silvers, silver tabbies, and smokes. At that time self-silvers were not supposed to have any black shadings or markings, but, as Frances Simpson observed, "no self-silver has yet been born or bred." Therefore, the most lightly shaded silvers—the cats that were called chinchillas—filled in the self-silver class; and the silvers with darker shadings went into the shaded class, which was

Cream-and-White Persian

eliminated in 1902 because judges were having too much trouble distinguishing between chinchillas and shaded silvers.

No one can deny that the chinchilla is the most glamorous of all colors. Except for the chest and belly, which are pure white, the coat should be tipped evenly in one eighth of an inch of black at the end of each hair. Though the chinchilla is finer in bone and not as extreme as other Persians, it more than meets the Standard in refinement. Massive dimensions would not enhance this cat. What's more, the large, emerald-green eyes with their black eye lining and the black-lined nose and lips produce a very theatrical look that sets the chinchilla apart from all other Persians.

Though CFA recognizes the chinchilla and the shaded silver, the latter is nothing more than a silver cat with longer tipping and heavier shading than the chinchilla; and some shaded silvers, after they have matured, should be reclassified as chinchillas. It would

Cream-and-White Longhair, bred in England

probably be well to combine these colors into one class—especially since the Standard offers little help in this regard. For the chinchilla silver it reads: "undercoat pure white. Coat on back, flanks, head, and tail sufficiently tipped with black to give the characteristic sparkling silver appearance. Legs may be slightly shaded with tipping. Chin, ear tufts, stomach, and chest, pure white."

And for the shaded silver: "undercoat white with a mantle of black tipping shading down from sides, face, and tail from dark on the ridge to white on the chin, chest, stomach, and under the tail. Legs to be the same tone as the face. The general effect to be much darker than a chinchilla." But how much darker is a light shaded than a dark chinchilla?

The other shaded colors—golden, cameo, and tortoiseshell—were added to the division (as the smokes were being removed from it) during the 1960s and 1970s. These new shaded colors do not present quite the same challenges in breeding as the shaded and chinchilla do. These silver challenges include:

avoiding a diminution in size, maintaining the correct green or blue-green eye color, and refining the silver personality so that the cats are as sweet as they look.

SMOKE PERSIANS

The smoke Persian was known in England as early as 1860, according to one writer, who also reports that a smoke was exhibited at a show in Brighton in 1872. By 1893 the smoke was granted its own breed classes. Smokes were originally thought to be "a mixture of three self-coloured breeds—black, white, and blue." (Remember, in England every Persian color constitutes a breed.) Yet it is impossible to produce smokes no matter how many breeds or colors you combine if you don't include in your calculations at least one cat that carries the smoke gene.

Seventeen years after being awarded its own color classes, the smoke had made little progress in England, and by the time GCCF was formed in 1910, there were only eighteen smokes recorded in the first stud book. Worse yet, during the years following the Second World War, the smoke just about disappeared in England. Fortunately that situation did not obtain in the United States, where the smoke classes, though small, were consistently high in quality.

The same cannot be said for smokes today. Even the best seem to fall short in overall quality compared to other Persians.

For many years smokes were part of the silver or shaded division, but since the smokes had better bone and head type, they won frequently over the silvers. Silver breeders eventually petitioned CFA to remove the smokes from the shaded division because smokes had copper eyes and were not compatible to the breeding of silvers. As a result we now have a smoke division, which includes black, blue, blue cream, cameo, and tortoiseshell smokes.

Flame Point Himalayan/Persian

Like the shaded colors, smokes belong to the *tipped* category, a general name that indicates a pattern of colored tipping overlying a pale undercolor. This effect is produced because each hair on a smoke is white at the roots, and every hair should display the white frill as well as the white undercoat. Even if you spread the fur on a smoke's legs or head, it should be white at the base. Never should a smoke's coat anywhere be solid in color.

PARTICOLOR PERSIANS

Tortoiseshells have existed—in shorthaired classes at least—since the earliest days of the cat fancy, but it wasn't until the turn of the century that longhaired classes for torties were established. Many of the first torties probably did not endear themselves to the general public. Even today torties always seem to have a cross look and a temper to match. In addition, their muddled markings of red, black, and cream do not seem to give off the sweet expressions desired in the Persian. Perhaps this is why there were only eleven grand champion tortoiseshells during the first sixty-five years that CFA sponsored shows.

The tortie is a naturally occurring color achieved by combining black and red, which are both dominant colors, or by combining one of these dominants with the dilute of the other one—a black female with a cream male, for example. It is also possible, among other ways, to obtain torties by crossing tortoiseshell females with black, red, blue, or cream males, or by crossing blue-cream females with black or red males.

Tortoiseshell and blue cream are sex-linked colors. It is theoretically impossible to obtain males in these colors. Though such anomalies do occur infrequently, they are able to breed even more infrequently.

BICOLOR PERSIANS

For many years tortoiseshells and their dilute sisters the blue creams were the only particolored Persians in the fancy. Then in the early 1950s a New Jersey breeder of red and tabby Persians became interested in calico American Shorthairs, which were still called Domestic Shorthairs at the time. Calico was not then a recognized color in Domestic Shorthairs. Like many other Domestic breeders of her day, this woman used Persians off the record to improve type in her calicos while she was waiting for them to gain championship

recognition. In the meantime she came up with a few calico longhairs, which she registered as such according to the prevailing rules of open registration. Other breeders liked the old-fashioned, picture-postcard look of these cats and began crossing them to Persians. This interest eventually resulted in the acceptance of calico Persians in June of 1955, the same month that calico Domestic Shorthairs were accepted.

For the next fifteen years, however, bicolor males produced by the now-acceptable calico Persians were not eligible for registration. Many breeders were convinced that the acceptance of bicolors and their subsequent crossing with solid-color Persians would lead to a return of the buttons and lockets that breeders had worked for decades to eliminate from their solid-colored Persians. Eventually reason got the better of most breeders who realized that it was absurd to recognize the female of a sex-linked color—i.e., the calico—but not the male. Bicolored males were duly accepted, and they have not ruined the Persian breed in the meantime.

POINTED PERSIANS

On February 20, 1984, CFA incorporated the Himalayan breed into the Persian breed, making the former a color division of the latter. Absorbing one major breed into another forced many breeders and judges to rethink their ideas of what constitutes a breed.

Over the years there have been several attempts to produce Siamese cats with long hair. Or Persian cats with Siamese markings, if you will. This had been tried on the continent in the 1920s and in the United States in 1932. The attempt in that country was successful, but the accomplishment didn't inspire any sense of obligation in the cat fancy; and the idea went nowhere. In 1950 Margaret Goforth in the United States and Brian Stirling-Webb in England began working with Siamese-Persian crosses. They, along with Ben and Ann Borrett in Canada and Mrs. Harding in England, were the successful pioneers in developing the Persian-Siamese cross, which came to be known as the Himalayan.

When the Himalayan was accepted as a breed in 1957, CFA required four generations of like-to-like colorpoint breeding behind kittens being presented for registration. The association was very strict in its rules, and it was lucky to have one or two Himalayans at a show. As time went on and other associations passed CFA in the number of Himalayan entries they were drawing, CFA decided that since the Himalayan was a hybrid to begin with, it didn't matter if breeders used Persians in their Himalayan breeding programs. At once CFA began to see more and better Himalayans at shows, but the organization still refused to allow nonpointed cats from Persian-Himalayan crosses into the show ring. These cats could be used for breeding, but that was all.

Though one or two farsighted persons argued in the early 1960s that Himalayans should be recognized as colorpoint longhairs—as they are in England—that idea met with much debate and resistance in the United States. Interestingly enough, Siamese breeders, who are responsible for more experimental crosses than any other group, were the most vocal in their opposition to that move. Today, however, there should be no question that the Himalayan is indeed a Persian, for only color and point-restricted patterns were introduced to the Persian breed. What's more, Himalayans have enjoyed incredible success at the shows and have achieved a level of quality that should keep any Persian breeder from fearing a colorpoint or a colorpoint carrier in the pedigree.

As it should have done before, CFA also allows nonpointed Himalayans, known as colorpoint carriers, to compete in whatever division for which their color qualifies them. For many years before this became the rule, a number of these cats competed successfully as "Persians," thanks to their superior type and the creative paperhanging of their breeders and owners. As of early 1991, CFA and the American Cat Association were the only North American registries to incorporate the Himalayan breed into the Persian. All other associations still considered the Himalayan a separate breed. At least one group, the Canadian Cat Association, has separate classes for nonpointed Himalayan hybrids; and two registries, the Cat Fanciers' Federation and the Canadian Cat Association, have established a separate breed called the Kashmir for solid lilac and solid chocolate cats that result from Persian-Himalayan crosses.

EPILOGUE

Since the Persian Standard in this country has always been very progressive, there has been little change in it over the years, but there has been a tremendous change in the cat it describes. Beginning in the early 1970s American Persians have grown increasingly overtyped compared to longhairs in Great Britain. Yet we must remember that English breeders are renowned for producing many of the finest animals in the world. Their Persians remain less extreme than American cats because that is how the British prefer them.

Standard for the
PERSIAN

Courtesy of the Cat Fanciers' Association. Differences in the Standards of other registries are indicated at the end of the text.

HEAD: 30 (including size and shape of eyes, ear shape and set)	**COAT:** 10
	BALANCE: 5
	REFINEMENT: 5
TYPE: 20 (including shape, size, bone, and length of tail)	**COLOR:** 20
	EYE COLOR: 10

In all tabby varieties, the 20 points for color are to be divided 10 for markings and 10 for color. In all "with white" varieties (calico, dilute calico, bicolor, van bicolor, van calico, van dilute calico, and tabby and white), the 20 points for color are to be divided 10 for "with white" pattern and 10 for color.

GENERAL: the ideal Persian should present an impression of a heavily boned, well-balanced cat with a sweet expression and soft, round lines. The large round eyes set wide apart in a large round head contribute to the overall look and expression. The long thick coat softens the lines of the cat and accentuates the roundness in appearance.

HEAD: round and massive,[1] with great breadth of skull. Round face with round underlying bone structure.[2] Well set on a short, thick neck.

NOSE: short, snub, and broad.[3] With "break."[4]

CHEEKS: full.[5]

JAWS: broad and powerful.

CHIN: full, well developed, and firmly rounded, reflecting a proper bite.

EARS: small, round tipped, tilted forward, and not unduly open at the base. Set far apart, and low on the head, fitting into (without distorting) the rounded contour of the head.

EYES: brilliant in color, large, round, and full. Set level and far apart, giving a sweet expression to the face.[6]

BODY: of cobby type, low on the legs, broad and deep through the chest, equally massive across the shoulders and rump,[7] with a well-rounded midsection and level back. Good muscle tone with no evidence of obesity. Large or medium in size. Quality the determining consideration rather than size.

LEGS: short, thick, and strong. Forelegs straight.

PAWS: large, round, and firm. Toes carried close, five in front and four behind.

TAIL: short, but in proportion to body length. Carried without a curve and at an angle lower than the back.

COAT: long and thick, standing off from the body.[8] Of fine texture, glossy and full of life. Long all over the body, including the shoulders.[9] The ruff immense and continuing in a deep frill between the front legs. Ear and toe tufts long. Brush very full.

DISQUALIFY: locket or button. Kinked or abnormal tail. Incorrect number of toes. Any apparent weakness in the hind quarters. Any apparent deformity of the spine. Deformity of the skull resulting in an asymmetrical face and/or head. Crossed eyes. For pointed cats, also disqualify for white toes, eye color other than blue.[10]

PERSIAN COLORS
(See page 170 for a full description of the colors listed below.)

Particolor colors: Bicolors (black and white, blue and white, red and white, or cream and white), blue cream, calico, dilute calico, tabby and white, tortoiseshell, van bicolors (black and white, red and white, blue and white, or cream and white), van calico, van dilute calico. **Pointed colors:** blue lynx point, blue point, blue-cream point, blue-cream lynx point, chocolate point, chocolate-tortie point, cream point, flame (red) point, lilac point, lilac-cream point, seal lynx point, seal point, tortie point, tortie lynx point. **Shaded colors:** chinchilla golden, chinchilla silver, shaded cameo (red shaded), shaded golden, shaded silver, shaded tortoiseshell, shell cameo (red chinchilla), shell tortoiseshell. **Smoke colors:** black smoke, blue smoke, blue-cream smoke, cameo smoke (red smoke), smoke tortoiseshell. **Solid colors:** black, blue, chocolate, cream, lilac, peke-face red, red, white. **Tabby colors:** blue patched tabby, blue tabby (classic, mackerel), brown patched tabby, brown tabby (classic, mackerel), cameo tabby (classic, mackerel), cream tabby (classic, mackerel), peke-face red tabby, red tabby (classic, mackerel), silver patched tabby, silver tabby (classic, mackerel).

Persian allowable outcross breeds:[11] none.

[1] TICA: "Medium to large."
[2] CFF: "The full face should appear to be square."
[3] ACFA: " ... as broad as it is long."
[4] ACA, CFF: "There should be a decided indentation between the eyes, called the break."
[5] CFF: " ... with the impression of a shallow furrow starting from the inner corner of the eye and gently curving downward toward the outer corner of the lip line, giving the appearance of a sloping mustache."
[6] CFF, TICA: "The color must conform to the requirements for coat color."
[7] CFF: "The rump of the female tends to be rounder than that of the male."
[8] ACA, CFF, TICA: "Allowances should be made for seasonal variations in length and thickness."
[9] CFF: "There are two types of Persian coats allowable—long and flowing, or medium long and thick."
[10] CFA: "The above listed disqualifications apply to all Persian cats. Additional disqualifications are listed under `Colors.'"
[11] In all associations where the breed is recognized.

Ragdoll

ORIGIN

The patriarch of the Ragdoll breed was a mitted, seal point male named Daddy War Bucks, who was born in Riverside, California, in the mid-1960s. War Bucks' mother was a longhaired, free-running white named Josephine. His father, according to Ann Baker, who was Josephine's owner, was a Sacred Cat of Burma (Birman).

DEVELOPMENT

Baker developed the Ragdoll by crossing Daddy War Bucks' children—and their children—with one another. After naming the breed, she sought championship status for her cats. She founded the International Ragdoll Cat Association (IRCA) in 1971, but soon

Blue Mitted Ragdoll

afterward breeders who felt that IRCA guidelines were too restrictive formed the Ragdoll Fanciers' Club (RFC). Working with the established federations, RFC has obtained championship status for Ragdolls in every organization in this country except the Cat Fanciers' Association.

Baker and the RFC have always claimed that there are significant differences between Ragdolls and other cats. Ragdolls are bigger and more impervious to pain, and they go limp in a person's arms when held—a tendency that inspired their name. These attributes, says Baker, first appeared in Josephine's kittens after she had recovered from being hit by a car. They had not been noticeable in her preaccident kittens.

The RFC—which allows that not all Ragdolls go limp when held and that *high tolerance*, not *imperviousness*, describes their cats' reaction to pain—prefers to attribute these tendencies to a "fluke of nature." Yet one thing can't be argued, says RFC and that is the Ragdoll's size. Females should range between ten and thirteen pounds, males between fifteen and twenty. That makes the Ragdoll, RFC likes to boast, the largest breed of cat in the *Guinness Book of Pet Records.*

Standard for the
RAGDOLL

Courtesy of the Cat Fanciers' Federation. Differences in the Standards of other registries are indicated at the end of the text.

SCALE OF POINTS

Head & Neck: (20)
The head is a medium-sized, broad, modified wedge with the appearance of a flat plane between the ears. Muzzle is round, medium in length, with well-developed chin. Nose to have a gentle break between the eyes. Medium-sized skull. Neck is short, heavy, and strong.
Objection: Roman nose.

Ears & Eyes: (10)
Ears are medium sized, broad at base, slight tilt forward, with rounded tip and medium furnishings. Set of ears should be a continuation of the modified wedge. Eyes are blue, the bluer the better, in all patterns and colors. Eyes are large and oval. Outer part of aperture to fall in line with base of ear. Not oriental.
Objection: pointed ears. **Withhold wins:** eye color other than blue.

Body & Tail: (25)
Body is long, with a full chest, as broad at the shoulders as it is at the hindquarters. Muscular and heavy in the hindquarters.[1] Tail is long in proportion to body length, medium at the base, with a slight taper, and carried at an angle higher than the back.[2] Full weight and size are not expected for at least four years.
Objections: short tail or cobby body.

Legs & Feet: (5)
Medium long with heavy boning. Musculature to be medium heavy, with back legs higher than front. Feet are large and round, with tufts between toes. Fur on the front legs to be thick and short to medium in length. Fur on the hind legs is medium to long, thick, and featherlike. **Objections:** short or long, thin legs.

Color & Pattern: (20)
Full color is not obtained until at least two years of age.

Coat: (10)
Medium long to long, longer preferred. The coat lies with the body and breaks as the cat moves. The coat is longest around the neck and the outer edges of the face, giving the appearance of a bib. The coat is short on the face and increases in length from the top of the head down through the shoulder blades and back. Fur to be plush and silky. **Withhold wins:** short coat on any pattern.

Condition & Balance: (10)
Placid by nature. Calm, alert, affectionate, and intelligent. Gentle voice, but seldom used. Eyes bright. Solid and firm, giving the impression of graceful, flowing movement and subdued power.

PATTERN DESCRIPTIONS

Bicolor: the color may be seal, blue, chocolate, or lilac. The points (ears, mask, and tail) to be well defined. Mask to have a white, inverted "V"; stomach, all four legs, feet, and ruff to be white. The color on the body to be a shade lighter than the points, and may have various markings of white and color patches. **Nose leather and paw pads:** pink. **Eyes:** blue, the bluer the better. **Objections:** white on ears and tail. Color patches on stomach or area designated white. **Withhold wins:** any dark marking on white area of mask; whiskers other than white.

Colorpoint: the color may be seal, blue, chocolate, or lilac. The points (ears, mask, legs, and tail) to be darker and well defined. Body color to be sound to the roots. Body color to be lighter than point color. Chest, bib, and chin areas may be somewhat lighter in color. Soft shadings of color are allowed on the body. Allowance to be made for uneven shading for a cat under two years of age. **Eyes:** blue, the bluer the better. **Objection:** chin darker than ruff. **Withhold wins:** any white.

Mitted: the color to be seal, blue, chocolate, or lilac. The points (except feet) to be well defined. A broken or evenly matched white blaze of even dimension on nose and/or between eyes to be acceptable. White mittens on front legs to be evenly matched and scalloped. Back legs should be entirely white, extending no higher than midthigh. White must go around the hocks entirely. White stripe, varying in width, extends from the bib and runs down the underside between the forelegs to the underbase of the tail. The body is a shade lighter than the point color. **Eyes:** blue, the bluer the better. **Objections:** lack of white stripe running down the underside to base of tail. Any dark spotting on white mittens or underbelly. **Withhold wins:** lack of white chin.

RAGDOLL COLORS

BLUE POINT: body should be an even, platinum gray of bluish tones, shading gradually to a lighter color on the belly and chest. Points should be a deeper, grayish-blue tone, all points being as nearly the same shade as possible. Flesh tone of nose leather and paw pads to be dark blue gray.

CHOCOLATE POINT: body color should be ivory all over; shading, if at all, to be in the color of the points. The points should be a warm, milk-chocolate color. The ears, mask, legs, paws, and tail to be as even as possible. Allowance should be made for incomplete mask, etc. in kittens and younger cats. The ears should not be darker than the other points. As a result of diluted pigmentation of the points, the flesh tones show through the tip of the nose leather, resulting in a burnt-rose tone, while the foot pads have a salmon-pink color.

LILAC POINT:[3] body color should be an even milk-white color; shading, if any, in the color of the points. The points should be a lilac gray of pinkish tone, the dilute pigment permitting the flesh tones to show through, resulting in a delicate, peach-blossom tone in the inner surface of the ears. The foot pads have a coral-pink color, and the nose leather presents a translucent, old-lilac hue at the tip.

SEAL POINT: body color should be an even, pale fawn or cream, shading gradually into a lighter color on belly and chest. Points should be dense, deep seal brown, and all of the same shade. Flesh tones of nose leather and foot pads to be a dark brown, almost black, color.

Ragdoll allowable outcross breeds:[4] none.

---

[1] ACFA: "There is a tendency for a 'fatty pad' on the lower abdomen (greater Omentum)."
[2] ACA: "Back level, not arched."
[3] ACFA calls this color a frost point.
[4] In all associations where the breed is recognized.

Russian Blue

ORIGIN

For the first forty-one years that cat shows were held in Great Britain, all shorthaired blue cats, regardless of origin, competed in the same class. Some of those cats were blue domestic shorthairs from Great Britain, others were foreign-born cats that were variously called Archangel cats, Russian blues, Spanish blues, Chartreuse blues, and even American blues. The cats from Archangel, said cat lover Harrison Weir, "were of a deeper, purer tint than the English cross-breeds."

The Archangel cats "had larger ears and eyes, and were larger and longer in the head." They had been named after the city of Arkhangelsk, a port on the White Sea about 150 miles south of the Arctic Circle, from whence they may have been carried by sailors to Western Europe in the 1860s.

Perhaps because the cobby, round-headed British

Russian Blue

133

cats dominated the blue shorthaired classes, the Russian entries were assigned to their own judging category, called the Foreign Blue, in 1912. Their fortunes improved after this, but as all other breeds did, they fell into decline during World War II. After the war, breeders in England seeking to revive their lines outcrossed to other cats whose color and type most closely resembled the Russian Blue's. Some English breeders chose the British Blue, which contributed a plush, pale-colored coat to the reemerging breed. Other breeders preferred to use blue point Siamese, which produced a more extreme, foreign body type.

During the late 1940s and 1950s Scandinavian cat fanciers began working to develop a Russian Blue of their own, crossing a blue cat from Finland with a blue point Siamese. And what wonderful heads they produced. Some of the Russian Blues in Scandinavia were as fierce as they were big, but they possessed a style that enhanced the breed, a look all its own, just the thing to separate the Russian from the other blue shorthairs. The coats on the Scandinavian cats, unfortunately, were short and tight as well as dark.

DEVELOPMENT

A few Russian Blues had reached the United States around 1900, but little is known about these cats beyond their names, and serious work with the breed did not begin until 1947 when a Texan named C.A. Commaire imported two Russian Blues from England. Dorothy Leck of Three Crown cattery imported several cats from the Swedish lines with their magnificent heads and emerald green eyes, and the subsequent combination of the English and Scandinavian lines eventually produced pale, silver-blue coats and graceful body type. Since there were no natural Russian Blues to be imported, hybridizing did not cease. Breeders did what they had to do in order to expand the gene pool and to improve temperament, for Russian Blues were not exhibited in great numbers, and their temperament left a good deal to be desired.

With the recessive pointed gene in the background, certain combinations of Russian Blues will produce what breeders call White Russians. They are not white at all. They are born white, as all blue point Siamese are; but these kittens, of course, are nothing more than the consequences of the blue point Siamese that have been used in their backgrounds.

Standard for the RUSSIAN BLUE

Courtesy of the Cat Fanciers' Association. Differences in the Standards of other registries are indicated at the end of the text.

HEAD and NECK: 20	**COAT:** 20
BODY TYPE: 20	**COLOR:** 20
EYE SHAPE: 5	**EYE COLOR:** 10
EARS: 5	

GENERAL: the good show specimen has good physical condition, is firm in muscle tone, and alert.

HEAD: smooth, medium wedge, neither long and tapering nor short and massive. Muzzle is blunt, and part of the total wedge, without exaggerated pinch or whisker break. Top of skull long and flat in profile, gently descending to slightly above the eyes, and continuing at a slight downward angle in a straight line to the tip of the nose. No nose break or stop. Length of tophead should be greater than length of nose. The face is broad across the eyes due to wide eye set and thick fur.

MUZZLE: smooth, flowing wedge without prominent whisker pads or whisker pinches.

EARS: rather large and wide at the base.[1] Tips more pointed than rounded. The skin of the ears is thin and translucent, with little inside furnishing. The outside of the ear is scantily covered with short, very fine hair, with leather showing through. Set far apart, as much on the side as on the top of the head.

EYES: set wide apart.[2] Aperture rounded in shape.[3]

NECK: long and slender, but appearing short due to thick fur and high placement of shoulder blades.

NOSE: medium in length.

CHIN: perpendicular with the end of the nose and with level underchin. Neither receding nor excessively massive.

BODY: fine boned, long, firm, and muscular;[4] lithe and graceful in outline and carriage without being tubular in appearance.

LEGS: long and fine boned.

PAWS: small, slightly rounded. Toes: five in front and four behind.[5]

TAIL: long, but in proportion to the body. Tapering from a moderately thick base.

COAT: short, dense, fine, and plush. Double coat stands out from body due to density. It has a distinct soft and silky feel.

DISQUALIFY: kinked or abnormal tail. Locket or button. Incorrect number of toes.

RUSSIAN BLUE COLOR

COLOR: even bright blue throughout. Lighter shades of blue preferred. Guard hairs distinctly silver tipped, giving the cat a silvery sheen or lustrous appearance.

A definite contrast should be noted between ground color and tipping. Free from tabby markings. Nose leather: slate gray. Paw pads: lavender pink or mauve. Eye color: vivid green.

Russian Blue allowable outcross breeds:[6] none.

[1] ACFA: "As wide at the base as they are tall."
[2] ACA: "Set at least one and one half eye widths apart."
[3] ACFA: "Almost round, just oval enough to show oriental slant. Set one eye width or more apart."
[4] ACA, ACFA, CFF: "Muscular in the manner of a swimmer rather than that of a wrestler."
[5] ACA, TICA: "Appears to stand and walk on tiptoes."
[6] In all associations where the breed is recognized.

Scottish Fold

ORIGIN

All Scottish Folds are descended from a white cat named Susie, who was born near the village of Coupar Angus in east central Scotland in 1961. Susie, whose parents were both straight-eared farm cats, owed her uniquely folded ears to a spontaneous mutation. Cat fanciers, who have long been enchanted by the Fold, owe the preservation of this breed to a shepherd named William Ross and his wife, Mary.

The Rosses lived near Susie's owners, a family named McCrae. After William Ross had noticed Susie playing in the McCraes' yard, he and Mary went to visit the McCraes, who promised that if Susie ever had fold-eared kittens of her own, they would let the Rosses know. Two years later, after Susie had had a litter by a farm cat, the McCrae's gave the Rosses one of her kittens, a female with a snow-white coat like her mother's. The Rosses named her Snooks.

DEVELOPMENT

When Snooks was a year old, she produced a white, fold eared male named Snowball, whose father was a red tabby farm cat. The Rosses then bought a British Shorthair female to breed to Snowball, and began visiting cat shows to see if anyone else was interested in fold-eared cats. They were introduced to Pat Turner, a lively English woman with an interest in cats and genetics, who obtained a fold-eared male from the Rosses and began a series of experimental breedings. She concluded that the gene responsible for folded ears is an incomplete dominant: i.e., if a kitten has one gene for folded ears and one gene for straight ears, it will always develop folded ears. Turner also discovered, as the Rosses had earlier, that Folds' ears look normal at birth. Around the age of fifteen to twenty-five days, when normal kittens' ears are beginning to straighten, Folds' ears begin going in the opposite direction.

According to the laws of chance, half the kittens from fold-eared/straight-eared crosses will have folded ears. Some breeders try to increase the number of Folds in a litter by breeding one fold-eared cat to another. This will produce, on the average, three Folds instead of two in a litter of four; but there is reason to suspect that this breeding strategy produces short, inflexible tails, and hocks that curve like the rockers on a rocking chair. Neither of these conditions is life threatening, nor is the fold-eared gene a lethal one; but there is

reason to question the existence of any breed in which you cannot mate like to like without putting kittens at risk. In fact, the GCCF does not recognize Scottish Folds in Great Britain, though the newer Cat Association of Britain does.

By 1970 three Scottish Folds had been sent to Dr. Neil Todd, a geneticist who operated the Carnivore Genetics Research Center in Massachusetts. Todd did not continue his Fold research very long, and one of his cats went to Salle Wolfe Peters—who bred Manx and American Shorthairs in her Wyola cattery in southeastern Pennsylvania. Thanks largely to the work of Peters and Karen Votava, a Fold breeder from Lubbock, Texas, Scottish Folds were accepted for registration in the United States in 1973 and for championship competition five years later.

Since Fold-to-Fold crosses were not considered safe (though they were never officially forbidden in this country as many people feel they should have been), Fold breeders are allowed to use British and American shorthairs in their breeding programs. There is really no reason why the American Shorthair should have been included. The American coat, which is too flat-lying, is all wrong for the Fold; and the American head, which is too long, does not enhance the folded ear. A rounded head lends a more pleasing balance to the Fold's ears, and a plush, stand-up coat is without question the most desirable for a Fold. Logically, the Scottish Fold should have been accepted as a variety of the British Shorthair, just as the Himalayan in now properly accepted as a variety of the Persian. By doing so, the problem of non-showable, straight-eared kittens would have been solved because they could have been shown—if good enough—as British Shorthairs.

Silver Classic Tabby Scottish Fold

Standard for the
SCOTTISH FOLD

Courtesy of the Cat Fanciers' Association. Differences in the Standards of other registries are indicated at the end of the text.

HEAD: (55)	Tail 20
Ears 25	Coat 10
Head shape, muzzle, neck, chin, profile 15	**COLOR:** (5)
Eyes 15	Color of coat and eyes 5
BODY: (40)	
Body structure of torso, legs and paws 10	

GENERAL: the Scottish Fold cat occurred as a spontaneous mutation in farm cats in Scotland. The breed has been established by crosses to British Shorthair and domestic cats in Scotland and England. In America, the outcross is the American and British Shorthair. All bona fide Scottish Fold cats trace their pedigree to Susie, the first fold-ear, cat discovered by the founders of the breed, William and Mary Ross.

HEAD: well rounded with a firm chin and jaw. Muzzle to have well-rounded whisker pads. Head should blend into a short neck. Prominent cheeks with a jowly appearance in males.

EYES: wide open with a sweet expression. Large, well rounded, and separated by a broad nose.[1] Eye color to correspond with coat color.[2]

NOSE: nose to be short with a gentle curve. A brief stop is permitted but a definite nose break considered a fault. Profile is moderate in appearance.

EARS: fold forward and downward. Small, the smaller, tightly folded ear preferred over a loose fold and large ear. The ears should be set in a caplike fashion to expose a rounded cranium. Ear tips to be rounded.

BODY: medium, rounded, and even from shoulder to pelvic girdle. The cat should stand firm on a well-padded body. There must be no hint of thickness or lack of mobility in the cat due to short, coarse legs. Toes to be neat and well rounded with five in front and four behind. Overall appearance is that of a well-rounded cat with medium bone; fault cats obviously lacking in type. Females may be slightly smaller.

TAIL: tail should be medium to long but in proportion to the body. Tail should be flexible and tapering. Longer, tapering tail preferred.

COAT: dense, plush, medium short,[3] soft in texture, full of life. Standing out from body due to density; not flat or close lying.[4] Coat texture may vary due to color and/or region or seasonal changes.

DISQUALIFY: kinked tail. Tail that is foreshortened. Tail that is lacking in flexibility due to abnormally thick vertebrae. Incorrect number of toes. Any evidence of illness or poor health.

SCOTTISH FOLD COLORS
(See page 170 for a full description of the colors listed below.)

Particolor colors: bicolors (black and white, blue and white, red and white, cream and white), blue cream, calico, dilute calico, tortoiseshell. **Shaded colors:** chinchilla silver, shaded cameo (red shaded), shaded silver, shell cameo (red chinchilla). **Smoke colors:** black smoke, blue smoke, cameo smoke (red smoke). **Solid colors:** black, blue, cream, red, white. **Tabby colors:** (in classic, mackerel, patched, or spotted patterns): blue tabby, brown tabby, cameo tabby, cream tabby, red tabby, silver tabby. **Other Scottish Fold colors:** any other color or pattern with the exception of those showing evidence of hybridization resulting in the colors chocolate, lavender, the Himalayan pattern, or these combinations with white.

Scottish Fold allowable outcross breeds:[5] British Shorthair, American Shorthair.

[1] CFF: "The overall appearance should be of innocence or surprise."
[2] ACA: "Any eye color allowed and of secondary importance."
[3] ACA, ACFA, CFF, TICA: "Short."
[4] CFF: "A double coat shall be penalized."
[5] In all associations where the breed is recognized.

Scottish Fold Longhair

ORIGIN

All Scottish Folds, regardless of coat length, are descended from a white, fold-eared cat named Susie: a shorthaired kitten with curious ears born near the village of Coupar Angus in east central Scotland in 1961. The breed Susie inspired was born in the United States during the next decade when Folds were accepted for championship competition. A decade later the second breed that Susie inspired, the Scottish Fold Longhair[1], took its place on the show bench.

From the start, longhaired kittens had appeared in Scottish Fold litters. Indeed, Susie and her daughter Snooks produced longhairs themselves, which indicates that genotypically the Scottish Fold was a dual-coated breed from the beginning. The potential of Susie, Snooks, and their offspring to throw longhaired kittens was complemented by the British Shorthairs used in Scottish Fold breeding programs. The British, too, carry a longhair gene because Persians are a legitimate outcross for British Shorthairs in England.

Silver· Classic Tabby-and-White Scottish Fold Longhair

139

DEVELOPMENT

The decision to pursue championship status for shorthaired Folds only was a practical, some would say a timid, one. William and Mary Ross, the breed's founders, were advised not to promote longhairs because they looked as if they didn't have any ears at all. The Rosses and other cat fanciers involved with Folds in the 1960s and early 1970s accepted this advice because they already anticipated some difficulty gaining recognition for their singular-looking breed. They were, of course, correct. The GCCF eventually rescinded the registration of Scottish Folds, though the breed is currently accepted by the Cat Association of Britain.

Though Fold breeders were not committed to promoting longhairs, no one seemed committed to stop producing them either. The first registered Fold in the United States was sired by an Exotic Shorthair, another breed that carries the longhair gene. Exotics and any shorthaired cats were legitimate outcrosses for the Scottish Fold until the latter was accepted for champion competition, at which point British and American shorthairs became the only sanctioned crosses. Exotics, however, remained a legitimate Fold outcross in CFA for one or two years after the Fold's acceptance, and they remain an illegitimate Fold outcross in all associations to this day.

"In retrospect," says one British cat fancier who was

Silver-patched Torbie Van Scottish Fold Longhair

present at the Fold's creation, "I'm not sure it was such good advice [telling the Rosses to work with shorthaired Folds only]. The longhairs I have seen have been just lovely."

A Fold breeder in America told *Cats* magazine in 1984 that "there is nothing prettier than a Scottish Fold with long hair. I wouldn't be surprised if they were eventually recognized. There are longhaired Manx, longhaired Siamese, and longhaired Abyssinians. I can't see that there aren't going to be Longhair Folds."

As of May 1, 1987, there were. In the preceding fall the Scottish Fold Breed Section of The International Cat Association voted thirty-nine to one in favor of accepting the Scottish Fold Longhair for championship competition beginning with the 1987-88 show season.

No one is certain where or by whom the first Longhair Folds were shown in new breed classes in TICA, but the name most frequently mentioned is Hazel Swadberg in Renton, Washington. She exhibited a number of Longhairs in the Northwest Region in 1982. The following year a *Cats* magazine contributing editor learned about the Longhaired Fold and with the help of two TICA judges was soon able to obtain recognition for these engaging cats.

Standard for the
SCOTTISH FOLD LONGHAIR

Courtesy of The International Cat Association. Differences in the Standards of other registries are indicated at the end of the text.

HEAD: 15	**EYES:** 15
EARS: 30	**BODY:** 10
TAIL: 20	**COLOR:** 10

RECOGNIZED CATEGORY/DIVISIONS/COLORS: traditional category, all divisions, all colors.

GENERAL: the Scottish Fold occurred as a spontaneous mutation in farm cats in Scotland. The breed has been established by crosses to British Shorthair and domestic cats in Scotland and England. In America, the outcrosses are the American and British shorthairs. All bona fide Scottish Fold Longhairs trace their pedigree to Susie, the first fold-eared cat, discovered by the founders of the breed: William and Mary Ross.

HEAD: well rounded with a firm chin and jaw. Muzzle to have well-rounded whisker pads. Head should blend into a short neck. Prominent cheeks with a jowly appearance in males.

EYES: wide open with a sweet expression. Large, well rounded, and separated by a broad nose.[2] Eye color to conform to coat color.[3]

NOSE: nose to be short with a gentle curve. A brief stop is permitted, but a definite nose break is considered a fault. Profile is moderate in appearance.

EARS: fold forward and downward. Small, the smaller, tightly folded ear preferred over a loose fold and a large ear. The ears should be set in a caplike fashion to expose a rounded cranium. Ear tips to be rounded.

BODY: medium,[4] rounded and even from shoulder to pelvic girdle. The cat should stand firmly. The body should be well padded. There must be no hint of thickness or lack of mobility in the cat due to short, coarse legs. Toes to be neat and well rounded. Overall appearance is that of a well-rounded cat with medium bone; fault cats obviously lacking in type. Females may be slightly smaller.

TAIL: tail should be medium to long but in proportion to the body. Tail should be flexible and tapering. Longer, tapering tail preferred.[5]

COAT: semilong; standing away from the body; ruff and britches desirable. The texture of the coat is soft and full of life.

PENALIZE: definite nose break.

DISQUALIFY: tail that is foreshortened. Tail that is lacking in flexibility due to abnormally thick vertebrae.

Allowable Scottish Fold Longhair outcross breeds:[6] British Shorthair, American Shorthair, Scottish Folds

---

[1] This breed is called the *Longhair Fold* in CFF and the *Highland Fold* in ACFA.
[2] CFF: "The overall appearance should be of innocence or surprise."
[3] CFF: "Eye color does not need to conform to coat color. Allowance should be made for development of eye color up to the age of eighteen months."
[4] CFF: "Medium to large in size."
[5] CFF: "... ending in a modified, blunt tip [and] with a full plume."
[6] In all associations where the breed is recognized,

Siamese

ORIGIN

From the earliest days of the cat fancy, the Siamese has been recognized—even by those who have no interest in cats—as a breed unlike any other. The first known reference to a cat with the Siamese pattern has been found in the *Cat-Book Poems*, a centuries-old manuscript preserved in the Thai National Library in Bangkok. This anonymous work contains verses that describe white-haired cats with black tails, feet, and ears—a recognizable portrait of today's seal point Siamese. The *Cat-Book Poems* was rescued from the ancient Siamese city of Ayudha, which was 417 years old when it was leveled by Burmese invaders in 1767. We can assume, therefore, that the Siamese breed is well over two centuries old, and perhaps a good deal older.

Another reference to cats with the Siamese pattern occurred in 1793 in the writings of the naturalist Simon Pallas. These cats, which Pallas had observed in central Russia, had darker extremities than the cats from Siam—and light chestnut bodies where the "Siamese" bodies were white. Pallas' cats may have descended from imported Siamese, or perhaps the recessive Siamese gene had mutated spontaneously in Russia, too. In either case, climate would have accounted for the differences in color between Pallas' cats and the ones in the *Cat-Book Poems*. The formation of pigment in the Siamese is directly related to temperature. The colder the environment, the darker the markings and body color.

Beyond these references to Siamese, all theories about the breed's derivation are just that, including the belief that Siamese originated in the Khorat province in northeastern Siam (now Thailand). Yet whatever its origin, the breed had arrived in England by 1871. Catalogs from the Crystal Palace shows for 1871 through 1887 list nineteen Siamese entries.

Not all the Royal Cats of Siam, as they were also called in those times, resembled the Siamese we know today. In 1889 Harrison Weir reported that "Mr. Young, of Harrogate, possesses a chocolate variety of this Royal Siamese cat." According to Weir, Young had purchased his cat—which had a rich, dark-brown body and darker points—from an English gentleman who had obtained the cat from Singapore. While allowing that "this peculiar color is very beautiful and scarce," Weir insisted that "the light gray or fawn color with black and well-marked muzzle, ears, and legs is the typical variety." For its part, Young's chocolate Siamese appears to have resembled the current Burmese, whose ancestors are also thought to have originated in Siam.

There is no doubt—and little wonder—that Siamese attracted the attention of royalty and the elite, for no breed of cat could then compare with the unique color and pattern of the Siamese. Even its voice and personality identified this as a breed apart. Siamese were treasured among wealthy and titled persons in Siam, who protected their cats by keeping them indoors and who were seldom willing to allow unaltered Siamese cats to leave the country. A Mrs. Vivian of Dover, England, who imported Siamese in 1885 and 1886, wrote that her cats were believed to have come from the King's palace in Siam, "where alone the breed are said to be kept pure." The first imported cats known to have originated in the King's cattery were Pho and Mia, two seal points who were presented by the King to Owen Gould, the departing British consul general, in 1884. Gould, in turn, gave these cats to his sister, a Mrs. Veley, who showed them at the Crystal Palace the following year.

DEVELOPMENT

Frances Simpson, a well-known English judge and author during the late nineteenth and early twentieth centuries, declared that Siamese were "perhaps the most difficult cat to breed and rear" in England. Another writer predicted that because of their delicacy Siamese were "never likely to be common." They were especially susceptible to enteritis and respiratory problems. Nevertheless, the Siamese' intelligence, personality, and distinctive appearance were sufficient to insure its popularity and proliferation.

For many years the seal point was the only variety of Siamese considered desirable. Blue points were not recognized until 1934, chocolate points in 1952, and lilac (or frost) points in 1955. Since the genes that produce these colors were present in the native Siamese population long before the breed became fashionable, the delayed recognition of the nonseal varieties must be blamed on snobbery and stubbornness. When a blue point was exhibited at an English show in 1896, the judge disqualified the cat. Whether this was a true blue point or a self-blue Korat—yet another

breed found in Siam—is not known; but there must have been some crossbreedings between Siamese and the self-colored blue cats in Siam, for blue point kittens appeared in many litters born to the earliest Korats imported to this country.

By the turn of the century interest in Siamese had spread to the United States, and the breed began to appear at American shows. Volume I of the Beresford Cat Club book, published in 1900, contains the names of Lockhaven Siam and Sally Ward, two Siamese that were owned by Mrs. Clinton Locke of Chicago, founder of the Beresford Cat Club, the first cat club in the United States, which later evolved into the American Cat

Seal Point Siamese

Association. The progress of the Siamese in this country mimicked its development in England. The breed appealed to the well connected and to persons of some station. Mrs. Locke acquired cats from Lady Marcus Beresford, a legendary fancier in Great Britain, and one Siamese was imported by the United States postmaster general. The Siamese also experienced the same health problems in this country as they had in England. According to Carlon Boren, a prominent Siamese breeder in the United States during the 1940s and 1950s, the first two Siamese to win championships in this country "both died in 1905, probably of enteritis."

When the Siamese arrived in this country, they didn't come cheap. "The earliest Siamese," wrote Boren, "cost not less than a thousand dollars, plus transportation charges and other fees." Second- and third-generation, American-bred stock sold "for two hundred dollars up to one thousand dollars." One cat who earned his keep was Champion Oriental Nanki Pooh of Newton, Imp., who lived to be seventeen and who sired more than thirteen hundred kittens. These numbers reflect the popularity and the problems of the Siamese in the United States during the first two thirds of this century. As recently as the 1960s, you could find scores of Siamese at shows. In fact, the number of Siamese entries was such—as many as sixty or seventy cats—that hip or belly spots were enough to eliminate cats from consideration.

Unfortunately, quantity did not equal quality in Siamese classes. "The breed was nearly loved to death," says one fancier, and by the 1950s and 1960s many of the Siamese found at shows were of doubtful merit, the results of indiscriminate importation and breeding during the preceding decades, when every traveler to the Orient seemed to come back with a pair of Siamese cats. Most of these cats had coarse bone, round eyes, short heads, stocky bodies, and questionable origins. Ironically, they descended on the fancy at the time when serious breeders had eradicated most of the kinked tails, crossed eyes, white lockets, and white toes that had plagued the Siamese in the earliest days of the breed. In addition, during the 1950s some breeders began producing Siamese with horselike heads, over-exaggerated chins that were much too heavy for a fine Siamese wedge, ears that were tilted forward and set too high on the head, bodies that were too thin, and poor muscle tone. Judges who thought this was the latest thing in Siamese put wins on these cats, in spite of the fact that the breed Standard had not been changed.

Regrettably, that vogue led to the beginning of the decline in the Siamese. For a number of years now Siamese have been losing popularity because of too many problems within the breed, too many surplus kittens being produced, too little demand relative to supply, and internal rivalries among Siamese breeders, including their stubbornness regarding the acceptance of new colors. Like their animals, Siamese fanciers are a breed apart. They are grimly dedicated to their breed—and they sometimes appear to be unaware that other breeds exist. They often suspect others are abusing Siamese in the development of new breeds, yet it was Siamese breeders themselves who were responsible for the initial use of outcrosses to strengthen their own cats.

Today the Siamese are desperately trying to make a comeback. Classes are small, and although the type is generally good, the cats seem to fall short in one area or another. Furthermore, the acceptance of eleven new shorthair breeds between 1964 and 1979 helped to diminish the status of the Siamese. It is still the most popular shorthaired cat (and the second most popular cat overall) in terms of new registrations; but it was overtaken long ago by the Persian, and it has conceded first place among shorthair breeds on the show bench to the Abyssinian.

Standard for the
SIAMESE

Courtesy of the Cat Fanciers' Association.
Differences in the Standards of other registries are indicated at the end of the text.

HEAD: (20)
Long, flat profile 6
Wedge, fine muzzle,
    size 5
Ears 4
Chin 3
Width between eyes 2

EYES: (10)
Shape, size, slant, and
    placement 10

BODY: (30)
Structure and size,
    including neck 12
Muscle tone 10
Legs and feet 5
Tail 3

COAT: 10

COLOR: (30)
Body color 10
Point color 10
Eye color 10

GENERAL: the ideal Siamese is a medium-sized, svelte, refined cat with long, tapering lines; very lithe but muscular. Males may be proportionately larger than females.

HEAD: long, tapering wedge. Medium in size, in good proportion to body. The total wedge starts at the nose and flares out in straight lines to the tips of the ears, forming a triangle with no break at the whiskers. No less than the width of an eye between the eyes. When the whiskers are smoothed back, the underlying bone structure is apparent. Allow for jowls in stud cats.

SKULL: flat. In profile, a long straight line is seen from the top of the head to the tip of the nose. No bulge over eyes. No dip in nose.

EARS: strikingly large, pointed, wide at base; continuing the lines of the wedge.[1]

EYES: almond shaped. Medium size. Neither protruding nor recessed. Slanted towards the nose in harmony with lines of wedge and ears. Uncrossed.[2]

NOSE: long and straight. A continuation of the forehead with no break.

MUZZLE: fine, wedge shaped.

CHIN and JAW: medium size. Tip of chin lines up with tip of nose in the same vertical plane. Neither receding nor excessively massive.

BODY: medium size. Graceful, long, and svelte. A distinctive combination of fine bones and firm muscles. Shoulders and hips continue same sleek lines of tubular body. Hips never wider than shoulders. Abdomen tight.

NECK: long and slender.

LEGS: long and slim. Hind legs higher than front. In good proportion to body.

PAWS: dainty, small, and oval. Toes: five in front and four behind.

TAIL: long, thin, tapering to a fine point.

COAT: short, fine textured, glossy. Lying close to body.

CONDITION: excellent physical condition. Eyes clear. Muscular, strong, and lithe. Neither flabby nor bony. Not fat.

COLOR: body even, with subtle shading when allowed. Allowance should be made for darker color in older cats as Siamese generally darken with age, but there must be definite contrast between body color and points. Points: mask, ears, legs, feet, and tail are dense and clearly defined. All of the same shade. Mask covers entire face including whisker pads, and is connected to ears by tracings. Mask should not extend over the top of the head. No ticking or white hairs in points.

PENALIZE: improper (i.e., off-color or spotted) nose leather or paw pads. Soft or mushy body.

DISQUALIFY: any evidence of illness or poor health. Weak hind legs. Mouth breathing due to nasal obstruction or poor occlusion. Emaciation. Visible kink. Eyes other than blue. White toes and/or feet. Incorrect number of toes. Malocclusion resulting in either undershot or overshot chin.

SIAMESE COLORS

BLUE POINT: body bluish white, cold in tone, shading gradually to white on stomach and chest. Points deep blue. Nose leather and paw pads: slate colored. Eye color: deep, vivid blue.

CHOCOLATE POINT: body ivory, no shading. Points milk-chocolate, warm in tone. Nose leather and paw pads: cinnamon pink. Eye color: deep, vivid blue.

LILAC POINT:[3] body glacial white with no shading. Points frosty gray with pinkish tone. Nose leather and paw pads: lavender pink. Eye color: deep, vivid blue.

SEAL POINT: body pale fawn to cream, warm in tone, shading to lighter color on the stomach and chest. Points deep seal brown. Nose leather and paw pads: same color as points. Eye color: deep, vivid blue.

ADDITIONAL SIAMESE COLORS

(See page 170 for a full description of the colors listed below.)

The following colors are recognized by some, but not necessarily all, the other registries in North America.

Lynx point colors: blue lynx point, blue-cream (or blue-tortie) lynx point, chocolate lynx point, chocolate-tortie lynx point, cream lynx point, lilac lynx point, lilac-cream lynx point, red lynx point, seal lynx point, seal-tortie lynx point. **Particolor point colors:** blue-cream (or blue-tortie) point, chocolate-tortie point, lilac-cream point, seal-tortie point. **Solid point colors:** cream point, red point.

Siamese allowable outcross breeds:[4] none.

---

[1] ACFA: " Pricked slightly forward as if listening."
[2] CFF: "No less than the width of an eye between the eyes."
[3] ACFA calls this color "frost."
[4] In all associations where the breed is recognized.

Singapura

ORIGIN

In 1971 Hal Meadow, a geophysicist who lived in New Orleans, was sent to Singapore on business. There he found four, brown-ticked cats in the Lo Yang district. He paid a crewman on a ship that was bound for the United States to transport these cats to his friend Tommy Brodie, a woman living in Houston, Texas. There were no import or export papers sent with the animals, nor was there any other record of their origin.

DEVELOPMENT

Meadow's friend Tommy Brodie had once bred Abyssinians and had also been a Cat Fanciers' Federation allbreed judge. Intrigued by the brown-ticked cats from Singapore, she allowed three of them to reproduce. The fourth had died in the meantime. She kept no records of these transactions because she did not intend to establish a new breed from these cats.

In short, but not necessarily chronological, order: Hal Meadow and Tommy Brodie were married; Hal and Tommy Meadow went to live for a while in Singapore after Hal Meadow had been transferred there on business; three of the original imports from Singapore produced children and grandchildren; and Hal and/or Tommy Meadow decided to establish a new

Singapura

breed from these cats. But the nature of Hal Meadow's work in Singapore in 1971 had been politically sensitive. Therefore, he insisted that Tommy not reveal the origins of the cats he had sent her.

When the Meadows went to Singapore in 1974, they took several cats with them. Three of these were grandchildren of the cats that Hal Meadow had found on the island in 1971. These grandchildren were called Tess, Tickle, and Pusse. When the Meadows left Singapore and returned to the United States in 1975, they announced that they had found Tess, Tickle, and Pusse on the streets in Singapore and that they intended to establish a new breed based on this unique, naturally occurring Singapore street cat.

Cat publications in the United States dutifully printed Tommy Meadow's articles about the origin of the breed she had founded. All the registries in North America duly recognized the Singapura for championship competition. The Meadows' revisionist history of the creation of their breed, which they maintain was warranted by the nature of Hal Meadow's work, would have remained the official story had not an American named Jerry Mayes gone to Singapore in the mid-1980s to find additional street cats to bring back to the United States.

When people in Singapore looked at Mayes peculiarly after he had asked them about Singapore street cats, he began to do some investigating. He discovered that the import papers filed by the Meadows when they had entered Singapore as husband and wife contained the singular names of three "brown Abyssinian" cats: the aforementioned Tess, Tickle, and Pusse.

Eventually Mayes brought this information to the attention of Sandra Davie, a reporter for the Singapore *Straits Times.* Davie phoned Tommy Meadow during the summer of 1990, and during their conversation, which Davie claims to have taped, Meadow admitted fabricating the story about finding cats on the streets of Singapore in 1974. She admitted the same thing to the Cat Fanciers' Association board of directors in an executive session in February 1991. Davie's interest in the story was prompted by the fact that the Singapore tourist board was about to launch a gigantic promotion based on these tiny cats. The board looked to have egg on its face if it turned out that the Singapura, newly designated mascot of its native land, had actually been bred in somebody's basement in the United States and then transported to Singapore, as some people in

Singapore and the States were beginning to suggest.

When the Meadows appeared before the CFA board in February 1991, they were able to substantiate with passports and visas Hal Meadow's presence in Singapore twenty years earlier. They did not substantiate, at least according to the minutes from the executive session, the existence of the cats that Hal Meadow shipped from Singapore in 1971.

There are some people who continue to question the origin of the Singapura, but there are more disturbing questions about this breed. They concern its future, not its past. To date, the Singapura has been derived from only four cats: the three that Hal Meadow shipped to America in 1971, and another import from Singapore that arrived later. There are no allowable outcrosses for this breed, and the Singapura registry is already closed in the Cat Fanciers' Federation, which means that no additional imports from Singapore can be registered. The registries in other associations—with the exception of the Canadian Cat Association and The International Cat Association—are virtually closed, too, because they require anywhere from a three-to a five-generation pedigree on cats imported from Singapore. No one has been breeding cats over there long enough to satisfy this requirement. Only CCA and TICA, which allow the registration of imported Singapuras, have a policy that will allow the needed expansion of this breed's gene pool. Meanwhile, the number of Singapura litters registered in CFA dropped from fifty-five in 1989 to twenty-eight in 1990.

Standard for the
SINGAPURA

Courtesy of the Cat Fanciers' Association.
Differences in the Standards of other registries are indicated at the end of the text.

HEAD: (25)
Ears 10
Head shape 4
Width at eye 4
Muzzle shape 4
Profile 3

EYES: (10)
Size and placement 6
Shape 3
Color 1

BODY, LEGS, and TAIL: (20)
Neck 3
Proportion 10
Legs and feet 5
Tail 2

COAT: 15

COLOR: 15

MARKINGS: 15

GENERAL: the appearance of an alert, healthy, small to medium-sized, muscular-bodied cat with noticeably large eyes and ears. Cat to have the illusion of refined, delicate coloring.

HEAD: skull rounded with rounded width at the outer eye, narrowing to a definite whisker break and a medium-short, broad muzzle with a blunt nose. In profile, a rounded skull with a very slight stop well below eye level. Straight line nose to chin. Chin well developed.

EARS: large, slightly pointed, wide open at the base, and possessing a deep cup. Medium set. Outer lines of the ear to extend upward at an angle slightly wide of parallel. Small ears a serious fault.

EYES: large, almond shaped, held wide open but showing slant. Neither protruding nor recessed. Eyes set not less than an eye width apart. Color hazel, green, or yellow with no other color permitted. Brilliance preferred. Small eyes a serious fault.

BODY: small to medium overall size cat. Moderately stocky and muscular. Body, legs, and floor to form a square. Midsection not tucked but firm.

NECK: short and thick.

LEGS and FEET: legs heavy and muscled at the body tapering to small, short, oval feet.

TAIL: length to be short of the shoulder when laid along the torso. Tending towards slender but not whippy. Blunt tip.

COAT: fine, very short, lying very close to the body. Allowance for longer coat in kittens. Springy coat a fault.

MARKINGS: each hair to have at least two bands of dark ticking separated by light bands. Light next to skin and a dark tip. Dark tail tip with color extending back toward the body on the upper side. Cat to show some barring on inner front legs and back knees only. Allowance to be made for undeveloped ticking in kittens. Spine line not a fault.

PENALIZE: dark coat coloring next to skin, definite gray tones, barring on outer front legs, necklaces, non-visible tail faults.

DISQUALIFY: white lockets, barring on tail, top of the head unticked, unbroken necklaces or leg bracelets. Very small eyes or ears. Visible tail faults.

SINGAPURA COLOR

COLOR: color to be dark-brown ticking on a warm, old-ivory ground color. Muzzle, chin, chest, and stomach to be the color of unbleached muslin. Nose leather pale to dark salmon. Eyeliner, nose outline, lips, whisker apertures, hair between the toes to be dark brown. Foot pads a rosy brown. Salmon tones to the ears and nose bridge not a fault. Warm, light shades preferred.

Singapura allowable outcross breeds:[1] none.

---

[1] In all associations where the breed is recognized.

Somali

The origin of the Somali begins with the origin of its shorthaired littermates, the Abyssinians. For many of their early years the Abyssinians were, of necessity, hybrid cats. By 1900, fewer than twenty years after the Abyssinian had been listed as a separate breed in England, many authorities concluded that it was simply the result of chance matings among ordinary ticked tabbies, and the name Abyssinian was replaced for a time by "Ticks" or "British Ticks" or "Bunny Cats." This decision was supported by records that subsequently appeared in the 1900-1905 stud book of the National Cat Club in England. Each of the twelve Abyssinians listed there had at least one parent of unknown origin.

It is certainly possible that some of those unknowns were either longhaired cats or shorthaired cats which had inherited the recessive longhaired gene from one of their parents. And it is probable that breeders in England, struggling to develop the Abyssinian, resorted to outcrossing as the easiest way to cope with limited stock and the setbacks occasioned by two world wars. Indeed, the list of stud cats in the 1947-48 GCCF records contains just four Abyssinian males, two of them unproven. Breeders looking to find mates for their females at that time obviously had to look elsewhere for eligible suitors.

DEVELOPMENT

Whatever the origin of the longhaired gene, there is no doubt that longhaired Abyssinian kittens were man-made. They were not the result of a spontaneous mutation as some Abyssinian breeders stubbornly insisted. Nor was England alone responsible for introducing this gene to the breed. American breeders also helped to enlarge the Abyssinian gene pool—and to enhance those qualities that needed strengthening—through outcrossing. Nevertheless, Abyssinian breeders behaved true to form as cat fanciers and refused to recognize their longhaired kittens as natural Abys. Such kittens were sold without papers as quickly and quietly as possible.

One day in 1969 a year-old longhaired Abyssinian named George—who had been given away at the age of five weeks—was brought by his fifth owner to a private shelter in Gillette, New Jersey. Evelyn Mague, the woman who operated the shelter, is an Abyssinian breeder. In fact, she later discovered that she owned the Abyssinian male that had sired the much-traveled George. Mague thought that George was "the most beautiful cat" she had ever seen, but he was not used to being around other cats; so she had him neutered and vaccinated, which no one had bothered to do for him yet. Then she placed him in a single-cat home.

Mague resented the way George had been treated. Although his parents had been pedigreed cats from some of the finest Abyssinian lines of that time, he was treated no better than a street cat because he had been born with long hair. Mague determined to find and show another longhaired Aby. Then she determined to start a campaign to get these cats accepted. When Aby breeders would not hear of calling these cats longhaired Abyssinians, Mague chose the name Somali because Somalia forms the eastern and southeastern borders of Ethiopia, which used to be called Abyssinia.

Finding another longhaired Aby was not difficult. In order for two shorthaired cats to produce a longhaired kitten, each of those shorthairs must possess a longhair gene. Since Mague had inherited George's mother when his breeder left the business of breeding cats—and since she already owned George's father—she was able to produce additional Somalis with little difficulty: one out of every four kittens on the average. Breeding Somalis to Somalis, of course, will produce nothing but longhairs.

After running an ad in *Cats* magazine for a year, Mague heard from a breeder in Canada who had

Ruddy Somali

bought some longhaired Abys from a Canadian judge and had been working with them for four or five years. Gradually Mague found other Aby breeders with longhairs, and in 1972 founded the Somali Cat Club of America (SCCA). Registration and championship status for the Somali soon followed. The now defunct National Cat Fanciers' Association was the first to recognize Somalis.

Genetically, the only difference between a Somali and an Abyssinian is one gene: that which determines coat length. There was little sense in creating a new breed for these cats. They should have been an Abyssinian variety. There is even less sense for insisting, as most associations do, that shorthaired kittens born from Somali-Abyssinian crosses have to be registered as Somalis and cannot be shown. At least one registry, The International Cat Association, currently allows all kittens from such sanctioned outcrosses to be shown as either Abys or Somalis, depending on their coat length.

Standard for the
SOMALI

Courtesy of the Cat Fanciers' Association. Differences in the Standards of other registries are indicated at the end of the text.

HEAD: (25)	**COAT:** (25)
Skull 6	Texture 10
Muzzle 6	Length 15
Ears 7	
Eye shape 6	**COLOR:** (25)
	Color 10
BODY: (25)	Ticking 10
Torso 10	Eye color 5
Legs and Feet 10	
Tail 5	

GENERAL: the overall impression of the Somali is that of a well-proportioned, medium-to-large cat with firm muscular development, lithe, showing an alert, lively interest in all surroundings, with an even disposition and easy to handle. The cat is to give the appearance of activity, sound health, and general vigor.[1]

HEAD: a modified, slightly rounded wedge without flat planes; the brow, cheek, and profile lines all showing a gentle contour. A slight rise from the bridge of the nose to the forehead, which should be of good size with width between the ears flowing into the arched neck without a break.

MUZZLE: shall follow gentle contours in conformity with the skull, as viewed from the front profile. Chin shall be full, nether undershot nor overshot, having a rounded appearance. The muzzle shall not be sharply pointed, and there shall be no evidence of snippiness, foxiness, or whisker pinch. Allowance to be made for jowls in adult males.

EARS: large, alert, moderately pointed, broad, and cupped at the base. Ear set on a line towards the rear of the skull. The inner ear shall have horizontal tufts that reach nearly to the other side of the ear; tufts desirable.[2]

EYES: almond shaped, large, brilliant, and expressive. Skull aperture neither round nor oriental. Eyes accented by dark lid skin encircled by light-colored area. Above each a short, dark, vertical pencil stroke with a dark pencil line continuing from the upper lid toward the ear.

BODY: torso medium long, lithe, and graceful, showing well-developed muscular strength. Rib cage is rounded; back is slightly arched giving the appearance of a cat about to spring; flank level with no tuck up. Conformation strikes a medium between the extremes of cobby and svelte, lengthy types.

LEGS and FEET: legs in proportion to torso; feet oval and compact. When standing, the Somali gives the impression of being nimble and quick. Toes: five in front and four in back.

TAIL: having a full brush, thick at the base, and slightly tapering. Length in balance with torso.

COAT: texture very soft to the touch, extremely fine and double coated. The more dense the coat, the better.

LENGTH: a medium-length coat, except over shoulders, where a slightly shorter length is permitted. Preference is to be given to a cat with ruff and breeches, giving a full-coated appearance to the cat.

PENALIZE: color faults—cold gray or sandy tone to coat color; mottling or speckling on unticked areas.

Pattern faults—necklaces, leg bars, tabby stripes, or bars on body; lack of desired markings on head and tail. Black roots on body.

DISQUALIFY: white locket or groin spot or white anywhere on body other than on the upper throat, chin, or nostrils. Any skeletal abnormality. Wrong color paw pads or nose leather. Unbroken necklace. Incorrect number of toes. Kinks in tail.

SOMALI COLORS[3]

BLUE:[4] coat warm, soft blue gray, ticked with various shades of slate blue, the extreme outer tip to be the darkest, with an ivory undercoat. Tail tipped with slate blue. The undersides and forelegs (inside) to be warm cream to beige to harmonize with the undercoat color. Nose leather: dark pink. Paw pads: mauve, with slate blue between toes, extending slightly beyond the paws. Eye color: gold or green,[5] the more richness and depth of color the better.

FAWN:[6] coat warm rose-beige, ticked with light cocoa brown, the extreme outer tip to be the darkest, with a blush beige undercoat. Tail tipped with light cocoa brown. The underside and inside of legs to be a tint to harmonize with the main color. Nose leather: salmon. Paw pads: dark pink, with light cocoa brown between the toes, extending slightly beyond the paws. Eye color: gold or green,[7] the more richness and depth, the better.

RED:[8] warm, glowing red ticked with chocolate brown. Deeper shades of red preferred. Ears and tail tipped with chocolate brown. Nose leather: rosy pink.

Paw pads: pink with chocolate brown between toes, extending slightly beyond paws. Eye color: gold or green,[9] the more richness and depth the better.

RUDDY: overall impression of an orange brown or ruddy ticked with black. Color has radiant or glowing quality. Darker shading along the spine allowed. Underside of body and inside of legs and chest to be an even ruddy tone, harmonizing with the top coat; without ticking, barring, necklaces, or belly marks. Nose leather: tile red. Paw pads: black or brown with black between toes and extending upward on rear legs. Off-white on upper throat, lips, and nostrils only. Tail continuing the dark spine line ending at the black at the tip. Complete absence of rings on tail. Preference given to unmarked ruddy color. Ears tipped with black or dark brown. Eye color: gold or green,[10] the more richness and depth of color the better.

(PLEASE NOTE: the Somali is extremely slow in showing mature ticking, and allowances should be made for kittens and young cats.)

Somali allowable outcross breeds[11]: Abyssinian.

---

[1] TICA: "The female being finer boned and usually more active than the male."
[2] TICA: "A thumbprint marking is desirable on the back of the ear."
[3] This breed is also recognized in lilac and cream by the American Cat Association.
[4] This color not recognized in ACFA.
[5] ACA: "Or hazel."
[6] This color not recognized in ACFA.
[7] ACA: "Or hazel."
[8] TICA calls this color sorrel (cinnamon).
[9] ACA: "Or hazel."
[10] ACA: "Or hazel."
[11] In all associations where the breed is recognized.

Tonkinese

ORIGIN

The one breed to originate in Canada, the Tonkinese is a hybrid cat that was first accepted for championship competition by the Canadian Cat Association in 1965. This breed was developed in the early 1960s by a Canadian cat fancier named Margaret Conroy, who decided to cross a seal point Siamese and a sable Burmese to create a cat with some of the qualities she liked best in each of the breeds. She hoped for a cat that would be intermediate in type and have a temperament falling between that of a Siamese and a Burmese. Conroy believed that Siamese were becoming too stylized and extreme for popular taste. Although Conroy could not have foreseen this, the Burmese would eventually acquire a new and controversial look, thereby creating a demand in the market for a cat like the Tonkinese, with some of the characteristics of the old style Siamese.

Nearly a decade before Mrs. Conroy "officially" developed her new breed, Milan Greer, a pet shop owner in New York City, had worked towards the same goal. Greer used colorpoint Siamese and Burmese in his plan and claimed to have produced five generations of cats that he called Golden Siamese before dropping the project. When Margaret Conroy began working on her Siamese-Burmese crosses, she also used the name Golden Siamese for a few years. Records indicate that *Tonkinese* (first spelled with an *a* instead of an *i*) was suggested later by cat fanciers who wanted to avoid any suggestion that this hybrid was either a Siamese or Burmese.

DEVELOPMENT

With help from breeders who shared her belief in the virtue of moderation—"I don't like to fool with Mother Nature; it bothers me," says one Tonkinese advocate—Conroy wrote a standard for an "intermediate" breed and presented this standard to the Canadian Cat Association. The cat described in her blueprint was neither slinky, like the Siamese, nor stocky, like the Burmese. Instead, the Tonkinese was designed with a medium torso, moderately slim legs, well-developed muscles, a head with a modified wedge, and medium ears set as much on the side as on the top of the head.

By the end of the sixties, Margaret Conroy was no longer breeding cats, but by then the Tonkinese had gained popularity in the United States, and in 1972 the now-defunct Independent Cat Federation became the

Platinum Mink Tonkinese

153

first registry to recognize Tonkinese for Championship competition. Eventually all the other registries in the United States followed suit.

In developing the Tonkinese, Margaret Conroy had virtually reinvented the wheel. In 1930 a female cat named Wong Mau, from whom all Burmese cats are descended, arrived in the United States. Wong Mau was a brown hybrid with darker points on her face, legs, feet and tail. Bred to a sealpoint Siamese, she produced both Siamese cats and other offspring that resembled her, with darker bodies than the Siamese and with less contrast between point color and body color. It was not until Wong Mau was bred to one of her sons, or when two of her offspring were bred together, that the uniform, sable-brown Burmese color appeared. It is obvious, therefore, that Wong Mau—in addition to being the matriarch of the Burmese breed—was also the precursor of today's Tonkinese. In fact, she was a Tonkinese cat long before the Tonkinese breed was invented, and the "light" phase kittens that Dr. Joseph Thompson, Wong Mau's owner, referred to in his writings were possibly the earliest examples of this strain.

Just as Wong Mau did not breed true for color neither does the Tonkinese today. Furthermore, not every color produced by Tonk-to-Tonk breedings is accepted for championship competition. All registries recognize the Tonk in natural mink, blue mink, platinum mink, champagne mink, and honey mink colors. A few other associations, most notably the American Cat Fanciers Association and The International Cat Association, accept Tonkinese in solid mink and pointed colors as well.

The addition of *mink* to the universally accepted Tonkinese colors is somewhat confusing. Though many people believe that *mink* describes the feel of the Tonkinese coat, Jane Barletta, who pioneered the breed in the United States, reports that *mink* actually describes the original Tonkinese pattern: a medium brown that shaded to a lighter hue on a cat's underparts and to a dark-brown color at its extremities. To obtain balanced Tonkinese colors, breeders are challenged by the necessity of restricting the expression of the gene for point coloration to a medium tone while avoiding any solid-color appearance that would make the Tonkinese look like a spoiled Burmese.

Although Siamese and Burmese breeders made pointed remarks at first about their cats' lookalike cousins with the soundalike name, "that sort of hostility has been toned down considerably over the years," says Tonkinese breeder and TICA judge Mark Fensterstock. "Most Siamese and Burmese people accept the Tonk as another legitimate breed. In fact, there are a number of people who breed both Burmese and Tonkinese."

For its part, the public has never shown anything but enthusiasm for the Tonkinese. "When I go to a cat show," says Fensterstock, "and people see my cats—especially if I have some pointed Tonkinese with me—they'll say, 'Oh, that's like the Siamese we had for fifteen years.' There's a big demand for Tonkinese among people who had its old style component breeds for a long time and now can't find them anymore. These are people who like the more moderate, less extreme look."

While the Tonkinese is an intermediate cat by design, there is one outstanding feature about the breed: its brilliant, aqua-colored eyes. This is one area where the Tonkinese prefers license to limitation. A distinctive "blend" of the blue Siamese and gold Burmese eye colors, the Tonkinese' aqua eyes range from aquamarine to turquoise.

Standard for the TONKINESE

Courtesy of the Cat Fanciers' Association. Differences in the Standards of other registries are indicated at the end of the text.

HEAD: (25)
Profile 8
Muzzle 6
Ears 6
Eye shape and set 5

BODY: (30)
Torso 15
Legs and Feet 5
Tail 5
Muscle tone 5

COAT: 10

COLOR: (35)
Body color 15
Point color 10
Eye color 10

GENERAL: the Tonkinese cat was originally the result of a Siamese-to-Burmese breeding. The ideal Tonkinese is intermediate in type, being neither cobby or svelte. The Tonkinese should give the overall impression of an alert, active cat with good muscular development. The cat should be surprisingly heavy. While the breed is to be considered medium in size, balance and proportion are of greater importance.

HEAD: a modified wedge, somewhat longer than it is wide,[1] with high, gently planed cheekbones; the brow, cheek, and profile all showing clean, strong contours. In profile there is a slight convex curve of the forehead, from the top of the head to just above the eyes. A slight stop at eye level.[2] Good width between the eyes.

MUZZLE: blunt; as long as it is wide. Slight whisker break, gently curved, following lines of wedge. In profile, the tip of the chin lines up with the tip of nose in the same vertical plane.

EARS: alert, medium in size.[3] Oval tips, broad at the base. Ears set as much on the sides of the head as on the top. Hair on the ears very short and close lying. Leather may show through.

EYES: open, almond shape.[4,5] Slanted along the cheekbones toward the outer edge of the ear.[6] Eyes are proportionate in size to the face.[7]

EYE COLOR: aqua. A definitive characteristic of the Tonkinese breed, best seen in natural light. Depth, clarity, and brilliance of color preferred.

BODY: torso medium in length, demonstrating well-developed muscular strength without coarseness. The Tonkinese conformation strikes a midpoint between the extremes of the long, svelte body types and the cobby, compact body types. Balance and proportion are more important than size alone. The abdomen should be taut, well-muscled, and firm.[8]

LEGS and FEET: fairly slim, proportionate in length and bone to the body. Hind legs slightly longer than front. Paws more oval than round. Trim. Toes: five in front and four behind.

TAIL: proportionate in length to body.[9] Tapering.[10]

COAT: medium short[11] in length, close lying, fine, soft and silky, with a lustrous sheen.

BODY COLOR: the mature specimen should be a rich, even, unmarked color, shading almost imperceptibly to a slightly lighter hue on the underparts. Allowance to be made for lighter body color in young cats. With the dilute colors in particular, development of full body color may take up to sixteen months. Cats do darken with age, but there must be a distinct contrast between body color and points.

POINT COLOR: mask, ears, feet, and tail all densely marked, but merging gently into body color. Except in kittens, mask and ears should be connected by tracings. Allowance to be made for slight barring in young cats.

PENALIZE: palpable tail fault. Extreme ranginess or cobbiness. Definite nose break. Round eyes. Crossed eyes.

DISQUALIFY: yellow eyes. White locket or button. Visible tail kink.

TONKINESE COLORS[12]

BLUE MINK: body soft, blue gray, shading to a lighter hue on the underparts. Fawn overtones permissible but not preferable. Points: slate blue, distinctly darker than the body color. Nose leather: blue gray (corresponding to the intensity of the point color). Paw pads: blue gray (may have a rosy undertone).

CHAMPAGNE MINK: body buff cream. Points: medium brown. Nose leather: cinnamon brown (corresponding to the intensity of the point color). Paw pads: cinnamon pink to cinnamon brown.

HONEY MINK:[13] body golden cream, preferably with an apricot cast. Points: light to medium, ruddy brown. Nose leather: caramel pink. Paw pads: caramel pink.

NATURAL MINK: body medium brown, shading to a lighter hue on the underparts. Ruddy highlights acceptable. Points: dark brown. Nose leather: dark brown (corresponding to the intensity of the point color). Paw pads: medium to dark brown (may have a rosy undertone).

PLATINUM MINK: body pale, silvery gray with warm overtones. Not white or cream. Points: frosty gray, distinctly darker than the body color. Nose leather: lavender pink to lavender gray. Paw pads: lavender pink.

Tonkinese allowable outcross breeds:[14] none.

---

[1] TICA: "Head and ears give impression of equilateral triangle."
[2] CFF: "A clearly defined nose stop."
[3] ACA, ACFA, TICA: "Pricked forward."
[4] ACFA, CFF: "Slightly rounded on the bottom."
[5] TICA: "Peach pit. Half almond on top, slightly rounded on bottom."
[6] ACFA, TICA: "Set at least an eye's width apart."
[7] ACA, ACFA: "Medium in size, in proportion to the head."
[8] TICA: "Back rises slightly from shoulder to rump."
[9] ACFA: "Medium to medium long, in proportion to body."
[10] TICA: " ... gently to a slightly blunted tip."
[11] CFF: "Short."
[12] ACFA and TICA accept the following additional Tonkinese colors: natural, blue, champagne, and platinum solid; natural, blue, champagne, and platinum pointed.
[13] ACFA does not recognize this color.
[14] In all associations where the breed is recognized.

Turkish Angora

ORIGIN

The Angora is certainly as recognizable as any other longhaired breed in the world; and even though its fortunes do not compare with the Persian's, the two cats share a parallel history. Nearly two and a half centuries ago Angora cats existed in the region surrounding the city of Angora, now called Ankara. At the same time another variety of longhaired cat was associated with the province of Chorazan in Persia.

According to early observers, there was virtually no difference between Angora and Persian cats then. The French naturalist Count de Buffon, writing in the mid-eighteenth century, observed that Persian cats, "except in color ... have a perfect resemblance to the cat of the Angora." Persians were all gray. Angoras occurred in black, white, deep red, light fawn, mottled gray, and even smoke colors.

White Turkish Angora

DEVELOPMENT

After Persians and Angoras had made their way to England in the nineteenth century, a certain contrast became evident between them. The Angora's head was smaller, more narrow, and less round; its eyes were less round; its bone was less substantial; its tail was more fanlike and pointed at the tip; and its coat was not so heavy as the Persian's.

Still, Persians and Angoras were judged by the same standard. Gradually, Persian type won out; and by 1903 Frances Simpson, an English cat breeder and judge, declared, "There are two distinctive breeds: the *Long-haired* or Persian Cats, and *Short-haired* or English and Foreign Cats." But the Governing Council of the Cat Fancy, formed in England in 1910, decreed that Persians should continue to be called *longhairs*, a practice that survives in England today. The same practice also survived in the United States until the mid-1950s, when all pedigreed longhairs became *de facto* Persians, and Angoras became all but extinct.

Though effectively disenfranchised for a while, the Turkish Angora would soon be revived. In 1962 Mrs. Liesa F. Grant imported a pair of Angora cats from the Ankara Zoo. These and subsequent importations by other American breeders comprised the stock used to reconstruct the Angora as a separate breed in the United States.

From the 1940s the Ankara Zoo has maintained a breeding colony of Angora cats, and for a time so did the zoo in Istanbul. Since the zoos were the primary and most reliable sources of Turkish Angoras, the Cat Fanciers' Association—the first registry in North America to recognize the Turkish Angora, would not register any Turkish imports not born in the zoo. What's more, CFA was unwilling to register nonwhite

Angoras until 1978, some time after the other associations had recognized the breed in a variety of colors. It is no surprise that 76 percent of the 2,108 Turkish Angoras registered by CFA in the United States between January 1, 1958, and December, 31, 1990, were white.

Because the Angora had not been subject to controlled breeding for at least fifty years before it was revived in the United States, the breed remained true to its original type. There was almost no difference between the Angoras of the 1900s and the ones imported to the United States in the 1960s. Now that breeders are making selective choices in their breeding programs, changes are occurring in Turkish Angoras that are not in keeping with the true Angora type. Modern Angoras are much too high on their hind legs, and have ultralong bodies. They are too fine in bone and have suffered a loss of coat length. Hopefully, the interest in other Angora colors will return proper type to the breed.

Standard for the
TURKISH ANGORA

Courtesy of the Cat Fanciers' Association. Differences in the Standards of other registries are indicated at the end of the text.

HEAD: 35	**COLOR:** 20
BODY: 30	**COAT:** 15

GENERAL: solid, firm, giving the impression of grace and flowing movement.
HEAD: size, small to medium. Wedge-shaped.[1] Wide at top.[2] Definite taper toward chin.[3] Allowance to be made for jowls in stud cat.
EARS: wide at base, long, pointed, and tufted. Set high on the head and erect.
EYES: large,[4] almond shaped.[5] Slanting upwards slightly.
NOSE: medium long, gentle slope. No break.
NECK: slim and graceful, medium length.
CHIN: gently rounded. Tip to form a perpendicular line with the nose.
JAW: tapered.
BODY: medium size in the female,[6] slightly larger in the male. Torso long, graceful, and lithe. Chest, lightly framed.[7] Rump slightly higher than front.[8] Bone, fine.[9]
LEGS: long. Hind legs longer than front.
PAWS: small and round, dainty. Tufts between toes.
TAIL: long and tapering, wide at base, narrow at end, full. Carried lower than body but not trailing. When moving, relaxed tail is carried horizontally over the body, sometimes almost touching the head.
COAT: body coat medium long,[10] long at ruff.[11] Full brush on tail. Silky with a wavy tendency. Wavier on stomach. Very fine and having a silklike sheen.[12]
BALANCE: proportionate in all physical aspects with graceful, lithe appearance.
DISQUALIFY: Persian body type. Kinked or abnormal tail.

TURKISH ANGORA COLORS

(See page 170 for a full description of the colors listed below.)

Particolor colors: bicolors (black and white, blue and white, red and white, or cream and white), blue cream, calico, dilute calico, tortoiseshell. **Smoke colors:** black smoke, blue smoke. **Solid colors:** black, blue, cream, red, white.[13] **Tabby colors:** blue (classic and mackerel), brown (classic and mackerel), cream (classic and mackerel), red (classic and mackerel), silver (classic and mackerel). **Other Turkish Angora colors:** any other color or pattern with the exception of those showing hybridization resulting in the colors chocolate, lavender, the Himalayan pattern, or these combinations with white.

Turkish Angora allowable outcross breeds:[14] none.

---

[1] ACFA: "Modified wedge shape."
[2] ACFA, CFF, TICA: "Top of skull is medium wide."
[3] ACFA, CFF, TICA: "No whisker pinch."
[4] TICA: " ... but in proportion to the head."
[5] ACA: " ... to almost round."
[6] ACFA: "Medium to small in females."
[7] CFF: "Chest to be narrow and deep, never rounded."
[8] ACA, ACFA: "Upper leg should lie at close angle to the body with the lower leg straight."
[9] TICA: "Medium to fine."
[10] TICA: "Semilong."
[11] ACFA: " ... and undersides."
[12] ACFA: "Seasonal variations in coat are acceptable."
[13] ACFA, CFF: "Color spot on whites is allowed up to two years."
[14] In all associations where the breed is recognized.

Turkish Van

ORIGIN

The Turkish Van is a mostly white, semilonghaired cat with a wide body, heavy bones, and a distinctive color pattern. The Van was named after the Lake Van district in western Turkey, but there is no evidence that the breed originated in this area, nor is it the only place in Turkey where Van cats have been found. "There is no repository of Turkish Van cats in Turkey," says one Van fancier, "and no one has ever found anybody in Turkey who bred for these cats specifically. In fact, the Turkish Van is really an Armenian cat. It is revered by the Armenian people, who settled in the Lake Van district and who pronounce *Van* to rhyme with *Don*, not *Dan.*"

Furthermore, while Turkish Vans have existed near Lake Van for centuries, if you went to this isolated region looking for a Van cat, you would be shown an odd-eyed white most likely a longhair that looks like the cat we know as the Turkish Angora. The reason for this confusion is a proclamation made by Mustafa Kemal Ataturk, who founded the modern Republic of Turkey in 1923. Ataturk declared that his successor would be someone who had been bitten on the ankle by an odd-eyed, white cat. This prediction understandably increased the popularity of odd-eyed white cats throughout Turkey.

DEVELOPMENT

The evolution of the Turkish Van as a breed began in 1955 when Laura Lushington and Sonia Halliday, two British women vacationing in Turkey, brought a pair of Van kittens back to England. These kittens differed in conformation as well as color from most of the Angora type cats around Lake Van. The Van kittens are substantially boned while the Angoras are delicate; Vans are heavily muscled while the Angoras

are lean; and the Turkish Vans' heads are a bit shorter and wider than the Angoras'.

The Van's most distinguishing feature—its unusual pattern—is caused by a piebald spotting gene. This dominant gene accounts for the presence of white in bicolored and tricolored cats. When the gene governing a trait is dominant, a kitten will exhibit that trait, e.g., a bicolored or tricolored coat, as long as the kitten inherits a copy of that gene from one of its parents. The van pattern, spelled with a lowercase *v*, is also found in other breeds, including Persians, Cornish Rex, Scottish Folds, and American Shorthairs.

When the two cats brought back to England by Laura Lushington and Sonia Halliday produced a litter of kittens that resembled their parents, the ladies were convinced they were working with a separate breed of cat, a breed for which they began to seek recognition. They imported two more Vans in 1959, and by 1969 Turkish Vans were accepted for championship competition in Great Britain. The following year the first Vans officially arrived in the United States. Other Vans may have arrived unofficially before that, brought into the country by military personnel returning from tours of duty at the American air base in Turkey. There is reason to believe that these unofficial Vans were frequently imported as Turkish Angoras and that some were bred into Angora lines here.

As of May 1, 1985, the Turkish Van was eligible for championship competition in The International Cat Association, the first—and so far the only—North American registry to accept this breed. The progress of the breed has been slow in the meantime. Part of the reason is the difficulty of finding Van cats in Turkey. Another factor is the temperament of the Turkish Van. Though much improved as the result of selective breeding in this country, the Van still suffers from a reputation for being somewhat troublesome in the show ring.

Red-and-White Turkish Van

Standard for the
TURKISH VAN

Courtesy of The International Cat Association. Differences in the Standards of other registries are indicated at the end of the text.

HEAD and EARS: 15	**COLOR and PATTERN:** 15
EYES: 10	**COAT:** 15
BODY: 15	**CONDITION:** 10
LEGS and FEET: 10	
TAIL: 10	

RECOGNIZED CATEGORY/DIVISION/COLORS: traditional category, particolor division, van pattern only. Red (auburn) and white, cream and white, black and white, blue and white, tortie and white, blue tortie and white, torbie and white, and blue torbie and white. (NOTE: Red and cream are to be heavily tabbied; black and blue may be tabbied or not. Tabby pattern may be either classic or mackerel.)

(See page 170 for a full description of the colors listed below.)

GENERAL DESCRIPTION: the Turkish Van is a semilonghaired white cat with distinctive markings, very broad through the chest, powerful and strong, but affectionate. The broad face tapers into a wedge with a slight break in the nose profile. Males have full ruff development. Ears are set further apart than the width of ear base, with the height equal to the amount of separation. Ears are pink and feathered internally. The head color may extend up the back of the ears.

The eyes are almond-shaped to almost round, set straight *to slightly oblique,* and are pink rimmed. Eye color is yellow to amber and gold, or blue, or odd-eyed. Large, expressive eyes preferred.

The body is long, broad, and muscular, with a solid feel. In males the shoulders are as broad as the head, tapering to the thighs. The females are more petite. The legs and feet are trim and muscular, set wide, and tapering to neat, round feet, with well-tufted toes.

The coat is an all-weather, semilonghair with no wooly undercoat. It lies relatively flat, and has feathering, britches and belly shag up to twice as long as the body coat. The facial hair is short. The coat is fuller and longer in winter.

The tail is a brush, with fur two inches or more long, continuous in color with the rump patch. The tail is darker above and lighter on the underside, more or less strongly ringed in the red or cream, and may not be ringed in the black, blue, or tortie.

The cat should be clean, parasite free, well groomed, gentle, and amenable to handling.

Allow for shorter summer coat, extended color on head and rump, random spots or blotches of color on the upper body, flanks, or outside of legs to the ankles, white spot at tip of tail.

COLOR: white with no trace of yellow. The markings are a blazed head patch, and a rump patch extending to the tip of the tail. One or more random spots of color are permitted on the upper body, flanks, and outside of legs to the ankles. The markings may be broken by patches of white. Nose leather and paw pads are pink.

EYE COLOR: eyes may be yellow to amber, blue, or odd-eyed, all with pink rims.

PENALIZE: yellowed white; color over 20 percent of the body; more than four spots of color in addition to those on head and rump; spots or blotches inside legs, feet, or lower body; lack of facial blaze.

WITHHOLD ALL AWARDS: color extending over more than 25 percent of body; adult males medium or small (fewer than twenty-eight inches long overall or under ten pounds); small adult females (fewer than twenty-five inches and eight pounds).

Allowable Turkish Van outcrosses:[1] none.

---

[1] TICA was the only association that recognized the Turkish Van as of January 1991.

American Curl

In June 1981 a black, longhaired, stray kitten with unusual, swept-back ears turned up at the house of Joe and Grace Ruga in Lakewood, California. Six years later the descendants of this kitten, whom the Rugas had named Shulamith, were competing in championship classes in The International Cat Association.

The Curl's ears are the product of a spontaneous mutation with incomplete dominant expression. If a kitten inherits one gene for curled ears and another for straight ears, that kitten will still develop curled ears.

In addition to its signature ears, the Curl can claim one other distinction: it is the only pedigreed cat that must be outcrossed only to nonpedigreed varieties. This has hampered the standardization of the breed. Setting type is difficult enough in a new breed that depends on established breeds for outcrosses. Trying to set type by crossing to cats obtained from shelters—or wherever else suitable, nonpedigreed cats might be found—makes the job ten times as difficult.

Black-and-White American Curl

Bengal

The present-day Bengal was created in the late 1970s by Mrs. Jean Mill of Covina, California, who wanted to reproduce the spotted pattern, colors, and facial qualities of the Asian Leopard Cat. Mill inherited eight females, the products of crosses between Asian Leopard Cats and domestic shorthairs, from a researcher at the University of California at Davis. She then added two male cats to this group: a feral, orange domestic with deep brown rosettes from a zoo in Delhi, India, and a brown—spotted—tabby domestic shorthair from a shelter in Los Angeles.

Ten years later there were two hundred Bengals in the United States, and the breed was being registered by The International Cat Association. Once TICA was satisfied that the Bengal exhibited a normal sterility profile and that it was no different on a cellular level from domestic cats, the breed became eligible to compete in championship classes as of May 1, 1991. Like the Ocicat, another man-made spotted variety, the Bengal does not always breed true for pattern.

Leopard-Spotted Bengal

Burmilla

When explaining the domestication of cats, zoologists often say that humans played a supporting role in that production. The cat, in its wisdom, found a vacant evolutionary niche and exploited it deftly.

In Great Britain in 1981, a chinchilla Persian male and a lilac Burmese female exploited a niche in their respective mating schedules to produce a mixed-breed litter of kittens. The youngsters—who developed comely green eyes and handsome black or brown tipping over a shimmering, silver base coat—were most attractive. As often happens, cat fanciers conceived of them as the foundation members of a new breed, which was duly christened the Burmilla.

Within three years of its inception the Burmilla was being championed by a breed club in England. In 1990 it advanced to preliminary status in its native land, where it is one of the most popular new breeds. Meanwhile, the Burmilla has also attracted the first stirring of interest abroad.

Black Tipped Burmilla

Javanese

Javanese are to Colorpoint Shorthairs what Balinese are to Siamese: the longhaired counterpart. The Javanese, accepted for championship competition beginning May 1, 1987, is one breed for which "new" implies no mystique, no clouded or gray area, and surely no chance for fantasizing. Nor does the name have anything to do with the cat's place of origin.

It is obvious how and why this breed should have appeared. When breeders crossed American Shorthairs to Siamese in order to produce new Siamese colors, a number of those Americans had long hair in their backgrounds. Consequently, Javanese have long hair in theirs.

Four registries do not make any distinction between the Javanese and Balinese breeds. In these registries any Siamese with long hair is called a Balinese. Efforts to combine the Javanese and Balinese breeds have always been voted down in the Cat Fanciers' Association and the Canadian Cat Association, however, because some Balinese breeders like to think that their cats are as pure as the Siamese. Therefore, they will not consider a merger of any kind, even though the coat texture, length, and feel of the Balinese and Javanese coats are identical.

Tortie Point Javanese

Oriental Longhair

Ebony Oriental Longhair

The Oriental Longhair, accepted for championship competition by The International Cat Association since 1985, is the final stage in the evolution of the Siamese cat. As we have seen, when Siamese were first shown in England during the nineteenth century, seal point was the only color acceptable. By the mid-1930s blue points were officially recognized. Twenty years later chocolate points and lilac points (sometimes called frost points) were added to the list.

While these "new" Siamese colors were being developed, some breeders were working with additional colors and also with longhaired Siamese variants. Known formally as Balinese, the latter were recognized by the Cat Fanciers' Federation in 1961 and in all other registries by 1970. Meanwhile, enterprising breeders in England and the United States were crossing Siamese to several other shorthaired breeds to produce the Oriental Shorthair: a cat of Siamese conformation whose color is not restricted to its extremities. Now accepted by all federations, the Oriental Shorthair was first recognized in 1976 by the Cat Fanciers' Association. Nine years later, TICA completed the Siamese evolutionary cycle by adding the Oriental Longhair to its list.

Despite some diehards' persistent lip service to natural mutations, the progression from Siamese to Oriental Longhair was no accident. For reasons discussed in other breed profiles, long hair and additional colors were added to the Siamese gene pool over the years by outcrosses to a number of other breeds. Finally, after the Oriental Shorthair had been developed,

a few breeders created the Oriental Longhair in the late 1970s and early 1980s.

To accomplish this, they crossed a Balinese and an Oriental Shorthair. This mating produces all shorthaired kittens unless the Oriental is carrying a longhaired gene, in which case, half the kittens will have short hair. By crossing two nonpointed, shorthaired Balinese-Oriental Shorthair hybrids, it is possible to arrive at the Oriental Longhair. It is also possible to reach this destination by crossing a nonpointed, shorthaired Balinese-Oriental Shorthair hybrid to a Balinese. In either case, some of the kittens may be pointed and some may have short hair.

The Oriental Longhair was a challenge to produce, and it remains a challenge to work with. Breeding to an Oriental Shorthair to improve type will produce all shorthaired kittens—and a lost generation—unless the Oriental is carrying a longhaired gene. Breeding to a Balinese to maintain long hair will produce Oriental Longhairs carrying a pointed gene, which could come back to haunt successive breedings. And if the Oriental Longhair is already carrying a pointed gene, half the kittens from a cross to a Balinese will be Balinese.

"There are so many variables to manipulate in producing Oriental Longhairs," one breeder observes, "that you can't flirt with this breed just because you're working with one of its parent breeds. You're either an Oriental Longhair breeder, or you aren't going anywhere." Which might explain why the Oriental Longhair, as of 1991, was recognized by only one association.

Snowshoe

The Snowshoe is a pointed cat with carefully drawn white markings on its face, chest, belly, and feet. This hybrid was developed in the late 1960s by Dorothy Hinds-Daugherty of Philadelphia. Though Mrs. Hinds-Daugherty disappeared from the cat fancy after working with the Snowshoe for several years, we can infer that creating this breed required a lot of patience and at least two matings between Siamese, bicolored American Shorthairs, and their offspring.

After she had created and named her new breed, Dorothy Hinds-Daugherty left its future in the hands of others. The first Snowshoe Standard was written by Vikki Olander of Norfolk, Virginia, who was influential in securing registration status for the Snowshoe in 1974 from both the American Cat Association and the Cat Fanciers' Federation. The breed has been recognized for championship competition by CFF since May 1, 1983.

Seal Point Snowshoe

Sphynx

A cat resembling the modern-day Sphynx was exhibited in the early 1900s as the New Mexican Hairless cat. Though cats without hair had appeared as spontaneous mutations in South America before that and in North America and Europe afterward, efforts to gain championship recognition for this breed were not made until hairless cats appeared in Ontario, Canada, in the 1960s.

The Sphynx reached provisional status in the Cat Fanciers' Association by 1970, but progressed no further because the CFA board was concerned about the breed's genetic difficulties–viz., its failure to develop an adequate immune system because of decreased T-cell function. The Sphynx was accepted for championship competition in 1971, however, by the now defunct Crown Cat Fanciers Federation.

Presently The International Cat Association is the only registry in North America in which Sphynx compete in championship classes. According to the TICA standard, the Sphynx has short, fine down on its body, and short, tightly packed, soft hair on its muzzle, tail, and feet.

Sphynx advocates claim that the cats being shown now are not subject to the same immune system deficiencies that once troubled the breed. It is perhaps too soon to make such claims, and even if the breed's health problems are no longer life threatening, its maintenance problems are troublesome. Since the Sphynx has no coat to absorb the natural oils a cat's body normally exudes, Sphynx must be bathed or towel washed frequently—or else you will always be able to tell by the grease spot where a Sphynx spent the night.

Blue Cream Sphynx

Color

Cats come in every color imaginable. Those colors officially permitted to accompany pedigreed cats into the show ring have formal, sometimes confusing names. The colors of nonpedigreed cats have simple, descriptive names—like *gray tiger*. Everybody knows what that means. Few people know what *chocolate tortie lynx point* means.

Breed Standards include a full description of all colors recognized by an association. For breeds like the Chartreux that occur in one color only, and for those like the Abyssinian that occur in few colors, we have printed complete color descriptions along with the breed profiles. For breeds that come in many colors, like the Devon Rex, Persian, and Exotic Shorthair, we have simply listed those colors, without descriptions, at the end of the breed Standard. If you would like to know more about any color that was not described fully in that section, consider the following.

There are roughly half a dozen basic cat colors. When one of those colors occupies the hairs on a cat from the tips to the roots, that cat is called solid or sometimes *self* colored. The hair shafts on some cats, however, are tinted to varying degrees along their tips while the rest of the hair shaft down to the cat's body is white. These cats are called shadeds or smokes, depending on how much of the hair shaft is occupied by color and how much is white. Still other cats have their color arranged in one of five tabby patterns. Furthermore, all of the above—solids, shadeds, smokes, and tabbies—can also occur with white. And some colors such as chestnut, red, and cream, which together equal a chocolate tortoiseshell—can occur with one another. Or with one another and with white. Finally, there are pointed cats, whose basic color is confined to their faces, ears, legs, and tails.

Space prohibits a full description of each of the colors found in Oriental Shorthairs, Maine Coons, Cymrics, and other multicolored breeds. Yet any of these colors in any one of those breeds will be understood by reference to the list of basic colors and patterns below.

For example, chocolate tortie lynx point is a Siamese color. By finding chocolate in the "Basic Colors" section, we learn that this is a rich, chestnut-brown color. The word *tortie,* short for *tortoiseshell,* turns up in the "Patterns" section, where we learn that tortoiseshells have unbrindled patches of cream and red mixed in with their basic color. The footnote for *lynx* in the "Tabby" section lets us know that there are tabby markings in this pattern, and *pointed* is our clue that the basic color on this cat is confined to its extremities—if *Siamese* hadn't already brought that to mind.

BASIC COLORS

BLACK: dense, coal black from the roots to the tips of the fur. Free from any tinge of rust on the tips, or smoke on the undercoat.

BLUE: even, pale blue from the nose to the tip of the tail. Sound to the roots. Though a light shade is preferred, a sound darker shade is more acceptable than an unsound lighter one.

CHESTNUT: rich, chestnut brown. Sound throughout.

CHOCOLATE: see chestnut.

CINNAMON: cinnamon, sound throughout.

CREAM: one level shade of buff cream without markings. Sound to the roots. Lighter shades preferred.

EBONY: see black.

FAWN: pale, pinkish fawn. Sound throughout. Lighter shades preferred.

LAVENDER: frosty gray with a pinkish tone. Sound throughout.

LILAC:[1] see lavender.

RED: deep, rich, brilliant red; without shading, markings, or ticking. Lips and chin are the same color as the coat.

WHITE: pure, glistening white.

SHADINGS

SHELL:[2,3] undercoat is white. The coat on the back, flanks, head, and tail is sufficiently tipped with the cat's basic color to give a characteristic, sparkling appearance. Face and legs may be very slightly shaded with tipping. Chin, ear tufts, stomach, and chest are white.

SHADED:[4] undercoat is white with a mantle of tipping in the cat's basic color that shades down from the sides, face, and tail from a deep hue on the ridge to white on the chin, chest, stomach, and under the tail. Legs are the same tone as the face. The general effect is much darker than a shell shading.

SMOKE: white undercoat, deeply tipped with the cat's basic color. Cat in repose appears to be that basic color (e.g., red, black, blue, etc.). In motion the white undercoat is clearly apparent. Points and mask of the primary color, with narrow band of white at the base of the hairs next to the skin which may be seen only when fur is parted.

CHINCHILLA GOLDEN: undercoat is a rich, warm cream. Coat on the back, flanks, head, and tail is sufficiently tipped with black to give a golden appearance. Legs may be slightly shaded with tipping. Chin, ear tufts, stomach, and chest, are cream. Rims of eyes, lips, and nose are outlined with black.

CHINCHILLA SILVER: undercoat is pure white. Coat on the back, flanks, head, and tail is sufficiently tipped with black to give a characteristic, sparkling-silver appearance. Legs may be slightly shaded with tipping. Chin, ear tufts, stomach, and chest, are pure white. Rims of eyes, lips, and nose are outlined with black.

SHADED GOLDEN: undercoat is a rich, warm cream with a mantle of black tipping that shades down from the sides, face, and tail from dark on the ridge to cream on the chin, chest, stomach, and under the tail. Legs are the same tone as the face. The general effect is much darker than a chinchilla. Rims of eyes, lips, and nose are outlined with black.

SHADED SILVER: undercoat is white with a mantle of black tipping that shades down from the sides, face, and tail from dark on the ridge to white on the chin, chest, stomach, and under the tail. Legs are the same tone as the face. The general effect is much darker than a chinchilla. Rims of eyes, lips, and nose are outlined with black.

PATTERNS

Tabby Patterns[5]

CLASSIC TABBY: markings are dense, clearly defined, and broad. Legs are evenly barred with bracelets coming up to meet body markings. Tail is evenly ringed. There are several unbroken necklaces on the neck and upper chest, the more the better. Frown marks on the forehead form an intricate letter "M." Unbroken line runs back from the outer corner of the eye. Swirls on cheeks. Vertical lines over the back of the head extend to the shoulder markings, which are in the shape of a butterfly with both the upper and lower wings distinctly outlined and marked with dots inside the outline. Back markings consist of a vertical line down the spine from butterfly to tail with a vertical stripe paralleling it on each side. These three stripes are well separated by stripes of the ground color. There is a large, solid blotch on each side, encircled by one or more unbroken rings. Side markings are the same on both sides. There is a double, vertical row of buttons on the chest and stomach. Hocks are the same color as the markings.

MACKEREL TABBY: markings are dense, clearly defined, narrow pencillings that encircle the body. Legs are evenly barred with narrow bracelets coming up to meet body markings. Tail is barred. Necklaces on neck and chest are distinct, like so many chains. Head barred with an "M" on the forehead. Unbroken lines run back from the eyes. Lines run down the head to meet the shoulders. Spine lines run together to form a narrow saddle. Hocks are the same color as the markings.

PATCHED TABBY: also called a torbie, this is a brown, silver, or blue tabby with patches of red and/or cream in its coat.

SPOTTED TABBY: markings on the body are spotted. They may vary in size and shape, but preference is given to round, evenly distributed spots. Spots should not run together in a broken mackerel pattern. A dorsal stripe runs the length of the body to the tip of the tail. This stripe is ideally composed of spots. The markings on the face and forehead shall be typically tabby markings. The underside of the body has "vest buttons." The legs and tail are barred.

TICKED TABBY: body hairs are ticked, but free of

stripes, or blotches, except for a darker, dorsal shading. Lighter underside may show tabby markings. Face, legs, and tail must show distinct tabby striping. Cat must have at least one distinct necklace.

Pointed Patterns

On pointed cats the basic color is confined to the face, ears, legs, and tail. The body is usually pale cream, fawn, or white. The latter may have either a bluish, creamy, ivory, or glacial overtone. Body color and point color are wedded in the pointed cat. For example, a blue point must have a bluish white, not a cream or a fawn, body.

NONTABBY POINTED COLORS

Blue, blue cream,[6] chocolate, chocolate tortie, flame (red), lilac, lilac cream, seal, tortie.

TABBY POINTED COLORS

Blue lynx, blue cream lynx,[7] chocolate lynx, chocolate tortie lynx, cream lynx, lilac lynx, lilac cream lynx, red lynx, seal lynx, seal tortie lynx.

Other Patterns

BICOLOR: a white cat with unbrindled patches of one of the following colors: black, blue, red, or cream. Also, a white cat with patches of blue cream, tortoiseshell, or one of the tabby, shaded, or smoke colors.

BLUE CREAM: blue with patches of solid cream. The patches are clearly defined and well broken on the body and extremities.

CALICO: a white cat with unbrindled patches of black and red. White predominates on the underparts.

DILUTE CALICO: a white cat with unbrindled patches of blue and cream. White predominates on the underparts.

TORTOISESHELL: unbrindled patches of red and cream combined with some other color such as black or chestnut. The patches are clearly defined and well broken on the body and extremities. A blaze of red or cream on the face is desirable.

VAN: a white cat whose color is confined to its head, tail, and legs. One or two small, colored patches are permitted on the body.

---

[1] The American Cat Fanciers Association calls this color frost.
[2] In the Devon Rex and Oriental Shorthair breeds this shading is called silver, which is not the same as the color chinchilla silver that is found in the Exotic Shorthair and the Persian.
[3] When the basic color is red, this color is also known as shell cameo or red chinchilla.
[4] When the basic color is red, this color is also known as shaded cameo or red shaded.
[5] When tabby patterns occur in point colors, the names of those colors contain the word *lynx*, as in *blue lynx point*.
[6] This color is called blue tortie is some associations.
[7] This color is called blue tortie lynx in some associations.

Addendum

HOW NEW BREEDS AND COLORS ARE ACCEPTED

A new breed or color must meet certain requirements before it can qualify for championship competition. First, the breed must be accepted for registration. In order for this to happen, a certain number of breeders (anywhere from six to twelve, depending on the association) must certify that they are working with the new breed, and a proposed Standard—along with several photos of representatives—of the breed must be submitted to an association's executive office. An association may also request that breeders bring cats from the new breed to a board meeting. If the board of directors is satisfied that the proposed new breed is sufficiently distinct from existing breeds and that it is free from genetic or health complications, then the board will grant registration status.

At this point most associations will allow the new breed or color to compete in the provisional class at shows. This gives judges a chance to become familiar with the breed, and it gives people involved with the breed a chance to do a little public relations work for their cats.

Finally, after a minimum number of persons (as many as twenty-five, depending on the association) is verifiably working with the breed, has registered anywhere from fifty to one hundred representatives of that breed, and the required number of cats has been shown in provisional classes, the breed is advanced, with board approval, to championship status. This process takes, on the average, from four to seven years, depending on the association.

CORRESPONDENCE BETWEEN COAT COLOR AND EYE COLOR

In several associations eye color must conform to coat color in breeds where more than one eye color occurs. When this rule is enforced, the following correspondences prevail:

American Shorthair/American Wirehair

Eye Color	Coat Color
blue	white
odd eyed	white
green/blue-green	chinchilla, shaded silver
green or hazel	silver tabby
brilliant gold	all other colors

British Shorthair

Eye Color	Coat Color
blue	white
odd eyed	white
green or hazel	silver tabby
gold or copper	all other colors

Cornish Rex

Eye Color	Coat Color
blue	white
odd eyed	white
green/blue-green	chinchilla, shaded silver
green or hazel	silver tabby
gold or copper	all other colors

Devon Rex

Eye Color	Coat Color
blue	white
odd eyed	white
green/blue-green	chinchilla
green or hazel	silver tabby
gold or copper	all other colors

Maine Coon Cat

Eye Color	Coat Color
blue	white
odd eyed	white
green, gold, copper	all other colors

Manx/Cymric

Eye Color	Coat Color
blue	white
odd eyed	white
green/blue-green	chinchilla, shaded silver
green or hazel	silver tabby
brilliant copper	all other colors

Persian/Exotic Shorthair

Eye Color	Coat Color
blue	white
odd eyed	white
green/blue-green	chinchilla, shaded silver, chinchilla golden, shaded golden
green or hazel	silver tabby
brilliant copper	all other colors

Scottish Fold/Scottish Fold Longhair

Eye Color	Coat Color
blue	white
odd eyed	white
green/blue-green	chinchilla, shaded silver
green or hazel	silver tabby
brilliant gold	all other colors

Turkish Angora

Eye Color	Coat Color
blue	white
odd eyed	white
amber	all other colors

Care and Housekeeping

BASIC SUPPLIES

According to Russian folk wisdom, a person who brings home a cat should throw it immediately onto the bed. If the cat settles down promptly, that means it will stay with its new owner. Perhaps this works in Russia, but cats are more apt to become homebodies if their new owners have laid in some basic supplies and have conducted a scrupulous safety check of the premises. First the supplies.

Litter pan. At least one. Roughly nineteen by fifteen by four inches. Litter pans come in several styles: open, enclosed, or outfitted with a raised, detachable rim that helps to contain litter when the feet hit the sand. Whatever the style, a pan should be steadfast, durable, and washable.

Litter. "Absorbent" and "dust free" are the buzzwords here. Most brands are. Some also contain deodorant—whose efficiency is in the nose of the beholder.

Litter scoop. At least one. The sturdier the better. Some of the thinner kinds snap too easily. Don't be caught without a spare.

Litter pan liners. Convenient for quick packaging and disposal of the entire contents of the pan. Optional at home; most desirable during motel stays.

Food and water dishes. Reusable plastic can retain odors even if it's washed carefully. Disposable plastic is a rude joke on the environment. Glass or metal dishes and bowls are the proper choice. Glass should be sturdy enough so that it won't break, crack, or chip if a cat knocks it over. Glass and metal should be solid enough so that they aren't likely to be tipped over. Vinyl place mats underneath food and water dishes will protect the surface where a cat eats.

Scratching post. Better than Scotch Guard for protecting furniture. Provides an acceptable fabric on which a cat can exercise its natural tendency to scratch. The post should be well anchored so that it won't tip over when a cat uses it, and tall enough so that cats can stretch themselves while scratching. The scratching surface should be made from a strong, stalwart material like sisal or hemp.

Grooming tools. A good currying should be part of every cat's routine—daily for some longhairs that are going to shows, less frequently for housebound shorthairs. Cats enjoy being groomed, especially if they're introduced to the routine when they're young. Cats also benefit internally from being groomed because the more dead hair that's removed from their coats, the less they'll swallow when they groom themselves, and the fewer hair balls they'll develop. Pet shops or vendors at cat shows carry a full arsenal of grooming aids: shampoos and rinses, nail clippers, brushes, combs, powders, ointments, sprays, hair dryers, grooming tables, Q-tips, cotton balls, and so forth. If the pet shop doesn't have Q-tips and cotton balls, the pharmacy will.

Toys. The pet shop, cat show vendor, and supermarket stock a generous selection of feline diversions. Cats especially like plastic balls with bells inside, but the ball should be sturdy enough so that the cat can't remove the bell and swallow it. A few of a cat's other favorite things include small stuffed toys, preferably in the shape of mice, and the occasional dose of catnip straight. Again, the cute, little eye on the toy mouse should not be loose, or it may wind up in the cat's stomach. A most popular toy is the Kitty Tease, which looks like a miniature fishing pole with a small bow tied to the end of the line. While the owner dangles the bow in the air, cats display their natural athletic ability by leaps and bounds.

Store-bought toys are not the only ones that cats enjoy. A crumpled piece of paper, an empty film canister, a cardboard box turned upside down with holes cut at either end, a plain-brown grocery bag, a pen sitting on a table . . . the possibilities are limited only by an owner's and a cat's imaginations. But store-bought or homemade, toys should not have

Grooming equipment for every coat length

dangling strings that cats might swallow or become entangled in, loose bits or pieces they can chew off and ingest, or sharp edges on which to get cut. Cellophane, plastic wrap, and aluminum foil should be avoided always.

Beds. Even when cats are given elaborate beds, they may want to sleep somewhere else—on a window sill

or comfortable chair or their owners' pillows. Many people wait until a cat has chosen the spot where it wants to sleep before buying a bed and putting it there.

Cage. The person with one cat has little need for a cage. The thoughtful, multiple cat owner scarcely needs cages either. The only times a cat might need to be caged are: from the time it's born until the time it's mastered toilet training, when it needs to be isolated because it's sick, or when it has just been brought into a new cattery and its owner wants to be satisfied that it isn't radioactive before letting it meet the other cats. Most breeders recommend a three-week isolation period in this case. If possible, sick cats or new cats in isolation should have the run of a small room—of which other cats cannot get within sniffing distance. Hands, dishes, and water bowls should be scrubbed and disinfected carefully after shut-ins have been petted or fed, and these cats should always be last in the feeding queue.

THE MENU

From a cat's perspective, food is *the* most important item on the shopping list. Before people bring a new cat home, they should find out what it has been eating,

Cats often find empty baskets inviting

and, if its diet has been sound, should continue with that product. If they choose to deviate from an established regimen, they should introduce new food a little at a time in increasing amounts for a week to ten days until the switchover has been accomplished without muss, fuss, or hunger strikes.

The supermarket or pet-supply store provides an extensive menu that will suit any cat's palate and nutritional requirements. Indeed, there are more than ninety brands of cat food available in the United States. Companies that manufacture these brands must satisfy an exacting set of conditions—mandated by the Association of American Feed Control Officials (AAFCO) and enforced by the states—with respect to identifying ingredients and substantiating nutritional claims made on pet food labels. Most cat foods provide 100 percent complete nutrition for a particular stage or for all

stages of a cat's life. Products not meeting either of these requirements are usually identified as suitable for intermittent or supplemental use only. Any food that delivers complete and balanced nutrition for all stages of a cat's life is a safe choice. It will provide the vitamins, minerals, and other nutrients a cat normally requires.

With so many products available, there is no excuse for a cat becoming addicted to one kind of food to the exclusion of all others. Owners should vary the menu from time to time, switching among beef, chicken, turkey, and fish entrees.

HOW MUCH TO FEED

Contrary to marketing clichés, cats eat to satisfy their energy needs first, not their finicky palates. Energy, while it is not a nutrient itself, is a vital property of the three classes of nutrients: proteins, fats, and carbohydrates.

Every cat should have its own feeding dish

Cats can neither create nor destroy energy. They can, however—through the series of chemical reactions known as metabolism—intercept, convert, and distribute the energy contained in food. The National Research Council estimates that the metabolizable energy[1] needs of cats range from 250 kilocalories per kilogram of body weight for ten-week-old kittens to 70 kcal/kg of body weight for sedentary adults fifty weeks of age or older. In plain English that's 113 Calories[2] of metabolizable energy per pound of body weight for kittens and 32 Calories per pound for couch potatoes. A more active adult requires 36 Calories of metabolizable energy per pound; pregnant females need 45. Despite some breeders' agitated endorsements of vitamin potions, nutritionists report that pregnant females need more Calories, not more vitamins.

People who add vitamins to canned food are not only wasting money, they also risk throwing the existing vitamin balance in the food out of kilter. This could prevent a cat from absorbing some of the essential vitamins that were already present in the food.

Among the three types of cat foods—dry, semimoist, and canned—there is more gross energy and, hence, more metabolizable energy by weight in dry food than in the others. Accordingly, a ten-pound, inactive, adult cat would satisfy its daily metabolizable energy requirements by consuming approximately 3.5 ounces of dry food, 3.8 ounces of semimoist food, or 11.9 ounces of canned.

Fresh water should be available to cats always. When most kittens reach twelve weeks, they have outgrown the need for milk. As they mature, they no longer manufacture the enzymes required to metabolize milk. Once this occurs, milk may upset most cats' stomachs.

Kittens should be fed three times a day until they are six months old, and twice a day until they are a year old. From then on, one meal a day is sufficient—especially if cats have dry food on which to nibble. If there is no one home to serve lunch to a kitten, set out

[1] Metabolizable energy is the difference between the gross energy that goes into a cat as food and the wasted energy that goes out of a cat in its feces and urine.

[2] Kilocalorie, when shortened to Calorie, is uppercased. For example, the five-hundred-plus calories (sic) in a fast-food cheeseburger are actually kilocalories and should be spelled Calories. A small *c* calorie, a thousand of which make up a kilocalorie, is the amount of heat energy needed to raise the temperature of one gram of water one degree centigrade.

a bowl of dry food next to the kitten's water bowl before leaving for work.

The amount of canned food given to kittens should equal the amount they will eat during the first thirty minutes after they have been fed. For a twelve-week-old kitten, that's two to three tablespoons of canned food at room temperature. Pick up and discard any food not eaten in thirty minutes. If it is more convenient to feed dry food exclusively, select a product with the lowest ash content to minimize the possibility that a kitten will develop urinary problems later in life. Again, be sure the dry food is nutritionally complete, and observe the feeding instructions on the package.

Food dishes should be washed after every meal. Water bowls should be washed daily.

THE CAT-PROOF HOUSE

Before bringing a cat home new owners should look at their houses the way they would if they were adopting an inquisitive two-year-old baby with super athletic ability. Cats are natural hunters. They are also natural explorers, wanting to investigate new objects, new openings, and whatever catches their eye in their domain. Therefore, the doors to any rooms that are off limits should be closed. Any small, breakable, or valuable items in the rooms a cat will be visiting should be safely out of reach. The cat should not have access to unscreened, open windows, and all window screens should be secure. Owners should see that no electrical cords are frayed; and if a cat develops a taste for them, they should be unplugged when not in use or wrapped in heavy tape or covered with plastic tubing, which can be purchased at an auto supply shop. Unused electrical outlets should be fitted with plastic, plug-in covers.

In the kitchen and bathroom, keep all chemicals, cleaners, and toilet articles in cabinets that can be locked or closed securely. Keep the hatches on all trash receptacles battened down. It is also a good idea to keep the toilet seat lid down. In the dining room, owners might want to take the table cloth off the table until a cat learns that climbing certain mountains is unacceptable.

In all rooms make sure there aren't any poisonous plants within the cat's reach. Some of the more common house plants that are poisonous to cats are: poinsettia, philodendron, caladium, dieffenbachia,

English ivy, hydrangea, Jerusalem cherry, mistletoe, and holly. A veterinarian can supply a more complete list.

WELCOMING A NEW ARRIVAL

After a person has bought every item on the shopping list and a few impulse items as well, has filled the litter pan with a couple of inches of litter, and has placed the pan in a convenient place, it's time to bring the new cat home. Whenever possible, this should be done at the start of a weekend or holiday when there's more time to spend with the newcomer.

Orientation can be a trying experience for a cat, and especially for a kitten. Normally a kitten has been taken away from mother, playmates, and the only home the youngster has ever known. Some cats adjust easily. After they've been taken from their carriers and placed in their new litter pans, they look around as if to say, "Nice place. What's for dinner?" But other cats—the majority, if the truth be known—are not so self-possessed. Don't be surprised if a cat acts timid at first, looks around, then dives under the sofa. Pull up a chair and a cup of coffee and go about watching television or reading the newspaper as though it were a normal day. The calm will be reassuring, and the cat's curiosity will prevail. No cat has ever permanently refused to come out from under a sofa. Once a cat has mastered the immediate surroundings—even if they comprise the underside of a couch—a natural instinct to explore will beckon. There's plenty of time for getting acquainted then.

The transition to a new home will go more smoothly if the cat's former owner can provide one of its favorite toys, a sleeping blanket, or even a small amount of soiled litter to sprinkle in the cat's new pan. These items give off familiar, comforting smells.

If there are other animals at home, do not include them in the welcoming party. Close the door to the room the cat will be exploring initially, or confine the other animals to another section of the house. Cats need to develop a sense of trust toward a new owner and a sense of comfort in new surroundings. This happens more easily if there are no distractions or challenges from other pets wanting to get acquainted with the cat.

A cat being introduced to a multipet household should spend the first few days and nights in a room or rooms with a closed door. Most breeders recommend that other cats should not even be allowed to sniff under the door and possibly transmit germs until three weeks have passed. Then allow the newcomer a few

The Household Cat: Nonpedigreed cats are judged in household pet classes, where beauty, cleanliness, and personality carry the day

more days to make the acquaintance of the other four-legged members of the house by exchanging greetings with them under the door. If they meet each other this way before they meet face to face, chances are the introductions will be less fraught with peril.

Young children can pose challenges to a cat's safety and sense of security. Explain to children that they should be careful to watch where they walk and play

when the cat is around. Caution them not to pick the cat up if they are not old enough to handle the cat properly. Cats should always be supported forward and behind when they are being held or carried. Explain, too, that cats are often frightened by loud, unfamiliar sounds. Ask children to speak and play quietly until the cat gets used to them. Reinforce this advice by setting a good example for the children to follow.

The first place a cat's feet should touch down in a new home is in the litter pan. Ninety-nine-point-nine percent of all cats have been thoroughly trained in the use of the pan by the time they are twelve weeks old, and even in unfamiliar surroundings a natural instinct for cleanliness will direct a cat to the pan—providing that he knows where it is. Always keep the pan in the same place, somewhere that is quiet and easy for the cat to find. For the first few days after its arrival, place the cat in the pan after meals and naps to reinforce natural instincts. And when the cat uses the pan, praise quietly.

If an accident occurs, clean the soiled spot with a non ammonia-based disinfectant cleaner and sprinkle a bit of vinegar on it to remove odor. A cat's attention span is about twenty seconds long, it will *not* serve any purpose to drag a cat to the spot for a scolding. If caught misbehaving, a stern *No!* is in order. When finished, the cat should be carried to the pan and shown where to conduct business. In the rare event that accidents are repeated, perhaps the litter pan is too far away for the cat's convenience. If your cat's territory covers more than one floor, there should be a litter pan upstairs and down.

Dirty pans are another cause of accidents. Cats are creatures of cleanliness and habit. All waste products, solid and moist, should be scooped out of the litter pan and disposed of each day. Replace discarded litter with a fresh supply as necessary. Once a week or sooner discard all litter in the pan, and wash the pan thoroughly with a mild, non ammonia-based cleanser.

Once a cat is comfortable with a particular kind of litter, stick with that brand. Switching litter products may upset the cat's reliance on the pan; and this, too, might result in accidents.

Accidents of another sort can be prevented by a little common sense. When closing any door in the house— the refrigerator door, closet doors, the door on the clothes dryer or oven—check to see that the cat isn't on the wrong side of it. Keep sewing supplies out of reach. After ironing, put hot irons out of harm's way. When cleaning, rinse all cleansers and chemicals thoroughly from any surfaces the cat may walk on. What gets on the cat's paws usually winds up in its stomach. Keep the bathroom door closed when drawing hot water for a bath. In general, keep an eye out for any potential accident waiting for a cat to make it happen.

Most often cats will have had their vaccinations before going to their new homes. Thus, trips to the vet will be limited, under normal circumstances, to visits for yearly checkups and booster shots. There might be times, however, when a cat becomes ill and a trip to the vet is advisable. (See chart on pages 187-88)

Once a cat has adjusted to a new home, everyone— including the cat—will settle into a comfortable routine that constitutes one of the more civilized and pleasant aspects of life. A cat having the run of the house will probably want to sleep where the owner sleeps. When people are reading, a cat will want to help turn the pages—or to sit on them; and when people are watching television, a cat will occasionally try to tag the characters on the screen. A cat will, in short, help to lighten the task of getting through each day. It is our responsibility—and it should be our pleasure— to return the favor.

WIELDING THE FINE-TOOTHED COMB

Grooming is an essential part of owning a cat, and should begin when kittens are young. Although cats deserve their reputation for cleanliness and personal hygiene, breeders have produced some varieties—viz., Persians and other longhairs—with profuse coats that are thicker and longer than nature would have designed. And regardless of coat length, virtually all breeds shed. Regular grooming removes dead hair from a cat's coat, and eliminates the necessity of removing that hair from the furniture—or from the floor in the form of a hair ball—later on.

A good way to get kittens used to being handled and to make it more pleasant to handle them is to start by clipping their nails. Hold the kitten's leg in one hand. Gently grasp the kitten's foot between thumb and forefinger. Press the top of the foot with the thumb, spreading the toes until the nails are extended. With the nails thus accessible, clip each one carefully to

THREE IMPORTANT QUESTIONS

Q: Should I have my cat altered?

A: Absolutely, unless the animal was purchased for breeding. When male cats reach maturity, they are inclined to spray their urine to attract females. This is an odor that no amount of vinegar will overcome. When female cats go into season, they will sometimes stop using their litter pans, and they will frequently keep the family awake at night with their calling. Most veterinarians recommend neutering or spaying when a cat is between seven and ten months old.

Q: Should I let my cat go outdoors?

A: Only if you have a completely closed-in yard that your cat cannot escape, other animals cannot enter, and fleas totally avoid. Otherwise your cat should remain indoors, where it's safe, dry, warm in the winter, cool in the summer, and is not likely to be hit by a car, victimized by a larger animal, or subject to the many accidents that befall outdoor cats.

Q: Should I get my cat declawed?

A: If it can be avoided, no. One way to save your cat's claws and your furniture is by training the cat to use a scratching post. Training should have begun when the cat was four weeks old; but you didn't have the cat then, so if no interest is shown in the scratching post you bought, you'll need to do some remedial training. Wave a toy directly in front of the scratching post so that your cat's nails dig into the post as they grab for the toy. Two or three times after realizing how good it feels to sink its claws into the post, the cat will get the idea. Then wave the toy farther up the post so that the cat is encouraged to climb up to reach it. Play this game two or three times a day for a few days, and the cat will soon be climbing the post like King Kong going up the Empire State Building.

avoid cutting into the quick—the visible, pink vein in the nail.

Giving the ears a light dusting with boric acid powder keeps them clean and protects them from ear mites. This remedy, which has been passed on by breeders since the 1940s, is still effective today.

Owners of shorthaired cats often think it is not so necessary to bathe their cats, but all cats do better with a good bath from time to time. With Persians and other longhairs, of course, it is important to comb and bathe more frequently.

Don't expect to get by with surface grooming just because you're going to bathe the cat afterward. Thoroughly brush and comb from the base of the coat outward until there is no dead hair coming off in the comb or brush. It is important in the Oriental breeds and the Burmese, where the hair is supposed to lie close and tight, to remove any loose hairs from the coat. Usually a rubber brush and hand stroking will do wonders.

Wirehaired cats need to be groomed also, but care must be taken not to strip their coats. Since the hairs are crimped and hooked, they could be pulled out with too fine a comb. A wire pin brush, the kind used on a delicate-coated show dog, is best here. Apply the brush carefully while blow-drying the cat after a bath. This will help to lift the hairs without removing them.

Never bathe a matted animal, as washing a matted cat will intensify the mats, creating more of a problem. When small tangles or mats develop in the coat, they can usually be broken up and removed with the fingers and the wide end of a metal comb. Never try to cut mats out with a pair of scissors. Most often it is the cat that gets cut. If a mat is too large to work out by hand, clip it off with a pair of electric clippers.

Place the cat in a sink or tub that has a drain and a spray-hose attachment. Never leave a cat sitting in a tub of dirty water. Gently wet the cat all over from the head down, then apply shampoo. Tearless shampoo is the safest to use. Lather the cat thoroughly—let the shampoo stand if the label says to—then rinse repeatedly until all shampoo has been removed from the coat. The quickest way to develop a dander or flakey condition on the coat is to leave dried soap (shampoo) particles behind—which never seem to brush out. Towel dry the cat to get as much water out of the coat as possible. This will cut down on drying time. Use a hair dryer, preferably one with a stand, and a metal comb to finish drying the cat.

New cat owners frequently ask how often they should bathe a cat. In fact, most novice exhibitors don't bathe their cats often enough. There is no harm done to the coat if a cat is bathed weekly. The coat actually improves with each bathing. All the loose, dead hair is gone, new growth is free to develop, and the cat remains in its show coat longer than it would have otherwise. Reluctance to bathe a cat often enough is a carryover from the days when breeders worried that too much bathing would remove hair from the coat. Only dead hair is removed by bathing. By not bathing

Frequently handled kittens become more sociable

Cats should always be supported from the front and the back

frequently enough, breeders were allowing the build up of dead coat. When they finally gave a bath, they produced a bag full of hair all at once, leaving the cat sparsely coated in many areas.

It is generally best to bathe a cat the day before a show. The concern about taking natural oils out of the coat by bathing is not well founded. Oils are intended to protect those animals who live outdoors from moisture and rain.

After bathing a cat, a little white talcum powder can be used to help keep the hairs separated. This must be brushed out carefully until there is no powder left before a cat is presented for judging. The use of colored powders is not ethical since they constitute an attempt

GROOMING A PERSIAN

Clip a cat's claws before clipping the cat. Never attempt to clip a cat before testing the cat's reaction to the sound of the clipper. Hold the cat securely and hold the clipper away from the cat when you turn it on. If the cat remains calm, clip a small portion of the fur on its back, while holding the cat so that it's facing away from you. Always clip with the lie of the coat. Use a number 10 or number 15 blade for clipping. Start with a number 10 **blade** and switch to a number 15 if you find that there are some areas of the cat where the number 10 is not working as well as it should. Generally, a number 15 clipper is better if you are trying to remove a mat that is tight to the skin.

Clipping always proceeds more quickly if there are two people working. Since the cat is somewhat thin skinned, be sure to stretch the skin properly so that it is flat with the blade, or else you might nick the cat while you are clipping. Most breeders leave a tuft of hair at the end of the tail and on the lower legs.

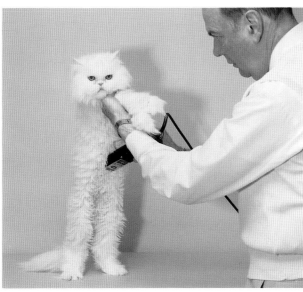

to deceive the judge. Using colored hair dyes and powders or any artificial means to alter the cat to fit the standard is another dishonest practice. What one achieves by misrepresenting a cat is a total mystery. The cat can't reproduce the alterations, so how could a person have any real feeling of accomplishment with an artificial win?

After the show season is over, many Persian breeders prefer to clip their cats down into a lion cut. A number 10 and number 15 blade on an electric clipper are the most efficient way to do this. Clip the entire neck, body and tail, leaving a pom-pom on the end of the tail. The cat is more comfortable this way, and there is no hair to mat or contribute to the formation of hair balls. What's more, the house is free from the tumbleweeds of hair that cats dig from their coats during the shedding season.

With any longhaired cat one must always be sure to keep the hair cut away and combed out on the hindquarters so that the cat can eliminate freely. Many cats have suffered severely from an impacted bowel because of matted-over hair, which shows a serious neglect on the part of the owner.

Once cats are cleaned and ready for the show, they should be kept in a cage on clean towels and bedding—at home and in their carriers as well. After spending all that time on preparation, one would not want to turn a cat loose and undo all that hard work.

COPING WITH EMERGENCIES

For all the modifications and improvements that breeders have made in the appearance of the cat, they have yet to produce a maintenance-free model. 'Til death do you part, there will be times—other than the yearly checkup—when you will have to take your cat to the veterinarian: when a cat begins sneezing or coughing and continues to for several hours; when a cat has an unusual discharge from the eyes or nose; when it scratches or licks a spot on its skin repeatedly and you notice hair loss and scaly, irritated-looking skin in that area; when it refuses to eat for more than two consecutive meals; when it has continuing attacks of vomiting or diarrhea; when it becomes listless or feverish or cries when it is picked up; when it urinates frequently or urinates outside the pan.

Since feline urologic syndrome (more bluntly known as *blockage*) occurs most frequently in older, neutered males, any deviation in their routine around the litter pan should be cause for concern. When older males begin visiting the pan more frequently than usual—and when they seem to be staying in the pan longer than they normally do—they may be suffering from urinary tract blockage. Owners who notice this behavior should check the pan to see if their males have produced a smaller-than-usual wet spot. If so, they should waste no time getting their cats to a veterinarian, for urinary blockage is painful and sometimes fatal.

Some people are disinclined to visit the doctor even when they are in great pain. This stubborn, it'll-be-all-right-in-a-while attitude should not be imposed on a cat. Indeed, it is better to err in the direction of hypochondria than grim-lipped stoicism where a cat is concerned. Thus, a good practice to follow if any troubling sign becomes evident in a cat is this: When in doubt, call a vet.

CAT OWNERS AND VETERINARY CARE

The most recent study published by the American Veterinary Medical Association (AVMA) indicated that cat owners have become more conscientious about taking their cats to the veterinarian. In 1987, 59.5 percent of the cat owners in the United States sought veterinary care for their animals. This represented a healthy 26 percent increase over the number of owners who took their cats to a vet in 1983, the last time before 1987 the AVMA had collected such information. Unhappily, the AVMA study also revealed that two out of every five cats in the United States did not receive medical attention in 1987—not even for an annual booster shot and physical examination.

WHEN TO CALL THE VET

SYMPTOM	AT ONCE	NEXT DAY
Any deep wound or wound still bleeding after pressure has been applied	x	
Seems drowsy after ingesting a foreign substance	x	
Stops breathing after chewing on a poisonous plant	x	
Temperature elevated beyond 105	x	
Temperature between 103 and 105, and other signs of illness present		x
Increased water intake coupled with excessive urination, diarrhea, lethargy, or elevated temperature		x
Decreased appetite coupled with coughing, vomiting, diarrhea		x
Sudden weakness in hindquarters	x	
General lameness in any leg lasting more than three days		x
Red, ulcerated sore on the lips or other part of the body	x	
Abscess that is warm and painful to the touch	x	
Any general swelling that is warm and painful to the touch		x
Runny nose accompanied by elevated temperature, pale gums, weakness	x	
Runny nose accompanied by lethargy, pus in the eye, or rapid breathing		x
Coughing accompanied by elevated temperature, difficult breathing, depressed energy level		x
Foul breath accompanied by increased water intake, increased urination, excessive appetite, lethargy		x
Evidence of trauma accompanied by shortness of breath, elevated temperature, pale gums, lethargy	x	

SYMPTOM	AT ONCE	NEXT DAY
Vomiting accompanied by lethargy, frequent attempts to urinate, elevated temperature, bloody stools	x	
Diarrhea accompanied by bloody feces, elevated temperature, vomiting	x	
Diarrhea accompanied by dehydration		x
Constipation accompanied by straining and failure to defecate	x	
Abnormally thin stools accompanied by elevated temperature		x

Reproduction

FIRST CONSIDERATIONS

Breeding a beautiful, well-mannered cat can provide joy, satisfaction, and the feeling of achievement that accompanies any creative endeavor, but there is a great responsibility attached to this enterprise. Too many unwanted kittens are produced by irresponsible, uncaring people who breed cats for the wrong reasons: to feed their own competitive egos, to make a fast buck, or to let their children observe the mystery of birth. Instead they should take their children to an animal shelter and let them observe the mystery of homeless animals and euthanasia. With as many as one hundred thousand purebred cats winding up in shelters each year, and with millions of healthy mixed-breed cats being destroyed annually for want of responsible owners, the decision to bring more kittens into the world is not one to be made lightly. For most people it is not one that should be made or even considered at all.

Persons inclined to breed cats should ask themselves what they plan to do with the kittens. If their answers include winning fame and fortune in the cat world, they should consider a hobby that does not involve living creatures. Competition in the show ring is such that few breeders become overnight sensations, and the laws of genetics are such that few, if any, litters are filled with nothing but show-quality kittens. Nor is it realistic to expect to make money selling kittens. *The time and expense required to raise animals almost always exceed the monetary return.*

We produce kittens not only for the joy they add to our lives, but for the kind of lives we can provide for them. If we cannot make them as happy as they make us, we shouldn't set about making them in the first place. The responsible breeder never produces a litter for which he or she does not already have good homes—or the resolute intention of providing one. Do not include among these good homes the promises from family members or friends who say they want a kitten. These promises rarely become reality, and the people who made them will offer a dazzling variety of reasons why they can't take a kitten when the time comes.

If you have not skipped to another section of the book by now, perhaps you are the rare individual who is responsible and serious enough to accept the stewardship of raising kittens. You don't need an associate degree in animal husbandry to do so, but you should understand that much is often lost in the translation of reproductive theory into live births. Breeders, therefore, need a working knowledge of the behavioral, gonadal, and endocrine relationships involved in reproduction as much as they need good stock and good fortune in their breeding programs. They need to know what can go wrong in a planned mating, and to realize that what can go wrong most likely will. They also need to know what to do when nature's plans are at variance with theirs.

THE ESTRUS CYCLE

As the days begin to lengthen following the winter solstice, the cat's eye—in a way not yet understood—responds to the increase in light by sending a neurochemical message to the brain. The brain then signals the hypothalamus to discharge gonadotropin releasing hormone (GnRH). This substance, in turn, signals the pituitary gland to release two additional hormones.

One is called follicle stimulating hormone (FSH). It travels through the bloodstream to the ovaries, where it prompts the development of follicles and the maturation of eggs within them. Once the FSH level in the bloodstream is elevated enough to cause follicle development—generally two to four follicles per ovary per estrus—ten to fifteen days pass before the follicles reach maturity.

The second hormone released by the pituitary gland

is called luteinizing hormone (LH). A small amount of this hormone, which is also dispensed per instruction from the hypothalamus, is needed to insure the final development and maturation of the ovarian follicles. As those follicles begin developing, the ovaries secrete estradiol-17B, also known as estrogen, the hormone primarily responsible for the behavior of a cat in season.

ESTRUS BEHAVIOR

Female cats, unlike dogs, display little if any swelling of the vulva and scant vaginal discharge when they go into season. Therefore, breeders have to rely on other clues to determine when females are ready to be bred. Those clues commence with the arrival of *proestrus,* a one- or two-day interval during which female cats behave as if they have spring fever. They become listless and more vocal than usual, flirt with other cats of either sex, and tread intermittently with their hind feet. In proestrus, cats often respond superaffectionately toward humans and the occasional table leg. If they were introduced to male cats at this time, females might allow those males to mount them, but penetration would generally be proscribed.

With the arrival of full-scale estrus, the female is

ready for serious courtship. Willing, eager, and frequently demanding, she will accept a mate without much preamble. She advertises her intentions by howling endlessly, or so it seems, and by going about most of the day in the lordosis posture: front end down, back end up, tail swept recklessly to the side. She remains in this agitated, sometimes comical, state for six to ten days, on the average, going out of season if she is not bred or if she is bred and does not conceive.

This cycle is repeated several times through March, when, for reasons not yet known, many females stop cycling for a spell. By June, unbred females resume cycling and continue doing so until autumn if they do not become pregnant. Toward mid-September most unbred queens are out of season. They remain in this fallow state, which is called anestrus, until nature inaugurates the reproductive cycle once more the following January.

OVULATION

Unlike all other mammals save the mink, ferret, and rabbit, the cat is an induced or reflex ovulator: females do not ovulate without copulatory stimulation. When the male achieves sufficient penetration, a signal is dispatched from nerve endings in the cervix to the brain via the nervous system. This signal is received by the hypothalamus, which then releases GnRH, causing the subsequent release of LH from the pituitary. When LH arrives in sufficient strength at the ovaries, it causes the follicles to rupture, releasing their eggs. This generally occurs between twenty-five to thirty-six hours after the mating-induced release of LH from the pituitary gland, but it can occur as many as fifty hours later. Once they have been released, eggs make their way into the fallopian tubes toward the waiting sperm.

SELECTING A MALE

After a female begins cycling, i.e., going into and out of season regularly, she ought to be spayed or else bred in due course. If she is allowed to continue cycling without intervention, she might develop cysts on her ovaries, and from those she might develop cancer.

The only females that should be considered for breeding are healthy, well-adjusted, show-quality females that have been in season at least once, are beyond ten months of age, and have done well enough at shows to convince their owners—and the judges

The Queen's Cycle

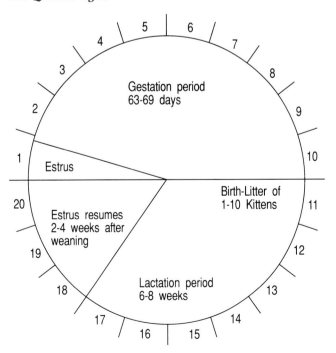

who have given them awards—that they have a contribution to make to their breeds.

There are several ways to locate the cat of your cat's dreams: visiting shows to see the cats being produced by today's studs; pouring over the yearbooks published by cat associations; or scanning the advertisements in various cat magazines and newsletters.

No matter what the source, two genetic principles guide the selection of a stud. He should be from a family or line of cats that has crossed well with the female's line in the past, and he should be accomplished in producing those qualities the female lacks. There's little chance of improving eye color in a female's kittens if the male she's bred to produces mediocre eye color as a rule.

Genetics being the gamble that it is, there is no way to guarantee top-quality kittens in any breeding venture. The best a breeder can do is minimize the chances of failure. Toward this end, the chosen stud should be at best a grandfather because it's easier to gauge a male's reproductive quality by looking at his children and their children as well. Too many people rush out to breed to the latest winner. This cat may develop into a top producer one day, but for now it's more reasonable to assume that his father already has.

While breeders have little jurisdiction over a cat's genes, the practical aspects of reproduction are more easily controlled. An owner should not send a female out for breeding to any cattery that does not request a current health certificate for that cat and additional proof that all her vaccinations are up to date. Nor should an owner send a female to a cattery that is unwilling to provide those same assurances regarding its stud.

The stud-service contract is another document that should accompany all breeding transactions. This

Somali mother with her kittens

needn't be a lengthy manuscript filled with meaningless words, but it should spell out the fee involved, the responsibilities of the stud owner while the queen is in his or her care, the length of time the stud owner is willing to keep the queen, what happens if the queen is not bred during that time, what happens if the queen is bred but loses her kittens prematurely after she returns to her owner, what happens if the queen has only one live kitten, and any other contingency that either party feels strongly enough about to put in writing. Such a contract, freely signed by both parties, is a legally binding document. Oral agreements are also considered legally binding, but, as the saying goes, they're not worth the paper they're written on.

GESTATION

The cat begins life as a one-cell being approximately 1/250th of an inch in diameter. Three days later that cell divides in two. Those cells divide seven more times in the next two days, at which point the cat has become a blastocyst. Eleven or twelve days after fertilization, the blastocyst attaches itself to the uterine wall. Though it is only four millimeters long, the blastocyst now contains the oxidative enzymes necessary to assimilate a variety of nutrients supplied through the tissues in the uterine wall.

Days thirteen through seventeen are a time of maximum sensitivity in kitten embryos, when 90 percent of all congenital malformations that are going

Kittens greeting their first mouse. From Harrison Weir's Our Cats and All About Them *(1889).*

to happen start to happen. Most of these malformations are caused by genetic, spontaneous, or teratogenic mishaps. There isn't much breeders can do about genetic or spontaneous misfortune once they've bred their cats, but teratogens—extrinsic influences that disrupt normal embryonic development—do fall under a breeder's control. Griseofulvin (an antifungal medication), modified-live panleukopenia vaccines, excess Vitamin A, and some steroids are among the substances that are always potentially harmful to the developing embryo. They are especially threatening from days thirteen through seventeen of gestation.

Though statistics are few regarding cats, we know that as many as two thirds of all fertilized human ova fail to survive the first two weeks of life. There is no reason to suspect that the odds are more generous to feline ova. Nevertheless, when the embryo enters the period of greatest vulnerability to outside influences, nature instructs it to begin setting aside the cells that will be used to form gametes when and if the embryo grows up to be an adult cat. These cells, which seem to participate only in the formation of gametes, appear in the embryo about the fourteenth day of gestation and are sequestered outside the embryo in a region attached to the gut. They soon migrate to that place in the embryo where gonads will develop, entering the gonads about the twentieth day of gestation. The pregnant female carries not only her children but also the seeds of her grandchildren.

About three weeks after conception, a female's nipples will begin to swell and to turn rose blush in color—a process which the British call *pinking up.* Soon afterward the female begins pinking up all over, radiating contentment and good health. As her nipples are beginning to glow, a mother's children are scarcely more than half an inch long. Yet they contain the earliest recognizable form of the liver, respiratory system, limbs, sense organs, skull, urogenital structures, and tail. By this time the period of maximum vulnerability for the entire embryo has passed. Also passing are the critical periods for the brain and spinal cord, days twelve through twenty-one, and the heart, days fourteen through twenty-three. By day thirty-six the critical periods for the skull and vertebrae, sense organs, limbs, palate, and reproductive organs have passed, too.

During this miraculous development the breeder is little more than a spectator, impatiently marking the

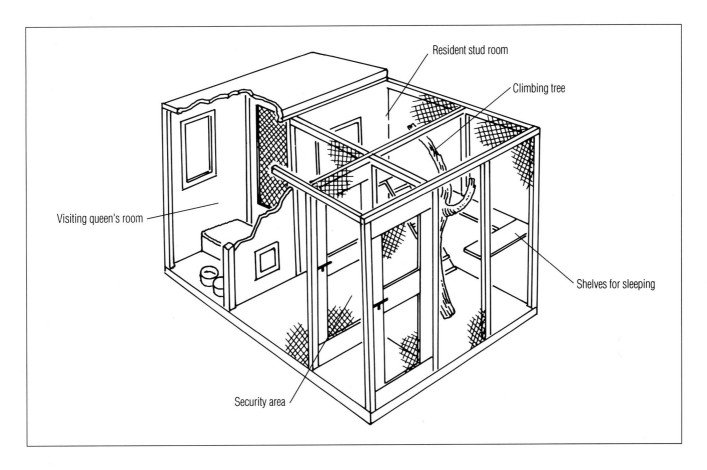

Resident stud room

Climbing tree

Visiting queen's room

Shelves for sleeping

Security area

days on the calendar. Somewhere between sixty-three and sixty-nine days following conception, on the average, the first kitten will make its way into the birth canal. Until this blessed event, there is little that breeders need to do outside their normal routine of feeding and caring for their animals. A pregnant cat does not need extra vitamins, though she may well demand extra food, and will always appreciate a little extra loving at this time.

GHOSTS IN THE MACHINES

With luck and the cooperation of a competent stud owner, a novice breeder will become a grandparent without tribulation. Unhappily, problems can affect the first-time queen; and predictably, those breeders who produce subsequent litters will eventually have to cope with several difficulties.

To begin, some queens keep their seasons to themselves. When their hormones come calling, these females act as if they are much too refined for outward response. Or any response at all. Other females, especially first-time breeders, suddenly go out of season

A spacious, multicompartment stud house

when they are sent to a male's residence to be bred. Still other queens, after breeding with one male by whom they produce nothing but pet-quality kittens, decide to bond with this mate for life. There are also females who mate willingly, but fail to become pregnant.

If females can not conceive of a way to frustrate the breeders' attempts at producing kittens, males are happy to oblige. A stud previously known to breed anything that moved—and a few things that did not—suddenly becomes discrete. Of course, the females he rejects are the ones he produced the best kittens with the previous year. Or a stud might continue to breed, but his conception rate will approach single digits.

THE SILENT HEAT

Ordinarily the signs that a female is in season are difficult to miss. But for some females a heat cycle is like the perfect crime, they leave no clues.

There is one straightforward solution to this problem. Allow the female to live with her intended until their union has been consummated. This is more easily done by those experienced breeders who keep their own males. There are other, more scientific, ways of coping with silent seasons if extended cohabitation is not convenient. These include interpreting vaginal smears to identify changes in vaginal cytology that occur during the estrus cycle; radio immunoassays to measure changes in hormone concentrations in the blood; and the direct viewing of the reproductive tract with a laparoscope. This latter technique has been used to monitor ovarian activity only with cats in laboratory-controlled reproductive studies. Vaginal smears and radio immunoassay may warrant consideration by the skilled breeder trying to cope with a valuable, top-winning female who gives no sign when she is in season.

THE STUD CAT

If breeding cats is a hobby, with a small *h,* and if you are fortunate enough to live close to someone with a superior stud that your female(s) get along with, you might breed a good cat or two each year and have fun showing them without having to own a male at all. But for several reasons, most of them having to do with convenience and with safeguarding their catteries from infection, many breeders choose to keep their own stud. The cautions exercised in choosing a mate for a female (see page 191) should be exercised to the *nth* degree in purchasing a male kitten, in buying or leasing a proven stud, or in keeping a kitten that you have bred for use in a breeding program. In addition, a new breeder should not select a male that is too closely bred, that is, one with the same cats appearing over and over in his pedigree.

Male cats produce an especially high proportion of abnormal sperm cells, 25 percent on the average, compared to males in other species. If a bull had more than 10 percent abnormality in his sperm, for example, he might not be considered a suitable prospect for stud. The more highly inbred a strain of cats, the more abnormal sperm the members of that strain will produce. Sperm samples collected by electroejaculation

A carpet helps breeding cats to maintain their footing and their concentration

The male often 'pedals' with his hind legs immediately prior to mating

from one inbred strain of lions revealed an abnormality rate approaching 75 percent.

With few exceptions, stud males cannot be permitted to have free run of the house. When they reach sexual maturity—generally between eight and sixteen months of age, depending on the breed—they begin to spray their urine to mark territory and to attract females. While female cats find something powerfully enchanting about male spray, humans simply find it overpowering. Thus the need to keep males confined. And to clean, deodorize, and disinfect their quarters daily.

The reason for confining a male is obvious, but there is no reason confinement should be abrupt. It is thoughtless to allow a young male to sleep in bed at night then to carry him into the basement one day and stick him into a pen. Far better to allow young kittens between weaning age and six or eight months of age

to run free in the house during the day and confine them at night in the quarters that will someday be their full-time home.

It is vital to provide a suitable pen for a stud male. At very least he deserves a large, walk-in enclosure outfitted with a cat tree and shelves to climb, plenty of room to play and jump, adequate natural light, and a window from which to view the world. Remember that a male is destined to be confined for the duration of his breeding career, and perhaps his entire life. Think about this—and about how you would like to spend the rest of your life in a comparable space—when deciding how much room to give your male. Having been denied his freedom in order to serve his breeder's interests, a male cat should not be denied any comfort that can be made available to him. In fact, whenever possible a breeder should provide a stud male with an outside run.

BREEDING MANAGEMENT

In a cattery in which the stud male is not kept in solitary confinement, he will know the other cats in the house, and there should be little fuss involved when it is time for him to romance one of his ladies in waiting. When a new cat is introduced to the household or when a strange female is brought in for stud service, breeders must be far more vigilant chaperons.

Before placing a strange or a painfully shy female with a male, be sure to introduce them gradually. Coy, retiring, or aggressive females may need to be conditioned to accept a male's presence before they will accept his advances. They may also need to be protected from males who would rather fight than frolic. And this being the age of liberation, we should also mention that some males who suffer performance anxiety may need time to get used to the idea of having a new female in their living quarters.

These difficulties can most easily be surmounted if the cats are introduced to one another before the female is in season. There is no law against placing inexperienced breeders together. We have all heard stories about the nine-month-old male who impregnates the six-month-old female with whom he was running about the house. But many breeders prefer to have an inexperienced cat learn biology from an experienced one. Most often the male will be the teacher and the female the pupil in this situation.

School could begin with the female being caged for a few days in the male's quarters while the male is permitted to make her acquaintance through the bars of her cage. If the male's quarters are not large enough to accommodate a cage, the female could be placed in a large pen next to a male's, or be allowed to run loose in the room where his pen is. However the introduction is accomplished, the idea is to fit the female into the male's routine, not to make his majesty feel dethroned.

This conditioning should start a week or so before the female is expected to come into season. When you feel the time is right—and after you've clipped everyone's claws—allow the two cats to interact without restraint for fifteen to twenty minutes. Retire to a neutral corner during this time, but have a blanket and a broom handy just in case.

For many cats this is a very stressful time. Much understanding from the stud and the stud owner are necessary to bring about a successful mating. Some stud males and queens will tolerate a helping hand from humans. Others do not want any restraint or guidance, and some do not want people around at all. Contrary to normal procedure in the dog fancy, many cat matings are never witnessed, only heard.

HOW OFTEN IS ENOUGH?

If a female in season is compatible with her suitor, they should be left to their own devices whenever possible for three days. Queens respond to mating stimuli in a random fashion, and researchers have yet to determine whether one mating is sufficient to effect ovulation in all cats. It appears to be for some females, but it most likely is not for the majority of queens. What's more, cats who ovulate in response to a single mating this season may not do so the next.

Researchers further suspect that the vigor of copulatory motion and the number of copulations per estrus influence the strength of the message sent from the cervix to the hypothalamus, telling it to release the

Tabby mother with her kittens showing the variable coat colors of the domestic cat

hormone necessary to bring about ovulation. Cats who do not ovulate after one mating were, perhaps, not sufficiently stimulated, and hence the hypothalamus was never told that it was time to release additional hormone. Or perhaps the hypothalamus did release the necessary LH, but its level in the bloodstream did not remain elevated long enough to insure ovulation.

In a study conducted in the late seventies, four groups of twelve females were allowed to mate once on either the first, second, third, or fourth day of estrus. Their conception rates were: 8.3 percent for the day-1 group; 16.6 percent for the day-2 group; 25 percent for the day-3 group; and 33.3 percent for the day-4 group. When three additional groups of females were allowed to mate three times a day on either the first, second, or third day of estrus, the conception rate was 83.6 percent in each group. Therefore, the suggestion is that males and females be allowed to breed ad libitum, if possible, for at least three days.

If a male is being used frequently in a cattery, and sexual exhaustion is a concern, a mating regimen in which cats were allowed to breed three times a day at three-or four-hour intervals during the first three days of estrus has produced conception rates between 90 and 100 percent in several studies. This timetable insures that functioning sperm, which only remains functional for two or three days, will be present in the reproductive tract in sufficient quantity when the female ovulates.

When two cats attempting to mate are not getting anywhere but tired—and the only result will be exhaustion on everyone's part—it is wise to separate them and wait until they are well rested before allowing them to try again. Some studs for some peculiar reason will attack a particular queen. In this case it is unlikely they will ever be compatible, and another stud should be chosen. Very often young, unproven males will attack a female or be too aggressive with their mates. It is important to supervise these early matings and to remember that it is never wise to use your hands or your feet to pry a male cat loose during a conflict. More than one stud owner has experienced a male's severe retaliation, and has ended up being bitten by her own cat. Such behavior is most frequent from the foreign shorthair breeds, which are more hyper and excitable during breeding. Keeping a wide broom in reserve for emergencies is not a bad idea.

ESTRUS-INDUCING HORMONES

Breeders dissatisfied with nature's progress are often tempted to intervene in her affairs. Technologies are available for influencing the reproductive activities of female cats, and some breeders have experimented with various hormones designed to bring a reluctant queen into season. There are no formally approved pharmacologic therapies for stimulating estrus in female cats. Nevertheless, synthetic hormones have been used in the laboratory—and occasionally without—to stimulate follicle growth and maturation and to bring about estrus behavior. Two synthetic gonadotropic hormones that appear safe and effective *if* they are used judiciously in consultation with a veterinarian are pregnant mare serum gonadotropin (PMSG), a potent compound obtained from the serum of pregnant mares, and follicle stimulating hormone pituitary (FSH-P), which is obtained from the pituitary glands of certain domestic animals.

These remedies are not for the beginner or for most experienced breeders, either. Reluctance is nature's way of telling us that some females should not be bred. The side effects of synthetic hormones are the drug manufacturers' way of telling us to be careful if we decide to use them. Treatment with FSH-P should not extend beyond five days because prolonged use might result in the formation of cystic follicles and interfere with ovulation. If the five-day treatment fails to produce a ripsnorting heat, the process should not be repeated, if at all, for another five or six weeks. A major problem with PMSG is that potency estimates of different preparations can vary significantly from one commercial lot to the next. There is, in addition, no available data concerning the safety of repeated PMSG use with the same queen.

Females can also be made to ovulate by exogenous stimulation. Two compounds effective in this regard are human chorionic gonadotropin (HCG) and gonadotropin releasing hormone (GnRH). The former is purified from the urine of pregnant women. The latter is a synthetic hypothalamic hormone. Neither substance will improve conception rates in queens receiving adequate mating stimuli, but they can be used in the cattery to insure maximum ovulation in queens that didn't conceive in the past after being bred or with queens who produced only one or two kittens last year even though they had been observed breeding enthusiastically for several days. In these circumstances a person might want to take a female to the vet's for an injection of hCG as a safety measure after that female has been bred normally. The trick is to make sure you know when she is first bred so you can administer hCG right away. This is important because the female will still take at least twenty-four hours to ovulate, and you don't want sperm to go stale in the meantime. Normally you shouldn't need a second injection of hCG, but if you want to be safe, another shot could be administered twenty-four hours after the first one. Of course, you should allow a cat to continue mating after hCG has been administered.

CONCLUSIONS

In times past the activities of cat breeders were little noticed by the outside world except when the local club put on its annual show and a club member's cat got its picture in the newspaper. But times have changed, and with the increased concern over the surplus-animal population, some animal-welfare groups and municipalities are beginning to ask whether a person has the right to keep and produce as many cats as he or she pleases. They are also beginning to suggest that limits be placed on the number of animals per household, and that licenses and periodic inspections be required of people who wish to keep more than three or five or some minimal number of pets.

So far the cat fancy's reaction to these suggestions has been to remove breeders' names and addresses from show catalogs so that animal-health inspectors cannot locate catteries that easily. One suspects that a stronger, more positive reaction ought to be forthcoming. For one thing, the cat fancy is still largely composed of individuals who breed cats on a limited and sensible basis. In 1990, most of the 19,871 people who registered litters with the Cat Fanciers' Association— 68 percent to be precise—registered just one or two litters. This level of activity should not be objectionable to any municipality. On the other hand, municipalities have the right—and cat federations have the obligation —to ask why anybody needs to produce more than twenty litters per year, as 229 people felt obliged to do in 1990, according to CFA figures. If registries take the lead in policing their own members, as some registries are considering, the cat fancy will be spared the imposition of regulation from without.

DELIVERING KITTENS

The kittening box is a roll-up-your sleeves, get-your-hands-messy workplace where the faint of heart or the mildly curious need not apply.

Anyone with patience enough can learn to groom a cat. Lots of fanciers can recite pedigrees the way a minister quotes the Bible. Many people can buy a decent cat. But the person who makes the cat fancy go around is the one who is willing to get up every hour and a half during the night to check on a queen that's due to deliver; who is willing to miss a party or a relative's wedding to stay home with an overdue mother; and who is determined enough to work for three quarters of an hour to get a weak kitten's heart going. It is sometimes the breeder's lot to cradle new life in a towel at three a.m. while a veterinarian pulls kittens out of an anesthetized female with a freshly made incision in her abdomen— and to get up every two hours around the clock to feed and clean kittens until they're old enough to take meals and use a litter pan on their own if their mother is unable or unwilling to nurse them.

During 1990 many thousands of people owned or leased females that produced litters of pedigreed kittens. No doubt most of these births were routine, as much as anything so miraculous can be routine, but it's the unexpected for which cat breeders have to prepare.

About the fifty-fifth day after a queen is first mated, she ought to be confined to a single room— preferably her owner's bedroom. Two or three days later, after she has settled in there, she ought to be confined to a cage in that room and be given generous periods of supervised free time. Left to her own instincts, a queen will sometimes want to have kittens in all the wrong places. If a queen needs assistance during delivery, a breeder shouldn't waste time coaxing her out from under a bed to provide it.

According to several textbooks, the standard gestation period ranges from sixty-three (or sixty-four) to sixty-nine days. Many experienced breeders begin taking their queens' temperatures on the sixty-first day after first mating. If the temperature is where it should be for a day or two—around 101.5 degrees—then suddenly drops to 98 or 99 degrees, kittens will most likely arrive within twelve hours. Should the temperature be elevated two or three degrees, call the vet at once.

The queen's delivery cage should be outfitted with one half of a large carrier or a cardboard box with three sides intact and the other side cut down so that only a two- to three-inch strip is left at the bottom to prevent kittens from crawling out. Either of these makes a good nest in which the queen can raise her kittens. Both should be sprayed with a safe disinfectant and wiped dry before being placed in the cage.

Some breeders use cloth towels to line the kittening box, others use newspaper or paper towels. When they put this box into the cage, some breeders switch from litter to newspaper strips or paper towels in the litter pan in case a queen decides to start having her kittens there while the breeder is out of the room.

Queens beginning to get serious about delivering kittens signal their intent with a discharge caused by the passing of a placental plug. This discharge is followed before long by rapid breathing, panting, deep purring, kneading with the paws, or frequent attention to the genital region. Breeders with longhaired cats should have clipped this area in advance. All breeders should have clipped their queens' nails about the time they were confined to their delivery cages.

Involuntary contractions soon follow the passing of the plug. When the queen begins to supplement these by bearing down in an effort to deliver, the breeder should note the time carefully. If the first kitten has not been born within an hour, call the vet and have a clean, towel-lined carrier ready.

When all goes normally, a dark, greyish-colored bubble will emerge from the vagina. Once that bubble of new life appears, the clock should be reset to thirty minutes. If the queen cannot pass the kitten on her own by that time, take her promptly to the vet.

Sometimes a breeder can help pull the kitten free. Sometimes a breeder can damage the kitten in trying to do so. Never pull between contractions. Always pull with the contraction, and always pull gently.

Some breeders recommend giving the queen a shot of oxytocin at this point. This should be done only if a breeder has discussed the possibility with a veterinarian in advance. Oxytocin should never be administered before a kitten is visible in the vaginal opening. A queen can die of a ruptured uterus is she's hit with a shot of oxytocin before her cervix is fully dilated, and it's no easy matter for a nonprofessional to tell when dilation has occurred. "I never administer oxytocin before the first kitten is born," says one breeder. "If I have any problems before then, I'm off to the vet's."

Once a kitten is "on the ground," as breeders say, the queen should begin licking it vigorously to clean it and to remove the placental membrane—or sack—surrounding the kitten. If the mother doesn't remove the sack from the kitten's face at once, do it for her so the kitten can begin breathing. The membrane should break and peel away if you rub the top of the kitten's skull gently with a small piece of clean cloth. If the membrane breaks, clean it away from the kitten's face. If it doesn't, take a pinch of membrane at the base of the skull between thumb and forefinger and pull it away carefully.

Hold the kitten face down in one prewashed and sterile hand while rubbing its back with a small, clean cloth. If the kitten is wriggling about and making a racket, give it back to its mother.

If the kitten is breathing with difficulty or not breathing at all, fasten a hemostat on the umbilical cord about six inches from the kitten. Grasp the cord on the side of the hemostat closer to the mother and pull gently. If the mother doesn't expel the placenta at once, don't waste time fussing with it. Cut the cord on the mother's side of the hemostat, remove the hemostat, dip the severed end of the cord into a bottle of white iodine, and try to revive the kitten. Aspirate any fluid in the kitten's mouth. Then hold the kitten in the palm of one hand, face toward you.

Make sure that the kitten's head is secure and immobile between your thumb and forefinger. Place your other palm over the kitten's underside, with your forefinger over the kitten's heart.

Holding the kitten securely in both hands, swing your hands down abruptly a distance of two or three feet, massaging the rib cage over the kitten's heart with your forefinger as you do. Repeat this two or three times. Aspirate the kitten again, swing it downward abruptly between your hands two or three times more, aspirate, swing, aspirate—as often as you need to until the kitten begins breathing—or until it is sadly obvious that the kitten is not going to begin breathing at all. Do not think about throwing in the towel until at least half an hour has passed.

When the swing method does not revive a kitten after five or ten minutes, some breeders dip the kitten up to its neck into a bowl of very cool water and then into a bowl of very warm water in hope that the shock will kick start its breathing mechanism. Breeders who have discussed the possibility with a veterinarian before hand sometimes put a drop of Dopram-V under the kitten's tongue to stimulate breathing at this point.

If a weak kitten does begin breathing on its own, give it back to its mother, but watch it carefully. If the kitten starts breathing slowly again or if it begins to feel cool to the touch, aspirate it again if necessary, massage it, and place it on a heating pad in a small box to keep it warm. Give it back to its mother in half an hour, but continue to monitor it carefully.

Meanwhile, the queen will normally be busy with other deliveries. Some queens chew the umbilical cords and eat every afterbirth compulsively. If not, cut the cords for them after five minutes or so, sterilize the severed end of the cord that is still attached to the kitten, and dispose of the afterbirth.

Be sure that all placentas are present and accounted for. A retained placenta can cause serious infection, may have to be removed surgically, and could mean that the breeder instead of the queen must raise the litter.

When the last kitten has been delivered, the queen will give an almost palpable sigh of relief and settle in to nursing her brood. At this point some breeders recommend giving the queen a shot of oxytocin to expel any placental material that might have been retained during the delivery. Ask the veterinarian in advance about the advisability of doing this.

Monitor the kittens and their mother for another hour or so to make sure all kittens are nursing normally. If any are not, consult a veterinarian or a good text on supplementary feeding and proceed accordingly.

THE DELIVERY SUPPLY LIST

1. The veterinarian's emergency number
2. A generous quantity of soft cloths
3. An equally generous supply of towels
4. Small hemostat (presterilized in boiling water)
5. Scissors (presterilized in boiling water)
6. White iodine
7. Aspirator
8. Heating pad
9. Small box
10. Oxytocin
11. Dopram-V
12. Several syringes
13. An eye dropper
14. A clean, towel-lined carrier
15. A good text on supplementary feeding
16. Coffee

Showing

FINDING A SHOW AND OBTAINING AN ENTRY FORM

Prospective exhibitors who have never been to a cat show should visit one without their cats to see what showing is like. *Cats* or *Cat Fancy* magazines, which are available at many newsstands, contain lists of shows throughout the United States and Canada. Cat registries can provide this information, too, if the local news dealer does not have these publications.

Owners who decide that they and their cats are ready for competition should write or phone the entry clerk to request a show flyer and an entry form for the show they've selected. Among other things, the flyer discloses the entry fee, show hall location, slate of judges, and closing date for entries. The flyer also reminds owners that all their cats' inoculations should be current. Shows often reach their quota before the advertised closing date, so it's best to enter at least two or three weeks prior to this deadline.

FILLING OUT AN ENTRY FORM

On the entry form, the exhibitor provides the name of the cat and that of its owner(s), its breed, color, registration number, date of birth, parents, sex, eye color, the class the cat will compete in, and the name of the person, if any, with whom the exhibitor would like to be benched. If questions arise when an exhibitor is completing an entry blank, entry clerks are happy to answer them at a reasonable hour. Once the form is completed, the exhibitor mails it and the entry fee ($30 to $55 for a two-day show, depending on the number of times a cat will be judged) to the entry clerk. If confirmation isn't received within two weeks, the exhibitor should phone the entry clerk and ask politely if the entry has been received.

ENTRY CONFIRMATION

When the mail carrier delivers the exhibitor's entry confirmation, it will contain a facsimile of the cat's listing in the show catalog, directions to the show hall, a list of motels near the hall, and other information the show committee deems pertinent. The exhibitor should check the confirmation to make sure that all names are spelled correctly, that the cat's registration number is accurate, and that the cat or kitten is entered in the correct class.

PRESHOW GROOMING AND PREPARATION

"A cat kept in clean surroundings, well fed and cared for, needs very little preparation for the show pen." This counsel, written in 1909, remains true today. Yet cats usually need bathing before a show. Some breeders prefer to bathe a cat several days in advance of a show to give the natural oils in the animal's coat—which may be removed by bathing—a chance to reappear. Others bathe their cats the day before a show. There is merit in both methods, and the way to find out which is best for a cat is by giving it a full-dress-rehearsal bath several weeks before the show and observing the cat for the next couple of days. If its coat looks great the day after its bath—and continues to look great for the next several days—the cat could be bathed between Tuesday and Friday of show week. If the coat looks dry or lifeless for a day or so after a bath but then regains its luster, the cat should be bathed no later than Wednesday. If the cat looks fine the day after a bath but not so fine two days later, bathe as near to showtime as possible, preferably on Friday. Whenever a cat is bathed for a show, the owner should clip its claws on all four feet. Show rules and the judges' safety require this.

PROVISIONS FOR A SHOW

No matter how carefully a cat or kitten is bathed, it will need touch-up grooming—at least for its owner's peace of mind—at the show. Therefore, exhibitors should pack an assortment of combs, a brush, if it's part

A typical cat carrier

of the normal grooming routine, Q-tips, cotton balls, paper towels, facial tissues, grooming powder, if applicable, eye drops, and any other accoutrements normally used in grooming sessions at home.

All entries are assigned to a benching cage where they remain when they are not being judged. Exhibitors are expected to bring curtains for the sides of the cage and a rug or towel for the cage floor. Cage size may vary from show to show, but most single cages are twenty-two inches long, wide, and tall.

Single cages are also uncomfortably small. For an extra $10 to $20 the thoughtful exhibitor orders a double cage when he or she sends in the entry blank. This allows the cat more room to stretch out and affords the exhibitor an extra chair on which to prop his or her tired feet. The approximate dimensions of a double cage are twenty-two inches deep and tall and forty-four inches wide.

The National Cat Club Show in Britain. At British shows the judges go from pen to pen accompanied by their steward to assess cats

In North American shows, cats are brought to the judging ring, where they are evaluated while exhibitors and spectators look on

The curtains people choose to fit those dimensions vary with individual taste, budget, accessibility to sewing talent, and sense of style. Some exhibitors' cages resemble florid palaces with plush, hand-sewn curtains and precious, little four-poster beds; others look like military barracks with bath towels held in place by safety pins. A few exhibitors bring their own cages, which may resemble the tour buses of country-and-western singers or miniature intensive-care units. Whatever the choice, minimum requirements dictate that cage curtains should be fastened securely inside the cage so that they cover both the sides and the back of the cage.

Just as styles in cage curtains vary, the number of incidental items packed for a show is a matter of personal comfort. Some exhibitors arrive with enough provisions for a month in the Kalahari Desert. Others bring only themselves, their cats, cage curtains and rug, a few grooming aids, a pen to mark the catalog, and a good book. A few of the possible additions to that list include pipe cleaners for fastening any loose corners of the benching cage, a small, TV-dinner-sized table for grooming, a towel to cover the table, a can opener, adhesive tape, a first-aid kit, and the cat's favorite toy and food. Show committees always provide litter, and they usually provide litter pans as well; but it's wise to carry a small, disposable, cardboard litter pan just in case.

AT THE SHOW

Cats should be transported to shows in airline-approved carriers, which are available at wholesale pet supply dealers, pet shops, and shows. The cat's journey will be more pleasant—especially if it is long or the cat is young—if the owner tapes a small litter pan to the floor inside the carrier. The rest of the carrier floor should be covered with a towel or disposable diaper. In cold weather many exhibitors cover the outside of their carriers with fitted, quilted bonnets that resemble toaster covers. These covers, which shield the traveler from the cold, are available at shows or from companies that advertise in cat magazines. They can also be sewn at home, if the exhibitor is so inclined.

New exhibitors should arrive early for check-in to obtain their cats' cage number and a catalog, set up the benching cage, and get their cats and themselves settled in their new environment. The first order of business is arranging the benching cage, then finding out where the litter and litter pans are stored and getting a necessary supply. Once the cage is decorated, outfitted with a litter pan and the cat's favorite toy, and the top has been double checked to insure that it's fastened securely, the exhibitor should place the cat or kitten into the cage and take an admiring step back. Some exhibitors feed their cats as soon as the cats have finished exploring their cages. Other exhibitors, who fed their cats before bringing them to the show hall, wait until later in the day to provide food. Water should be available throughout the day—or offered to the cat at periodic intervals.

The judging schedule is printed in the back of the show catalog or on a separate sheet provided with the catalog. Exhibitors should note when their cats are scheduled to be judged. They should also check the catalog to be sure their cat's name and all its biographical data are correct. If there are any mistakes, the master clerk should be told about them immediately.

JUDGING

Cats are summoned to the rings via the public address system. When the first numbers of a cat's class are called, exhibitors should begin listening carefully for their cat's number. While carrying a cat to the appropriate ring, an exhibitor should have a secure grip on the animal. When the exhibitor arrives at the ring, the cat should be placed in the judging cage that has its number on top, and the door of the cage should be fastened securely before the exhibitor takes a seat in the gallery.

As Mark Twain said, it is difference of opinion that

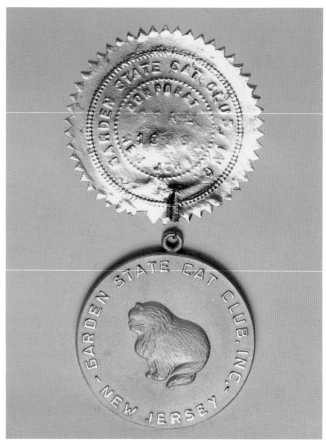

Besides rosettes, medals are sometimes awarded to owners of winning cats

makes horse races. The same is true of cat shows. Persons entering a show are simply paying to learn what several judges think about their cat on a particular day. Those exhibitors who keep this in mind and who remember that win or lose their cats will still love them tomorrow, will find that a cat show is a pleasant way to spend a weekend.

The plate (left) was awarded for a top regional win. The bowl (right) was presented to the owner of the best cat in the show

ON WITH THE SHOW

A cat show is composed of a number of separate, concurrently running, individual shows held in various judging rings throughout the show hall. Every cat in the hall may compete in every individual show—each of which is presided over by a different judge who presents awards independent of the decisions of other judges. Hence, a cat that is chosen best in show by the judge in Ring 1 may not always be given the same award—or any award at all—by the judge in Ring 2.

Individual shows are classified as either *allbreed* or *specialty*. In an allbreed show all cats entered compete for awards. In a specialty show only those cats of similar coat length—or type, depending on the association—compete against each other.

Whether an individual show is allbreed, longhair specialty, or shorthair specialty, competition is held in the following categories: championship, altered, kitten, provisional, and household pet.

Championship competition is for unaltered, pedigreed cats at least eight months old. The altered competition is for neutered or spayed pedigreed cats that are eight months of age or more. Kitten competition is for pedigreed youngsters between the ages of four and eight months. Provisional competition is for those breeds that have not gained championship status. Household pet competition is held for all mixed-breed, non-pedigreed cats—at least in theory. Today many people are showing pet-quality, pedigreed cats as household pets. No matter what their origin, household pets older than eight months must be altered before they can he shown.

Final Awards

After a judge has examined all the cats competing in the ring, it is time for finals—the curtain call in which the judge presents the top ten cats in that particular ring. During this ceremony, the judge introduces the cats, usually in ascending order of merit, until the best cat in show has been held aloft to generous applause.

Titles

Adult cats compete for titles whose names vary somewhat from one association to the next. All federations offer champion and grand champion titles, and most confer other titles beyond that.

An international set of championship medals

Champion, the lowest-ranking title, can be earned in most associations even if a cat is the only entry in its class. Titles beyond champion are earned by defeating specified quantities of other cats, usually other champions, in competition.

Altered cats compete for the same titles in their classes as championship cats do. In most associations, household pets also compete for titles, but those titles frequently have different names from the ones earned by championship or altered cats. Cats in provisional classes and kittens do not compete for titles.

Judging

The men and women who officiate at cat shows have demonstrated skill at breeding cats and a talent for exhibiting them. Prospective judges must have at least five to seven years consecutive breeding experience, depending on their association's requirements, before applying for admission to the judging program. They must serve on show committees in several capacities and acquire their initial show-ring experience by clerking for judges at shows. Once accepted into the judging program by their association's board of directors, judging trainees must pass examinations on breed Standards and show ring procedures and apprentice successfully with certified instructors at a specified number of shows.

During a show, judges[1] spend between one and two minutes evaluating each cat. They are often obliged to make more than two hundred of these ninety-second assessments per show, record their decisions in the judges' book, keep their impressions of the best cats straight in their minds—with the aid of a note pad—and pick the ten best cats in the show according to those ninety-second impressions. For this they are paid anywhere from forty cents to a dollar per cat—and all expenses—depending on their rank. Exhibitors who disagree with their decisions sometimes complain that a judge's opinion is not even worth that.

By the time they carry a cat half a dozen steps from its cage in the show ring to the judging table, judges have already determined much about that animal. They know whether its coat feels dirty and tacky, or silky and clean. They know whether a cat is down on weight or too stout. They know whether it has the feel of an animal in peak show condition.

This author always has a quick look at a cat before taking it out of the cage. From then the judging process—a routine that does not vary from one cat to the next—is designed to confirm whether the first impression will be the final one. While standing the cat on the judging table, the author quickly runs one hand along the cat's spine from the shoulders to the base of the tail and from there to the end of the tail, feeling for kinks in the tail as he does. The tail length on most breeds that have tails should be equal to the length of the back. This quick, hands-on assessment reveals whether it does. Some judges bend the tail around to measure it against body length, but they lose some length in the tail in doing so.

Once judges put their hands on a cat, they should not move them more than necessary, for when they do, a cat is able to collect himself if he's in a mood to be difficult. Over the years the author developed a style of holding one of a cat's hind legs—the one farthest from the author's body—between the middle finger and forefinger of his left hand, palm facing inward, and one of the cat's front legs between the same fingers of the right hand. This enables the author to hold a cat at arms length to judge the top line and the belly line of its torso, to see whether its legs are in proportion to its body, and to roll the cat over in his hands while the cat is still in the air to check its underbelly and paw pads. Since cats do not always stand still to show off their finer qualities, the judge must put the cat into a position that allows the easiest examination.

As judges are handling a cat, they're constantly making evaluations, comparing that cat to its Standard, a document that describes the ideal specimen in the breed (see Breeds section, page 37). Although each breed Standard contains a scale of points that assigns a numerical value to eye color, coat, head type, etc., those points are more of a guide to breeders trying to create a top-quality cat than they are to judges trying to evaluate one. No judge stands in the ring figuring how many points to award for each part of the cat.

---

[1] It is difficult to describe something as personal as the judging process—which is unique to every judge—within the confines of the third person narrator's voice. Whenever it becomes necessary for this writer to distinguish personal preference from general counsel, he will make that distinction by referring to himself as the author.

IDEAL SPATIAL RELATIONSHIPS IN PERSIAN AND SIAMESE HEAD TYPE

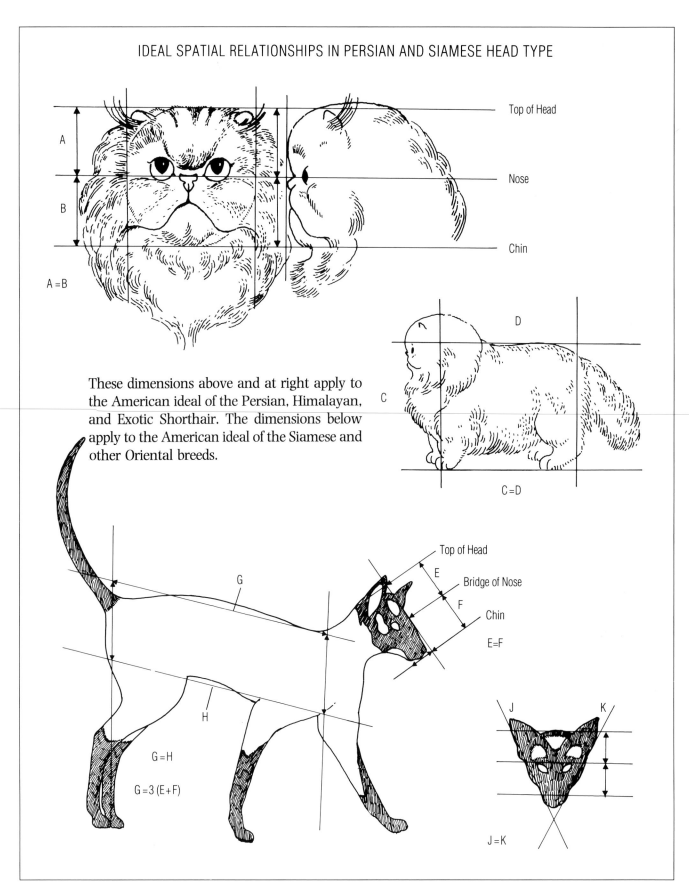

These dimensions above and at right apply to the American ideal of the Persian, Himalayan, and Exotic Shorthair. The dimensions below apply to the American ideal of the Siamese and other Oriental breeds.

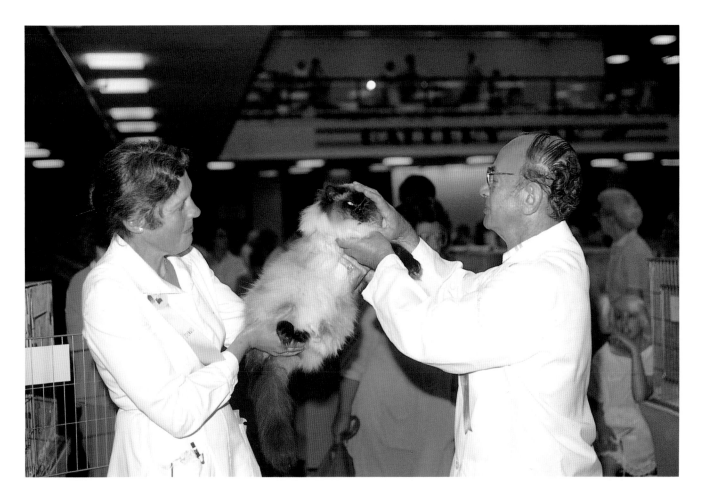

At a British show, a steward holds an entry while the judge assesses it

Anyone who did would end up being terminally confused.

This author believes it is easier to look for faults rather than virtues in judging a cat: not only the faults that are cause for disqualification according to the Standard, but general flaws in the type or conformation of the cat. One assumes that the cat being presented to a judge meets the breed Standard. It is the judge's job to discover where an individual cat's characteristics may not meet that Standard precisely. Then, if one cat has two faults and another cat has three, the two-fault cat is the winner.

With so many cats of exceptional quality being shown today, it doesn't take much to separate them this way. For example, many Persians have tiny, narrow noses with their nostrils pointing straight out; but according to the Standard, the nose is supposed to be broad and flat. The full coat on some Persians might cover a multitude of flaws, including large ears, long legs, and less-than-massive bone structure. Or perhaps a cat's eyes are too deeply set, or the eye aperture slants too much toward the ear. If judges look closely enough, they'll find these shortcomings and evaluate the cats accordingly.

Sometimes grooming is the tie breaker. A cat that is well presented has the best chance of advancing, and if all other things are equal, grooming can make the difference between a blue ribbon and a red one. This isn't to say that everyone who shows a cat has to be an artist with a comb and brush. Occasionally older fanciers can't groom the way they could before, or newer exhibitors have not learned all the skills they need.

Grooming is temporary, type is not. It's unfair to penalize one cat that's obviously superior to its competition simply because it isn't as well groomed.

Because cat judging is an art, not a science, there is room for subjectivity in judges' decisions, especially when they select the top ten cats in show. Unlike

The author presenting a Persian cat in finals

Standard might see that the silver is short in the face, has a wide, flat nose, and round eyes—all of which the Standard mandates. Nevertheless, the silver might not be as extreme or as massive as a blue Persian. In deciding which of those cats to place in the final—or which should be placed above the other for best longhaired champion, perhaps—judges must consider how difficult it is to produce a silver with a decent break to the nose.

If a judge believes that it was more difficult to achieve the quality of the silver than it was to achieve the quality of the blue—even though the blue is more extreme and massive than the silver—that judge could justify putting the silver over the blue. Another judge might not see it the same way, but that's what exhibitors are paying for—each judge's opinion. Unless judges encourage people working with cats in the more difficult or newer breeds, these breeds are never going to develop.

In addition to type, conformation, and presentation, there is one other critical attribute of a show cat: temperament. When this author started judging cats in 1953, they were much more difficult to handle than they are today. Indeed, their quality was frequently exceeded by their ferocity. It was not uncommon to see an owner put on heavy, leather gauntlets before placing a cat into the judging cage. Fortunately, cats were judged only twice during a show in those days, compared to the six to twelve to sixteen judgings (in some three-day shows) that exhibitors subject them to today.

Many judges believe that temperament and its chief component, charisma, are what separate the great cats from the good ones. Great cats just stand out. They are different enough to be unique, and yet still fit the Standard; and there is always that little extra something about them, that air of self-possession. Great cats have presence. They display themselves properly. They show off well enough to accentuate their best qualities.

Like type and conformation, temperament is inherited—from the people around a cat as well as its ancestors. Invariably people who are high strung and nervous have nervous cats. When a cat acts like a spoiled brat and is sassy and jittery, it's often because the personality of its owner is much the same. Unfortunately, when some people acquire cats that don't have a temperament problem, it doesn't take long for those cats to develop one.

picking best of breed, an intramural competition, choosing cats for finals involves comparing apples and oranges, Siamese and American Shorthairs, Persians and Turkish Angoras. It's one thing to decide which of five Tonkinese fits the Standard most closely, but it's quite another to decide if the best Tonkinese comes closer to meeting its Standard than the best Exotic Shorthair does.

This decision is further complicated because some breeds are older, more established, and more highly refined than others. In fact, within some breeds there are certain colors that are generally superior to others. Therefore, judges have to weigh the relative merit of achievements when they compare one breed to the next. The silver Persian is a case in point.

Judges who compare a silver Persian to its breed

Given the constraints under which they have to work, judges must become adept at thinking on their feet. They also have to have the courage to make their own decisions in the ring. Sometimes there are judges—though they don't constitute a great number—who are influenced by the reputation of the person showing the cat. These judges aren't necessarily dishonest, but if they don't know a breed well enough themselves, they assume that because a cat's owner is prominent, it must be a good cat.

Judges need to have a good, solid background—to have spent time showing cats and handling them—because the more judges know, the less influenced they are likely to be by the person showing the cat, or by other judges' opinion of that cat. When a judge knows cats, it is not in his or her heart to make an undeserving cat a winner.

In many regards judges are like appraisers. They put a value and a demand on a cat. Frequently, exhibitors who are uncertain of a kitten's value may enter that kitten in a show, hoping that the judges' decisions will determine whether the exhibitor should keep the

THE CAT FANCIERS' ASSOCIATION, INC.
World's Largest Registry of Pedigreed Cats
1309 Allaire Avenue ● Ocean NJ 07712 ● 201-531-2390
BREED/DIVISION AWARDS ● 1990-1991 Show Season
Page 1 of 2

Show: *Empire*

Date: *Feb 10-91*

Judge: *Richard Gebhardt*

Master Clerk: *Jim Williams*

LONGHAIR	BEST	2ND	BEST CH
BIRMAN	78	71	71
EXOTIC SH	81	—	—
MAINE COON	85	89	85
OLID PERSIAN	95	99	102
SHADED PERSIAN	114	113	113
SMOKE PERSIAN	115	—	—
TABBY PERSIAN	116	—	116
PARTI-COLOR PERSIAN	126	124	126
BI-COLOR PERSIAN	129	128	128
HIMALAYAN PERSIAN	132	134	132
TURKISH ANGORA	—	—	—

SHORTHAIR	BEST	2ND	BEST CH
ABYSSINIAN	140	146	139
AMERICAN SH	150	148	150
AMERICAN WH	—	—	—
BALINESE	155	—	—
BOMBAY	—	—	—
BRITISH SH	157	—	—
SABLE BURMESE	—	—	—
DILUTE BURMESE	—	—	—
CHARTREUX	—	—	—
COLORPOINT SH	162	160	162
CORNISH REX	166	163	163
CYMRIC	—	—	—
DEVON REX	167	—	—
EGYPTIAN MAU	—	—	—
HAVANA BROWN	168	—	—
JAPANESE BOBTAIL	—	—	—
JAVANESE	170	169	169
KŌRAT	—	—	—
MANX	—	—	—
OCICAT	174	172	172
ORIENTAL SH	177	178	177
RUSSIAN BLUE	180	—	
SCOTTISH FOLD	183	181	181
SIAMESE	186	185	—
SINGAPURA	—	—	—
SOMALI	190	189	187
TONKINESE	191	192	—

A page from a judge's book, showing the numbers of the best and second-best cats and the best champions in various breeds and divisions

kitten or sell it. Judges are also arbiters of taste. People breed to the winning cats, not to the losers, and the judge's opinion is a certification of value. That is why judges are responsible for seeing to it that sound, healthy cats with the greatest likelihood of carrying on their breeds become the winners.

Besides their knowledge of breeds and standards, judges must bring to their task an air of professional comportment. Their dress and behavior should not call attention to themselves, for the cat is the star in the show ring. During a show, a judge should not fraternize with exhibitors in an attempt to be one of the gang. Nor should a judge make "insider" comments to some exhibitors while a class is being judged. If this were allowed to happen, other exhibitors would have a right to feel resentful if their cats were not to do well, even if the judge's decisions were made impartially. Judges cannot expect every exhibitor to agree with their decisions, but their conduct should be such that every exhibitor respects them—and leaves the show feeling that the awards are earned by the cats, not their owners.

Judges also have a responsibility both to the letter and the spirit of the breed standards on which they base their evaluations. A judge is hired to apply, not interpret, the standards; and personal preference, while seldom entirely absent from a judge's considerations, ought never to be the deciding factor when it is time to give awards.

(Below) In Great Britain, Grand Challenge Certificates are awarded at Championship shows to cats of exceptional merit. Only cats who are already Champions/Premiers are eligible to enter these classes. Grand Challenge Certificates awarded by three different Judges at three different shows are needed for the cat to win the coveted title of Grand Champion/Premier.

The award of the Grand Challenge Certificate is not automatic. If the Judge decides that an exhibit is the best of all the cats entered, but not of sufficient merit to justify the award of a Certificate, it will only be given a first placing, and the Grand Challenge Certificate will be withheld. It is expected that the winner of one of these Certificates should be an almost perfect specimen of the breed.

Glossary

ACA: American Cat Association.

ACFA: American Cat Fanciers Association.

Agouti: the color between the stripes on a ticked or tabby cat; for example, the warm beige tone between the slate-blue stripes on a blue Abyssinian.

Allele: one of two or more genes—each governing a different physical characteristic—that can occupy a particular locus (position) on a chromosome; for example, the genes determining coat length--either long or short—are alleles.

Alter: 1) a cat that has been sterilized surgically; 2) to sterilize a cat by surgical means.

Anestrus: a period during which a female cat is not in season.

Any other color (AOC): any potential color—excluding those proscribed colors or patterns—that might occur in a breed.

Any other variety (AOV): a term used in some federations to describe any cat that is the offspring of two registered parents but is not eligible for championship competition because it does not conform to the requirements for coat length, coat color, eye color, or some other physical characteristic.

Awn hair: the coarser of the two types of secondary hairs; normally longer than down hair, but shorter than guard hair.

Back crossing: a form of inbreeding (see below) in which a cat is mated to its parent of the opposite sex.

Benching cage: in the show hall, the enclosure in which a cat remains when it is not being judged.

Best of breed: the cat which, in the judge's opinion, comes closest to meeting the breed Standard of all the cats in a given breed competing in that judge's ring.

Blaze: 1) in blue creams and tortoiseshells, a vertical division of two colors extending down the center of a cat's forehead and nose. When that arrangement is reversed on the cat's chin, the entire pattern is called a checkerboard; 2) in bicolors, a splash of white on the forehead and/or nose.

Bloodline (or line): the ancestors of a given cat; often used imprecisely to refer to any cat produced by a particular cattery.

Break: a distinct, unmistakable indentation affecting the bridge of the nose, occurring between—or at a moderate distance below a point in between—the eyes. The break is often more noticeable when viewed in profile.

Breed: cats with similar physical characteristics and, in most cases, some ancestors in common.

Brindling: the random mixture of hairs of different colors in a cat's coat; usually not a term of approbation.

Brush: 1) to groom a cat with a similarly named instrument; 2) the tail on a longhaired cat.

Carnivore: an animal whose diet consists primarily, if not exclusively, of meat.

Carry: 1) to possess a recessive gene (see below) or genes governing a physical characteristic that is not apparent to the eye; a shorthaired cat, for example, may be carrying a longhair gene; 2) to harbor the virus or bacteria that could transmit a disease while exhibiting no symptoms of that disease; 3) to be pregnant with kittens.

Cat fancy: the loose confederation of cat-registering bodies, breeders, and exhibitors dedicated to the care, welfare, promotion, and exhibition of pedigreed and other cats.

Catalog: a publication listing the entries for a cat show, together with the age, date of birth, title held (if any), parents' names, breeder's name, and owner's name for each entry. May also contain advertising, a list of exhibitors' addresses, and assorted information.

Cattery: a place where cats are bred and/or boarded.

Cattery name: the registered name of a place where cats are bred; may be used as a prefix by the breeder of a cat or as a suffix by a subsequent owner.

CCA: Canadian Cat Association.

Cell: the basic structural and functional unit of the body.

CFA: Cat Fanciers' Association.

CFF: Cat Fanciers' Federation.

Champion: a title that a cat earns, often but not always, by beating other cats in competition while striving to earn a more meaningful title such as Grand Champion (see below).

Chromosomes: minute, rod-shaped elements in the nucleus of a cell that control the inheritance of characteristics in the cell and in the entire cat.

Coarse: not smooth, refined, or harmonious in the arrangement of parts.

Cobby: close coupled; that is, short in the body, broad in the beam, and low on the legs.

Color breeding: mating cats of the same color and breed for at least three generations, or five, according to purists.

Condition: the state of a cat's well being; includes weight, muscle tone, cleanliness, radiant good health, and grooming.

Conformation: the configuration of a cat's torso, legs, and tail.

Congenital: existing at birth but not acquired by heredity.

Cross: 1) a mating between cats; 2) to mate or breed one cat with another which may not be related or may be of a different breed.

Dam: the female parent.

Depth of flank: the extent and substance of the flank—that area of the cat's side between the last rib and the hip. Most often used in reference to Manx and Cymric.

Dilute: a paler version of a basic color. For example, blue is the dilute of black, cream the dilute of red.

Division: a breed subdivision consisting of two or more color classes.

Doctoring: 1) a British term synonymous with neutering; 2) in the United States a term used to describe the illegal alteration of a cat's color or conformation.

Domestic: a nonpedigreed cat, usually a shorthair, indigenous to a particular country.

Dominant: prevailing over another. For example, the gene for folded ears is dominant over the gene for straight ears. Therefore, if a cat has one gene for folded ears and one gene for straight ears, the cat's ears will fold.

Double coat: a coat in which the awn hairs are as long as the guard hairs. Generally the awn hairs are intermediate in length between the longer guard hairs (see below) and the shorter down hairs (see immediately below).

Down hair: the shorter of the two types of secondary hairs, and the shortest hair in a cat.

Ear furnishings: hairs growing inside the ears.

Euthanasia: the act of humanely ending a cat's life.

Extreme: pronounced; possessing a desirable characteristic to an exaggerated extent.

Feral: when used properly, a term that describes a formerly domesticated cat—or the descendants of formerly domesticated cats—now living in a wild state. Often used imprecisely to denote any cat that doesn't seem to belong to anyone.

Final: 1) the ceremony in which rosettes or other honors are awarded to the ten best cats in show; 2) to qualify for that ceremony.

Follicle: 1) the indentation in the skin from which hair grows; 2) the sac on the female's ovary in which an egg develops.

Foreign: a moderately tubular body conformation. The Abyssinian has a foreign body; the Egyptian Mau, which is less tubular, has a semiforeign body.

Gene pool: the sum total of all the genes that exist in the cats of a given breed.

Genes: units of heredity that control the growth, development, function, and physical characteristics of the cat.

Genetics: the study of heredity.

Genotype: the genes an individual inherits from its parents; not to be confused with the individual's physical appearance (see phenotype).

Gestation: the period between conception and birth; normally lasts from sixty-three to sixty-nine days in cats.

Grand champion: a title earned by a cat (after it has become a champion) for defeating a specified number of other champions in competition. In The International Cat Association a titled earned by a cat after making a specified number of finals and earning a specified number of points in competition.

Ground color: the color occurring on the part of the hair shaft closest to the body.

Guard hairs: the outer—and longest—hairs in a cat's coat; sometimes called the primary hairs.

Heat: a period of sexual receptivity in a female cat.

Heterozygous: possessing a pair of dissimilar alleles (see above) for a particular trait.

Homozygous: possessing an identical pair of alleles (see above) for a particular trait.

Hormone: a chemical messenger sent into the bloodstream by a gland in order to affect development or function in another part of the body.

Hybrid: 1) a cat produced from a mating between cats of different breeds; 2) a breed derived by combining two or more breeds.

Hybrid vigor: an increase in health and vitality sought by mating one cat to another of a different bloodline or breed.

Inbreeding: a union between two cats that does not result in the introduction of any new genetic material to the offspring of those cats. Mother-son; father-daughter; and brother-sister matings constitute inbreeding. A knowledge of the traits—both good and bad—of the cats involved constitutes the wise use of inbreeding.

Kitten: for exhibition purposes, a cat between the ages of four and eight months.

Line breeding: a mating between related cats that have a common ancestor appearing at least once in the first three generations on both the sire's and the dam's side of the pedigree.

Litter: kittens born at the same time from the same mother.

Litter registration: enrolling a litter of kittens with a cat association.

Master grand champion: one of several titles awarded by some associations to designate show ring performance above and beyond the title of Grand Champion. Similar titles include Double, Triple, Quadruple, and Supreme Grand Champion.

Mutation: a genetic mishap—usually caused by environmental conditions or a glitch in the replication process—that alters the normal inheritance of a characteristic.

Neuter: 1) a castrated male; 2) to remove testicles from a male cat.

New breed or color: a competitive category for cats or kittens not yet accepted for championship competition.

Oriental: the most slim of the tubular body styles.

Outcross: 1) a breeding between two cats that do not have any ancestors in common for at least three generations; 2) a breed that can be used in the production of another breed of kittens. The Abyssinian, for example, is an allowable outcross for the Somali.

Papers: registration documents issued for a cat.

Pedigree: a document containing the known names, titles, colors, and registration numbers of the first three to five generations of a cat's predecessors.

Phenotype: a cat's physical appearance; always influenced by heredity and sometimes by environment (that is, vitamins, diet, and grooming), too.

Piebald: a pattern in which areas of white surround areas of color.

Pigment: coloration (or coloring matter) in a cat.

Pointed: a pattern in which a pale body color contrasts with darker color(s) confined to a cat's face, ears, legs, and tail.

Points: 1) the face, ears, legs, and tail of a pointed cat; 2) units earned in competition that count toward the attainment of a title or year-end award

Pricked: the upright or forward inclination of a cat's ears.

Provisional: a class for cats or kittens not yet accepted for championship competition.

Purebred: a cat whose ancestors are all of the same variety or allowable varieties; not a synonym for pedigreed.

Quarantine: a period during which a cat is isolated from other cats in order to prevent the spread of disease.

Queen: a female cat of breeding age.

Quick: the vein in a cat's claw.

Rangy: long in the body.

Recessive: 1) a characteristic that does not become apparent unless a cat possesses two genes governing that trait; 2) a gene governing a recessive trait.

Register: to enroll a cat, kitten, or litter with a registering body.

Registry: an association that records the lineage of cats, issues registration numbers, licenses shows, etc.

Ring: an area in which cats are judged at a show.

Roman nose: a nose characterized by low-slung nostrils and an arch.

Rosettes: gaily colored arrangements of ribbon that consist of a round centerpiece to which several long strips of ribbon have been affixed.

Rufous: a genetic factor that alters a color, generally for the better. The rufous influence can be seen in the ruddy Abyssinian, which would be a black agouti tabby otherwise.

Selective breeding: the purposeful mating of two cats in order to achieve a desired end or to eliminate an undesired one.

Self: solid; as in, "The father is a self-red cat."

Set type: to breed successive generations of cats containing a certain characteristic in the hope of producing cats that will not only possess that characteristic but will also pass it on to their offspring.

Sire: the male parent of a cat, the father.

Solid: all of one color (see self).

Spay: 1) a female cat that has been sterilized surgically; 2) to render a female cat sterile by surgical means.

Spotting: 1) white areas in a cat's coat; 2) the discharge of fluid by a pregnant cat.

Standard: a document that describes the ideal specimen in a breed.

Stop: a slight indentation in the bridge of the nose occurring between—or at a moderate distance below a point in between—the eyes (see break).

Stud: a siring male cat.

Stud book: a volume containing the names, sexes, registration numbers, and colors of cats and (when known) their ages, and dates of birth; also contains similar information (when known) about the cats' parents.

Titles: merit ranks earned by a cat in competition.

TICA: The International Cat Association.

Tuck up: the drawing up of the underline which may be created by a curved spine, as seen in the Cornish Rex and other breeds.

Type: the arrangement of the overall parts of the cat in accordance with breed specifications.

Undercoat: the wooly down hairs on a cat; also used to denote the down and the longer awn hairs together.

Variety: a cat—with two registered parents—that is not eligible for championship competition because it varies from the breed standard in eye color, coat length or color, etc.

Appendices

CAT REGISTRIES

A cat registry performs many functions for its members. In addition to registering cats and recording their lineage, federations charter clubs, sanction shows, license judges, enforce by-laws and show rules, award titles to cats that have earned them in competition, approve breed Standards, recognize new breeds and colors, publish breed Standards and show rules, present national and regional awards annually to the highest-scoring cats and kittens in the association, and publish newsletters, magazines, and an annual yearbook.

There are six cat registries in North America. Each one is an independent association, with its own registration and show rules, its own judges, licensing requirements, breed Standards, publications, and year-end award winners.

American Cat Association
8101 Katherine Avenue
Panorama City, CA 91402
818-782-6080

American Cat Fanciers Association
P.O. Box 203
Point Lookout, MO 65726
417-334-5430

Canadian Cat Association
83 Kennedy Road South
Unit 1805
Brampton, Ontario
Canada L6W 3P3
416-459-1481

Cat Fanciers' Association
P.O. Box 1005
Manasquan, NJ 08738-1005
908-528-9797

Cat Fanciers' Federation
9509 Montgomery Road
Cincinnati, OH 45242
513-984-1841

The International Cat Association
P.O. Box 2684
Harlingen, TX 78551
512-428-8046

NUMBER OF CAT SHOW ENTRIES

	1989-90	1988-89	1987-88
ACA	2,009	1,365	1,246
ACFA	20,073	21,000	20,346
CCA	3,298	2,972	2,817
CFA	82,814	72,281	70,807
CFF	6,207	7,389	4,941
TICA	33,483	32,990	28,139
UCF			1,560
TOTAL	147,884	137,997	129,856

AVERAGE NUMBER OF ENTRIES PER SHOW

	1989-90	1988-89	1987-88
ACA	134	114	125
ACFA	139	138	153
CCA	157	156	166
CFA	228	216	223
CFF	163	151	103
TICA	138	151	139
UCF			120
TOTAL	179	172	175

FELINE HEALTH AND WELFARE ORGANIZATIONS

The relationship between animal welfare societies and cat clubs is as old as the cat fancy. Clubs have long provided free tables at their shows, when space permitted, so that humane organizations could distribute information about responsible pet ownership and the importance of having animals neutered and spayed. What's more, cat clubs and individual fanciers have always contributed to support the research and the good work done by organizations such as the ones listed below.

Actors and Others for Animals
5510 Cahuenga Boulevard
North Hollywood, CA 91601
818-985-6263

American Humane Association
P.O. Box 1266
Denver, CO 80201
303-695-0811

American Society for the Prevention of
   Cruelty to Animals
441 East 92nd Street
New York, NY 10128
212-876-7700

Animal Welfare Institute
P.O Box 3650
Georgetown Station
Washington, D.C. 20007
202-337-2333

The Delta Society
Century Building, Suite 303
321 Burnett Avenue, South
Renton, WA 98055
206-226-7357

Friends of Animals
P.O. Box 1244
Norwalk, CT 06856

For information about FoA's low-cost, neutering-and-spaying program, call 1-800-631-2212

The Fund for Animals
200 W. 57th Street
New York, NY 10019
212-246-2096

Humane Society of the United States
2100 L Street, NW
Washington, D.C. 20037
202-452-1100

Morris Animal Foundation
45 Inverness Drive, East
Englewood, CO 80112-5480
1-800-243-2345

Robert Winn Foundation
1805 Atlantic Avenue
Manasquan, NJ 08726-1005

St. Hubert's Giralda
Geraldine Rockefeller Dodge Foundation
575 Woodland Road
Madison, NJ 07940

Bibliography

Beadle, Muriel. *THE CAT: A Complete Authoritative Compendium of Information About Domestic Cats.* New York, S & S Trade, 1977.

Carlson, Delbert G., D.V.M., and Giffin, James M., M.D. *Cat Owner's Veterinary Handbook.* New York, Howell Book House, 1983.

Carr, William H.A. *The New Basic Book of Cats.* New York, Charles Scribner's Sons, 1978.

Eustace, May and Towe, Elizabeth. *Fifty Years of Pedigree Cats.* London, Pelham Books Ltd, 1967.

Fireman, Judy. *The Cat Catalog.* New York, Workman Publications, 1976.

Fogarty, Marna Sharron. *The Cat Yellow Pages: The Cat Owner's Guide to Goods and Services.* New York, Charles Scribner's Sons, 1984.

Gebhardt, Richard H. (editor); Pond, Grace; and Raleigh, Ivor; *A Standard Guide to Cat Breeds.* New York, McGraw, 1979.

Greer, Milan. *The Fabulous Felines* (or Dogs are passe). New York, Dial Press, 1961.

Hawcroft, Tim. *The Howell Book of Cat Care.* New York, Howell Book House, 1991.

Jennings, John. *Domestic and Fancy Cats.* London, L. Upcott Gill, 1893.

Jude, A.C. *Cat Genetics.* Neptune, New Jersey, T.F.H. Publications, 1977.

Kelsey-Wood, Dennis. *Atlas of Cats of the World.* Neptune, New Jersey, T.F.H. Publications, 1989.

McGonagle, John and Vella, Carolyn. *In the Spotlight, a Guide to Showing Pedigreed and Household Pet Cats.* New York, Howell Book House, 1990.

Muller, Ulrike. New Cat Handbook: *Everything About the Care, Nutrition, Diseases, and Breeding of Cats.* New York, Barron, 1984.

Pond, Grace. *The Complete Cat Encyclopedia.* London, W.H. Heinemann, 1979.

Pond, Grace. *The Complete Cat Guide.* New York, Doubleday, 1977.

Richards, Dorothy S. *A Handbook of Pedigree Cat Breeding.* London, David and Charles, 1980.

Robinson, Roy. *Genetics for Cat Breeders.* London, Pergamon Press, 1977.

Sayer, Angela. *A Guide to Breeding and Showing.* New York, Arco Publishing, 1983.

Siegal, Mordecai, ed. *The Cornell Book of Cats.* New York, Villard Books, 1990.

Simpson, Frances. *The Book of the Cat.* London, Sir Isaac Pitman and Sons, 1903.

Soderberg, P.M. *Pedigree Cats, Their Varieties, Breeding, and Exhibition.* London, Cassell & Company Ltd., 1958.

Stephens, Gloria. *Legacy of the Cat.* San Francisco, Chronicle Books, 1990.

Taylor, David. *The Ultimate Cat Book.* New York, Simon and Schuster, 1989.

Weir, Harrison. *Our Cats, and All About Them.* New York, Houghton, Mifflin and Company, 1889.

Wilson, Meredith. *Cat Breeding and Showing.* New York, A.S. Barnes & Company, 1972.

Wilson, Meredith. *Showing Your Cat.* New York, A.S. Barnes & Company, 1974.

Wilson, Meredith. *Encyclopedia of American Cat Breeds.* Neptune, New Jersey, T.F.H. Publications, 1978.

Winslow, Helen M. *Concerning Cats.* Boston, Lothrop Publishing, 1900.

Wright, Michael and Walters, Sally, ed. *The Book of the Cat.* New York, Summit Books, 1980.

Cat Breeder and Owner List

The Publishers thank the following breeders and owners
for allowing their cats to be photographed for this book:

Silver Classic Tabby American Shorthair
Grand Premier Angiras Thomax
  of Grandcru
Bred by Barbara Courtney
Owned by Eric and Helena Thom

Ruddy Abyssinian
Grand Champion Shechinah Daniel
Bred by Chris Strom and
  Kathryn Whitten
Owned by Bob and Chris Strom

Brown Classic Tabby American Shorthair
Grand Champion Carocats Kubla Khan
Bred and owned by Carol and
  Michael Rothfeld

Silver Classic Tabby American Shorthair
Grand Champion Tylona's Gloriana of
  Grandcru
Bred by Barbara Goulding
Owned by Eric and Helena Thom

Calico American Wirehair
Champion Silva Wyte Filigree
Bred and owned by Richard Gebhardt and
  John Bannon

Red and White American Wirehair
Champion Silva Wyte Billy the Kit
Bred and owned by Richard Gebhardt and
  John Bannon

Blue Point Balinese
Grand Champion Mikaso's Moon Struck
Bred and owned by Kathryn and Michael
  J. Sokolis

Blue Point Birman
Grand Champion Oxdowne Love Bug
Bred and owned by Betty Cowles

Bombay
Grand Champion Road to Fame's
  Blackberry Brandy
Bred by Herb and Suzanne Zwecker
Owned by Robert Unangst

Blue-and-White Van British Shorthair
Champion Excalibur Edward Langtry
Bred by Pamela Barrett
Owned by Susan Ross

Blue British Shorthair
Ankara Appolonia Kelling
Bred and owned by Heidi and Dick Mullin

Sable Burmese
Champion Road to Fame's Extremely Bold
Bred by Herb and Suzanne Zwecker
Owned by Robert Unangst

Blue Chartreux
Champion Steppenbleu Echo
Bred by Stephanie Pendleton
Owned by Frederick Andrews

Seal Lynx Point Colorpoint Shorthair
Grand Premier Lebianco Nicholas of
  Quarry Hill
Bred by Josephine Quinzi
Owned by Anne Vanasse

Blue-and-White Cornish Rex
Grand Champion Blu Sprs Prince Tamino
Bred and owned by Ellen Weiss

White Devon Rex
Champion Briarmar Clair de Lune of
  Anuket
Bred and owned by Adele Gay and
  Omar Gonzalez

Silver Egyptian Mau
Premier Coonfederacy's Ptah of
  Chesterpeake
Bred by Dorie Eckhart
Owned by Thomas and Linda Getz

Brown Classic Tabby Exotic Shorthair
Grand Champion Jovan The Legend
Bred and owned by Cheryl
  and Bob Lorditch

Havana Brown
Champion Hav-a-Hill Prince Charles
Bred and owned by Phyllis Hill

Red-and-White Japanese Bobtail
Nekomo Nagusami of Kemage
Bred by Allen Scruggs and Douglas Myers
Owned by Mathis/Scruggs/Myers

Korat
Grand Champion and Double Grand
  Champion Petlar Li'l Bo Peepers of
  Si Sawat
Bred by P. Greuel and L. Jones
Owned by Daphne Negus

Brown Classic Tabby Maine Coon
Champion Bakerstmews Michael Milken
Bred and owned by Carolynn Holmes-Sgro

White Manx
Grand Champion Mendocino
  Bearelegance of Mayflower
Bred by P. and R. Webster-Powell/
  R. Denton
Owned by Muriel Slodden

Brown Mackerel Tabby-and-White
  Norwegian Forest Cat
Supreme Grand Champion Maineline's
  Tord
Bred and owned by Steve and
  Louise Clair

Cinnamon Ocicat
Grand Champion Luvadot's Megabyte
Bred by Robert Parker
Owned by Robert and Grace Parker

White Oriental Shorthair
Grand Champion Leggs Amapola of
  Mayflower
Bred by Lynn Von Egidy/Mallary/
  Gonzalez
Owned by Muriel Slodden

Calico Persian
Grand Champion Anz Maggie the Cat
Bred by Anne Waddington
Owned by Waddington/Hannon/Watkins

Copper-eyed White Persian kitten
Kitty Charms Icy Sensation
Bred and owned by Darlene and
  June Feger

Red Classic Tabby Persian
Champion Charo's Flash Fire
Bred by Charmayne Phillips
Owned by Gerald and Charmayne Phillips

Chinchilla Silver Persian
Grand Champion Diadem Pollyanna
Bred and owned by Janice Reichle

Black Smoke Persian kitten
Jolair's Break Every Rule of Roann
Bred by James Newly and Ann Gonzales
Owned by A. Gonzales and R. Gingerelli

Tortoiseshell Persian kitten
Skyhy Moonlight Sonata of Baramere
Bred by Glen and Pat McNeil
Owned by Barbara and Merle Phipps

Cream-and-White Persian
Grand Champion Anz Mr. Dickens of
    Bekah
Bred by Anne Waddington
Owned by Rebecca Beckley

Flame Point Persian
Grand Champion Sulltans Shocking Pink
Bred by Nancy Sullivan and
    Lauren Jacobs
Owned by Nancy Sullivan

Blue Mitted Ragdoll
Champion Flashback
Bred by Susan Stephens
Owned by Susan Marshall and
    Eric Freeman

Russian Blue
Grand Champion Tylona's Sparkle Plenty
Bred By Laurel and Barbara Goulding
Owned by L. and B. Goulding and
    T. Schreck

Silver Classic Tabby Scottish Fold
Champion Aberdeen Angus
Bred and owned by Terry Havel

Silver-patched Torbie Van Scottish Fold
    Longhair
Quadruple Grand Champion Wynsome
    Vanity Fair
Bred by Phil and Mary Ann Maggitti
Owned by Connie Webb

Seal Point Siamese
Grand Champion Shabou Shannon
Bred by S. McKeehen-Bounds and
    G. Bounds
Owned by S. McKeehen-Bounds and
    Marion Butler

Singapura
Grand Champion Changi's Sahaja of
angiras
Bred by Tommy and Hal Meadows
Owned by Bill and Barbara Courtney

Ruddy Somali
Grand Premier Roadraces' Stutz Bearcat
    of Grandcru
Bred by Carolyne Marriner
Owned by Eric and Helena Thom

Platinum Mink Tonkinese
Grand Champion Connacht's Shenanigan
Bred and owned by Frank Yaccino and
    Larry Rhinard

White Turkish Angora
Champion Cayman's Enchanting Princess
Bred and owned by Andrie Del Piano

Red-and-White Turkish Van
Champion Portacaeli Cabrera
Bred by A. Daly
Owned by Michael and Kitty Ann

Black-and-White American Curl
Supreme Grand Champion Carbon Copy
    of Fun Furz
Bred by Gerri Hamilton
Owned by Caroline Scott

Leopard-spotted Bengal
Champion Widwood Mustoflees of
    Belltown
Bred and owned by Roger and
    Karen Austin

Tortie-point Javanese
Champion Hunnapurr Sheezajehn
Bred and owned by Cathie Spina

Oriental Longhair
Talisyn's Chocolate Moose
Bred and owned by Steven Baylus

Seal-point Snowshoe
Cactus
Bred and owned by Jean Thompson

Blue-Cream Sphynx
Supreme Grand Champion Far from Pierrette
Bred and owned by Sandy Adler

Brown Spotted Tabby and White
St. Hubert's McKinley Domestic Shorthair
Owned by Marcy Zingler

Note: The titles presented here have been
earned in several of the major show-giving
federations.

The cats illustrated on pages 39, 64, 68, 87,
119, 122, 125, 164 were bred in Great
Britain and are all of Grand Champion or
equivalent status.

Photo and Illustration Credits

David Anstey 28, 29 and 193
Jane Burton 146
By courtesy of the Trustees of the British Museum 15
By courtesy of the Natural History Museum 14, 16
By kind permission of British Museum Press 196
Chanan Photography 38, 49, 102, 143, 166, 203
Richard Gebhardt 208
Marc Henrie ASC (London) 6, 7, 8, 39, 64, 87, 118, 119, 121, 122, 125, 164, 183, 184, 191, 194, 195,
    202, 209
Larry Johnson 42 153
Tetsu Yamazaki 94

INDEX